Work and inequality

SOCIAL POLICY IN MODERN BRITAIN

General Editor: Jo Campling

POVERTY AND STATE SUPPORT *Peter Alcock*
HEALTH POLICY AND THE NATIONAL HEALTH SERVICE
   Judy Allsop
THE VOLUNTARY SECTOR IN BRITISH SOCIAL SERVICES
   Maria Brenton
HOUSING AND SOCIAL JUSTICE *Gill Burke*
EDUCATION AS SOCIAL POLICY *Janet Finch*
WORK AND INEQUALITY *Susan Lonsdale*
FOUNDATIONS OF THE WELFARE STATE *Pat Thane*
THE ELDERLY IN MODERN SOCIETY *Anthea Tinker*
SOCIAL RESPONSES TO HANDICAP *Eda Topliss*
SOCIAL WORK, SOCIAL CARE AND SOCIAL PLANNING
   Adrian Webb and Gerald Wistow

WORK AND INEQUALITY

Susan Lonsdale

LONGMAN
London and New York

LONGMAN GROUP LIMITED

Longman House, Burnt Mill, Harlow
Essex CM20 2JE, England
Associated companies throughout the world

Published in the United States of America
by Longman Inc., New York

© Longman Group Limited 1985

First published 1985

BRITISH LIBRARY CATALOGUING IN PUBLICATION DATA

Lonsdale, Susan
   Work and inequality. — (Social policy
  in modern Britain)
  1. Industrial sociology — Great Britain
  I. Title   II. Series
  306'. 36'0941   HD6957.G7
ISBN 0-582-29629-3

LIBRARY OF CONGRESS CATALOGING IN PUBLICATION DATA

Lonsdale, Susan.
   Work and inequality.

  (Social policy in modern Britain)
  Bibliography: P.
  Includes index.
  1. Labor policy—Great Britain.   2. Great Britain—
Social policy.   I. Title.   II. Series.
HD8391.L66 1985   331.12'042'0941   84-12235
ISBN 0-582-29629-3

Set in Linotron 202 10/11 pt Plantin
Printed in Hong Kong by
Wing Lee Printing Co Ltd

CONTENTS

EDITOR'S PREFACE

This series, written by practising teachers in universities and polytechnics, is produced for students who are required to study social policy and administration, either as social science undergraduates or on the various professional courses. The books provide studies focusing on essential topics in social policy and include new areas of discussion and research, to give students the opportunity to explore ideas and act as a basis of seminar work and further study. Each book combines an analysis of the selected theme, a critical narrative of the main developments and an assessment putting the topic into perspective as defined in the title. The supporting documents and comprehensive bibliography are an important aspect of the series.

Conventional footnotes are avoided and the following system of references is used: the author, date and page number (Burke 1981: 46) in the text refers the reader to the corresponding entry in the references at the end of the book. Abbreviations are sometimes used as references, eg (MSC 1979); these are fully detailed in the list of abbreviations on p. viii–ix. A number in square brackets, preceded by 'doc' e.g. [docs 6, 8], refers the reader to the corresponding items in the section of documents which follows the main text.

In *Work and Inequality*, Susan Lonsdale looks at the unequal distribution of work in our society and some of the explanations for this. She documents some significant changes in employment, most notably the growth in female participation in the labour market, part-time employment and in unemployment, and the response to these trends by policy makers. A considerable part of the book provides us with evidence about the circumstances of groups in society who face discrimination and disadvantage in the labour market. The effectiveness of policies which are directed towards these groups are analysed and evaluated. The book concludes that a great deal of poverty and inequality still persists in Britain today as a consequence of the social division of labour and the concern of policy with efficiency rather than equity.

This book, which is particularly timely, upholds the long and reputable tradition in social policy of critically evaluating the effectiveness of policy and not eschewing the decisions and judgements that are required of a regulated process of policy making. In doing so, it begins to move beyond a simple concern with practical issues and solutions towards providing a long overdue analysis of the underlying social, political and economic forces which influence events.

Jo Campling

LIST OF ABBREVIATIONS

ACAS	Advisory, Conciliation and Arbitration Service
ADEA	Age Discrimination in Employment Act 1967
APA	Additional Personal Allowance
ATC	Adult Training Centre
CAITS	Centre for Alternative Industrial and Technological systems
CBI	Confederation of British Industry
CDPPEC	Community Development Project Political Economy Collective
CEP	Community Enterprise Programme
CI	Community Industry
CP	Community Programmes
CPAG	Child Poverty Action Group
CRE	Commission for Racial Equality
DE	Department of Employment
DHSS	Department of Health and Social Security
DRA	Dependent Relative Allowance
DRO	Disablement Resettlement Officer
DRS	Disablement Resettlement Service
DTS	Direct Training Services
EAS	Enterprise Allowance Scheme
EEC	European Economic Community
EOC	Equal Opportunities Commission
ERC	Employment Rehabilitation Centre
ESD	Employment Service Division
FIS	Family Income Supplement
ICA	Invalid Care Allowance
IEA	Institute of Economic Affairs
ILO	International Labour Organisation
ITB	Industrial Training Board

JRS	Job Release Scheme
MMA	Married Man's Allowance
MSC	Manpower Services Commission
NACEDP	National Advisory Council for the Employment of Disabled People
NCCL	National Council for Civil Liberties
NCIP	Non-Contributory Invalidity Pension
NEP	New Enterprise Programme
NHS	National Health service
OECD	Organisation for Economic Co-operation and Development.
OHE	Office of Health Economics
OPCS	Office of Population, Censuses and Surveys
OTP	Open Tech Programme
PEP	Political and Economic Planning
PER	Professional and Executive Recruitment
RADAR	Royal Association for Disability and Rehabilitation
SBC	Small Business Courses
SEPACS	Sheltered Employment Procurement and Consultancy Service
SIG	Sheltered Industrial Group
SPA	Single Person's Allowance
SPD	Special Programmes Division
SSRC	Social Science Research Council
TOPS	Training Opportunities Schemes
TSD	Training Services Division
TSP	Training for Skills Programme
TUC	Trades Union Congress
UVP	Unified Vocational Preparation
WEA	Workers Educational Association
WEEP	Work Experience on Employers Premises
YOP	Youth Opportunities Programme
YTS	Youth Training Scheme
YWS	Young Workers Scheme

ACKNOWLEDGEMENTS

A number of people have been very generous in reading and commenting on the manuscript. Their suggestions and comments have been invaluable and many have been unashamedly incorporated into the book. Responsibility for the way in which their ideas have been used remains entirely my own, as do any errors. Many thanks to Lesley Day, Christine Fowler, Emma MacLennan, Stan Newman, Chris Pond and Alan Walker. I especially want to thank Stan for his support and care, without which it might not have been done at all. I would also like to thank Jo Campling for all her patience and encouragement and Yvonne Cottam and Annette Oliver for their help in typing the manuscript.

Susan Lonsdale
January 1984

We are grateful to the following for permission to reproduce copyright material:

George Allen & Unwin (Publishers) Ltd for Document one from pp 128–129 (B Wootton 1962) and Documents five, seven and twenty-seven from pp 18–19, 254–256, 408–410 (W Beveridge 1944); Cambridge University Press for Document twelve p. 498 (Finch & Groves 1980); Commission for Racial Equality for Document twenty-six pp 10–11 *Employment Report* (Nov 1980); The Disability Alliance for Document twenty-two p. 3 (MSC 1981); Equal Opportunities Commission for Document ten from pp 5–6 (EOC 1981); the author, Jeanne Gregory for Document thirteen from pp 75–76 (J Gregory 1982); Heinemann Educational Books for Document twenty-five pp 63–64 (The Runnymede Trust and the Radical Statistics Race Group 1980); the Controller of Her Majesty's Stationery

Office for Document six from pp 497–499 (*Employment Gazette* 1980), Document sixteen from *The Guardian* and Document twenty from pp 4–7 (Tomlinson Committee 1943); the author, Janet Holland and the University of London Institute of Education for Document eleven from pp 37–38 (J Holland 1980); The Institute of Race Relations for Document twenty-four (B G Cohen & P J Jenner 1969); Dr C Littler for Document two from pp 15–16 (C R Littler 1982); Manpower Services Commission for Document nine from MSC *Annual Report* (1980/81), Document seventeen (MSC 1982) and Document twenty-one (MSC 1982); Office of Population, Census & Surveys for Document eighteen from pp 41–42 *Older Workers and Retirement* by S Parker (pub HMSO); Policy Studies Institute for Document eight from p. 1 (D Metcalf 1982) and Document nineteen from pp 174–176 (M Fogarty 1982) *Joint Studies in Public Policy No 5* Heinemann Educational Books for National Institute of Economic and Social Research, Policy Studies Institute, Royal Institute of International Affairs, 1982; Mr C Pond for Document fourteen from pp 11–12 (Low Pay Unit 1983) and Document fifteen from pp 10–13 (Low Pay Unit 1982); Professor A Sinfield for Document four from pp 1–3 (A Sinfield 1981); University of Cambridge for Document three from pp 77–78 C Craig, J Rubery, R Tarling and F Wilkinson (1982); Mr A Walker for Document twenty-three from pp 71–72 *Disability of Britain* by A Walker and P Townsend (eds), Martin Robertson (1981).

Chapter one
THE SOCIAL DIVISION OF LABOUR

The distribution of work is a major source of inequality in Britain. Not only do some people have it while others do not, but some are paid well for it while others are paid poorly or not at all. Differentials in work status and rewards abound. People entering the labour market face a differentiated job structure and their position within that structure depends not only on industrial and commercial factors but on socially determined criteria which serve to circumscribe the job choices available to some. What follows is not so much concerned with changes in the industrial and occupational distribution of employment nor with the growth and decline of different sectors, as with the distribution of work between different groups in society and the growth of a reserve of labour available for what appears to be a decreasing number of jobs. Social factors such as attitudes towards women and black people and beliefs about the capacities of people with disabilities help determine the constituents of this reserve. Certain groups are, therefore, in a weak position in the labour market, which has implications both for the individuals concerned and for policy making. Some reasons for their vulnerability will be suggested, showing how policy is often ineffective and reinforces their weaknesses rather than building on their strengths. This vulnerability is most often manifested in low pay and status, and unemployment.

Since low-paid workers are most susceptible to unemployment the two problems often go hand in hand and are 'part of the same continuum of labour market disadvantage' (Low Pay Review 1980). For most unemployed people being out of work is a temporary if frequent state of affairs which normally lasts only a few months (Metcalfe 1980; Daniel 1981a, 1981b). The unemployed as a whole tend to be drawn disproportionately from the unskilled and low-paid. In his study of poverty, Townsend found that the likelihood of unemployment rose sharply with falling occupational status and that unemployed men were twice as likely as continously employed men to have had poor working conditions and were more likely to have had a lower income (Townsend 1979: 604, 615). In addition, certain groups such as black people, young people, the elderly, the disabled, and women are over-represented among the unemployed relative to their size in the population. Consequently while individuals flow in and out of work, on aggregate they tend to be drawn from the same social groupings. In this sense they form a pool or a stock of accessible labour. The importance of the individual variation may explain why the unemployed do not easily rebel. It also belies the belief that the work ethic is conveniently fading away (Daniel 1981b). The concentration of unemployment on certain workers is not peculiar to Britain. A recent OECD report suggests that a deeply entrenched characteristic of OECD countries is that long-term and recurrent unemployment compounds 'the labour market problems of some members of the groups which traditionally bear an above average burden of unemployment, i.e. youth, older workers, migrants' (OECD 1982: 83, 93).

The amount of work available may be determined by economic demand and the ability to generate opportunities for employment but the allocation and organisation of work is influenced by institutional barriers which structure and stratify the labour force. People entering the labour market find that their position reflects a social hierarchy which determines their security or insecurity of employment. Various attempts have been made to explain inequalities in the labour market and hence at work. Two approaches will be examined here: human capital theory, which focuses attention on the effect of individual decisions on employment status, i.e. on the supply of labour, and structured or segmented labour market theory, which focuses on historical and institutional factors that influence the demand for labour. The concept of a dual labour market will be considered separately from segmentation theories which have been described as 'radical'. Within this second approach it will be argued that certain groups face discrimination in society which serves to confine and legitimise their position within those parts of the labour market which have greater insecurity, worse working conditions and lower pay. A brief discussion of the concept of a labour market will precede this.

A LABOUR MARKET

The concept of a labour market usually assumes that one can talk

of buying and selling labour and that there will be a demand for
and a supply of labour – both of which will affect and be affected
by the price of labour, i.e. earnings. Conventional theory suggests
that jobs are differentiated by the income they command and this
is determined by the quality of labour on offer, by the qualities
which each worker offers in terms of his/her skills, productivity and
so on.

Comparisons can be made with any market for a commodity
wherein workers represent the goods and their wages, the price. So
long as wages are flexible the market is held to be self-regulating.
However, the view of a competitive and perfectly functioning labour market no longer has much force in the face of government
intervention, trade union activity and employers' monopoly power,
all of which influence the buying and selling of labour. On a simple
level the market is not a free one and is influenced in a number of
different ways. First, the supply and demand for labour is not always easily and quickly adjustable. It can be restrained by: (*a*) a
lack of easy geographical mobility because of the nature of the housing market; (*b*) restricted entry into certain trades or professions;
(*c*) the need to undergo training for certain jobs; (*d*) being unable
to transfer certain rights which have accrued over time such as pension rights; and (*e*) a lack of child care or other facilities (Fulop
1971).

As a result of these factors governments can and have intervened
in the market to overcome these restrictions, e.g. by offering incentives to move geographically, by training facilities and in other
ways. This kind of intervention requires some forward planning
and projections of need and can also influence patterns of employment. More substantial government intervention includes the introduction of statutory minimum wages or statutory and voluntary
incomes policies.

Secondly, the contract that is made between the buyer and the
seller of labour reflects more than economic behaviour. The price
for work (and its products as well) is not only determined by the
interaction of supply and demand but by moral and social forces
(Routh *et al*. 1980: 4). Social values and conventions influence earnings paid, fringe benefits and working environments. This is nowhere better exemplified than in the pay and working conditions
of professional workers in contrast to, say, skilled workers. Wootton gives some useful examples of the esteem which doctors and
judges are accorded (Wootton 1962: 128) [doc 1].

Thirdly, the labour market is also an area where the struggle for control over labour takes place. Policies which mediate between employment and unemployment, e.g. the Redundancy Payments Scheme, the Job Release Scheme, the Young Workers Scheme and Equal Opportunities Policy (dealt with in detail in later chapters) both affect the supply and demand for labour and increase or lessen the vulnerability of certain workers. In promulgating various policies like these, the state responds to pressures both from labour to introduce protective, regulatory policies in the labour market and at work, and from employers to facilitate their control over the process of production, including the entry to and exit from work [doc 2].

HUMAN CAPITAL THEORY

Human capital theory is a useful example of the view that attributes disadvantage in the labour market to individual decisions or characteristics. Investments in the education and training required to enter certain jobs as well as innate ability are seen to determine the rate of return the individual receives from his/her job. The labour market is assumed to be competitive and functioning perfectly. In terms of this theory (which is usually most closely associated with Gary Becker) differences in earnings can be explained by seeing them as the return obtained on capital invested in acquiring certain skills and levels of education. It takes as its model rational 'economic man' who decides how much to invest in education, training and obtaining certain work experience – and who is subsequently rewarded or receives a return depending on the amount invested in the first place. Therefore wages or economic rewards for labour are determined by individual decisions and by innate ability. These 'investment' decisions can be said not only to influence future monetary rewards but one's propensity to unemployment. They include 'investments' in information about employment opportunities as well as in education and training. For instance, 'a better job might be found by spending money on employment agencies and situation wanted ads, . . . by talking to friends and visiting firms' as well as by moving geographically if necessary (Becker 1975: 39). In summary, certain forms of employment disadvantage can be attributed to lack of education or training or effort to obtain them. Undertaking such education and training is a cost which will be compensated for in higher earnings later.

Human capital theory makes two important assumptions which have been questioned. Firstly, all individuals are seen to have the same opportunities and are, therefore, at similar starting points. It has already been suggested, however, that social hierarchies severely restrict the freedom of opportunity of some people. The effect of poverty on the life chances of individuals has been well documented. Aside from this, Wootton suggests that, given the existence of free education and a free health service since the 1940s, more people should have been able to obtain human capital, thereby reducing differences in earnings. No such reduction, however, has occurred (Wootton 1962). A second assumption is that earnings are determined by economic forces. This suggests that differences in earnings should reflect only the differential required to compensate for the training undergone. Some North American evidence has shown this differential to be much greater, suggesting that differences in earnings need to be attributed to factors other than education and training (Atkinson 1975: 83–6). The equation between earnings and the level of skill have been shown to be misleading. They can be easily confounded by factors such as sexual and racial discrimination (Pond 1983). It is also extremely difficult to measure the productivity of a judge or the chairperson of British Steel against a skilled worker at British Steel, for instance, in order to arrive at an explanation of the very considerable wage differential between them. Neither does the high productivity of a whole enterprise appear to be reflected in the salaries and wages it pays. Instead, there appears to exist a 'culture' of earnings which is socially based and determined by factors such as class, sex, age or race.

DUAL LABOUR MARKET THEORY

In contrast to human capital theory, exponents of the dual labour market theory tend to pay more attention to the role played by the demand for labour in determining wages than to the supply of labour. Looking statistically at the distribution of earnings, they do not follow the patterns of most measures of 'ability' (such as IQ) or of educational achievement. A normal frequency curve is one where the majority of the things being measured are clustered about in the middle with a few extremes at either end. But the distribution of income or earnings is different. It is very unequally distributed and does not appear to reflect differences in either ability or education, as human capital theorists would have us believe. Moving on from these empirical observations, a number of writers then proposed an alternative theory to explain the way in which economic rewards for labour were so unequally determined. There are a number of theories that fall into this category, of which the dual labour market is one. The hypothesis of the dual labour market is that the allocation of job opportunities has to be understood in terms of a division of the labour market into a primary and a secondary sector. The primary sector contains good jobs which offer relatively high wages, good working conditions, substantial job security, chances of career advancement and a fair deal in the administration of work rules. The secondary sector has poor jobs which offer inferior social status, low wages and poor working conditions. The jobs are dead-end ones and insecure, often involving a capricious relationship between supervisor and worker. Particular groups such as women and ethnic minorities could find themselves in this sector (Bosanquet and Doeringer 1973; Doeringer and Piore 1975; Piore 1979).

A dual labour market is also associated with the concept of an internal labour market whereby on-the-job training requires entry into the labour force to be restricted to the lower levels. One explanation for the evolution of internal labour markets is that with increasing technological development certain firms are seen to require a labour force that is specifically and highly skilled and represents a valuable investment from the employer's perspective. The stability of such employees is, therefore, encouraged by high wages and good working conditions. In such firms, an internal labour market operates whereby recruitment and promotion occurs within the organisation. In contrast to this 'primary' sector is a 'secondary' sector in the economy which is not so advanced technologically and does not have such stable product markets. Relying on their competiveness and frequently sub-contracting from the primary sector, firms in this sector require a labour force that is flexible and inexpensive. These firms are characterised by paying low wages and offering poor working conditions (Doeringer and Piore 1971).

The hypothesis of a dual labour market was initially designed to explain the problems of ghetto labour markets in the USA in the 1960s. It was suggested that racial discrimination perpetuated the segmentation of the labour market into a primary and secondary sector by restricting certain workers to the latter. In other words they were not restricted because of their education or skills but because they were black (or female in some cases). The theory suggests that a dichotomy of the labour market has evolved over time into a primary and a secondary sector in which quite different rules apply. Initially applied to the United States by two economists, Michael Piore and Peter Doeringer, the theory has also been applied to parts of Europe and Britain (Piore 1980; Bosanquet and Doeringer 1973). Dual labour market theory was motivated by a need to explain a number of phenomena, among which were the persistence of poverty and income inequality, the failure of educational and training programmes to affect income or occupation, discrimination in the labour market, certain trends in unemployment and the growth of monopolies or market imperfections (Cain 1976: 1217–21).

The description of the two sectors does not answer the question of why they arose or developed in the first place, although a view of how the labour market works is implicit in the internal labour market theory. Piore suggests that the root of the dual labour market lies in the variability and uncertainty which is found in all modern industrial economies. It represents a way of solving or responding to this uncertainty by distributing its costs between certain groups. He suggests that in earlier times labour as a whole was made to bear the brunt of fluctuations in the economy and was simply hired and fired as needed, whereas nowadays a portion of the labour force shares the privileged position of capital and a smaller sector, the secondary sector, bears the brunt of periods when unemployment increases (Piore 1980). He argues that four principal explanations have been advanced to explain the origins of dualism (p. 383). These are a useful illustration of the very different implications which can be drawn from the concept of a dual labour market.

1. One argues that when employers invest in their workers, e.g. in training them, it becomes more efficient to keep them on as a stable force to maximise production. They then become a 'quasi-fixed' factor of production.

2. A second explanation sees the primary sector as developing out of a national employment contract in which employers, in return for certain wage concessions, agree to stabilise the variability of wages and employment.

3. Another argument is that this has been forced on employers by the efforts of trade union organisation and activity which have won for their members good conditions of work and high wages either through collective activity or through the political and legislative process.

4. A fourth interpretation is it results from employers' efforts to divide a united working class.

The bias of the first and second explanations is again rational economic behaviour that is based on a consensus about efficiency. The third and fourth, by contrast, implicitly suggest a more fundamental conflict of interest between workers and employers. The first argument implies that dualism arises because it is economically efficient. In this sense Piore argues that it can be compatible with human capital theory. Having initially espoused a view of dualism and internal labour markets which was consensus based, Piore's later study of the development of dualism in Italy, France and the United States leads him to reject it in favour of the third explanation. He suggests that labour militancy leads to the development and expansion of the secondary sector rather than the contract referred to in the second explanation. This development occurs in the following way: in depressed economic conditions, as well as in periods of labour unrest, job security, such as control on dismissal, the right to organise and the negotiation of seniority rights, becomes a central bargaining issue. Such rights, however, lead employers to search for a means of restoring the flexibility they need so that wage costs can be adjusted in periods of economic fluctuation. Methods of work such as sub-contracting, hiring temporary workers and plant decentralisation lead to the development of a secondary sector. Employers also become active in recruiting certain kinds of labour – 'acquiescent' workers such as women, youth, migrants and rural workers – to ensure that the secondary sector is viable. According to Piore

The migrants – foreign and domestic – the rural workers, and the women are attractive precisely because they belong to another socio-economic structure and view industrial employment as a temporary adjunct to their primary roles. They are willing to take temporary jobs because they see their commitment to these jobs as temporary, and they are able to bear the flux and uncertainty of the industrial economy because they have traditional economic activities upon which to fall back.

It is at this point that Piore comes close to implying that the development of a secondary sector is again a rational response to economic fluctuation at the same time serving the needs of certain workers. The characteristics of secondary workers are seen to be something the economic system makes use of but is not responsible for. Similarly, in an earlier work he refers to the bad habits and attitudes of secondary workers such as poor timekeeping. Others have viewed the secondary workforce as being partly a product of the system itself and as being manipulated in order to stabilise and legitimise the economic structure with all its inequalities, providing the flexibility required to be able to extend or discard the workforce

9

as the market is prosperous or depressed. Rubery, for instance, also argues that increased specialisation breaks down traditional barriers of skill, making for the threatening potential of a workforce with common interests. Labour market segmentation is one of the ways of dividing the workforce under the new circumstances. These later theories of the labour market are more thoroughly grounded in a view of conflict between employers and employees. They attempt to 'place the dual labour market theory in an historical and ideological framework' (Rubery 1978). It is to a consideration of these that we now turn.

'RADICAL' AND STRUCTURED LABOUR MARKET THEORY

Certain writers originally associated with dual labour market theory began to integrate the idea of a segmented labour market into what they termed a more radical economic analysis. This was done by looking at the historical and institutional causes of segmentation. 'Radical' and structured labour market theory has come to be associated with two schools of thought on either side of the Atlantic: David Gordon and his colleagues in the United States and the Labour Studies Group at the University of Cambridge in England. Both groups dispute the neoclassical view of the operation of the labour market that gives the relative efficiency of labour predominance in explaining the pay and position of individuals. Gordon *et al*. explain segmentation almost wholly in terms of it being a strategy for control of labour which is critical in understanding the forces affecting earnings. The British group are concerned with segmentation mainly as an explanation for the permanence and pervasiveness of low pay. Because of the different ways in which both groups approach segmentation they will be dealt with separately.

The movement beyond a dual labour market analysis represents more than a simple replacement with a description of a multiplicity of segments. According to Gordon, six clusters of generalisations or hypotheses about capitalist economies underlie the new 'radical' approach to labour market analysis. Firstly, all societies are characterised by a mode of production which reflects the social relations between people resulting from their connection with the process of production. Secondly, this social division of labour creates a division of society into economic classes, membership of which constrains an individual's activities. However, there are objective divisions among the working class' production experience. Thirdly, there is a driving force by owners of capital to increase their share

The social division of labour

of capital which dominates human need, i.e. capital accumulation. Fourthly, a set of institutions in society, such as the wage system, define and determine the nature and content of social relations among individuals. Fifthly, the state is dominated by the capitalist class and operates ultimately to serve its interests. Finally, there are certain contradictions within capitalism that generate tendencies which are fundamentally in conflict with the laws upon which it is based. These include worker alienation from his/her product and the individualistic ideology which induces workers to compete when the division of labour requires them to co-operate (Gordon 1972: 56). The segmentation of jobs serves the first two hypotheses by limiting the spread of working-class consciousness and solidarity. The hierarchies it creates at work establish an alternative incentive of status to replace the wage incentive. These general hypotheses, however, do formulate a radical theory of income determination and distribution, according to Gordon, and of the distribution of the work itself.

Gordon *et al.* argue that the emergence of monopoly capitalism early this century was accompanied by an increasingly homogeneous and proletarianised workforce which led to an upsurge of labour unrest. To meet this threat of strong worker organisation employers, they argue, actively and consciously fostered labour market segmentation. This was done by establishing a rigidly graded hierarchy of jobs, entry into which was controlled by internal labour markets – supported by union demands for seniority rights. In addition, concentration of ownership gave large corporations power to control and stabilise product market competition. This enabled them to offer greater stability of employment which in turn allowed corporate managers to 'organise job tasks more systematically in order to permit more control, greater differentiation among workers' tasks and greater fragmentation of informal work groups' (Gordon *et al.* 1982: 173). This control, dominance in product markets and greater planning capacity increased even further after the Second World War. Bureaucratic control was improved to ensure as much 'worker compliance and productivity' as possible (p. 187). The characteristic large corporation is called a 'core' firm. Small firms working in restricted markets are called 'peripheral' firms and are those providing secondary jobs. They survive because they are unprofitable for the large firms to acquire but profitable as areas to which large firms can transfer business risks. Some advantages are that 'sub-contracting to the periphery increases the potential flexibility of operations; the periphery provides a low-cost alternative

11

for the maintenance of excess productive capacity in slack periods; and core firms can avoid potential union problems and save on employee fringe benefits (p. 191). Gordon *et al.* state that their theory of dualism refers to units of capital, not to whole industries. Because labour market divisions represent historical tendencies, jobs cannot be exhaustively categorised into two or three segments. Therefore, many jobs occupy either intermediate positions or are as yet unaffected by segmentation. The hypothesis they advance is that 'the evolving structure of labor processes and labor markets [creates] increasingly differentiated labor segments' (Gordon *et al.* 1982: 166).

The Cambridge group are concerned with the strong emphasis given by Gordon *et al.* to the actions and motivations of employers in explaining the development of a structured labour market and the relative neglect of the role of worker organisations. They acknowledge the important role played by attempts to control the labour force but suggest that the analysis must be carried out in terms of a continuous struggle for control between employer and worker (Rubery 1978: 244). This entails a consideration of efforts to control labour at the level of the firm or industry (such as the introduction of new technology) rather than seeing the capitalist class as intent on devising a long-term strategy to divide and rule. They suggest that stratified employment systems are as much the result of worker strategies to create secure working conditions as employer strategies to divide and control the labour force. An attempt is made by the British group to develop an analysis of labour market structure in which the role of worker and professional or other organisations is given greater due. This has led to greater concern about the supply of labour and control over the supply of labour which worker organisations attempt. This control is affected by many of the policies dealt with in later chapters, such as the inhibiting effect of the family wage on female labour (Ch. 5) and the restrictions on immigrant labour (Ch. 9). The displacement of labour as skills become redundant and monopoly capitalism develops destroys jobs and skills. The competition for jobs reduces the bargaining power of labour. In acting defensively to protect themselves, unionised workers may act to the detriment of other unorganised workers. At the same time monopoly capitalism is seen to create an increasing number of low skilled, low productivity occupations (Rubery 1978: 266–7).

According to the Labour Studies Group, segmentation needs to have various multi-causal explanations based on 'the structure of technology, product markets, control over the labour process and labour supply conditions' (Rubery and Wilkinson 1981). The primary and secondary sectors as outlined by Piore are seen to be 'ideal types' of different industrial sectors distinguished by modern and traditional technologies, stable and declining product markets and market power and weakness respectively. In reality, both sectors are seen to have a share of monotonous, unskilled jobs. No simple dichotomisation of the labour market based either on job content or worker characteristics is made. The main distinction between the two sectors, it is suggested, is possibly simply a strongly organised workforce and the ability of the firm to pay high wages (Craig *et al.* 1982: 80).

In their study of five industries, Craig *et al.* posit two causes of low pay and status. The first cause is to be found in the industrial structure. The intensity of product market competition for some products constrains the ability of the industry to pay good wages. (The corollary of this would be higher paying industries which are characterised by considerable concentration of ownership. The power of large firms in their product market permits them to pay consistently above what a notional labour market might dictate – not because their labour has above average productivity but because the firm has above average revenue per unit of output.) Secondary firms cannot insulate themselves from a decline in demand. Primary firms do so by shifting risks to sub-contractors or by moving into other product markets. The second cause of low pay is said to be found in the low labour market status of the workers employed. Although 'the number of good jobs in the economy is mainly determined by the development of the industrial and technological structure largely independent of labour supply' (Craig *et al.* 1982: 77), social processes are at work generating a supply of labour for secondary sector employment. This structures the supply of labour to meet the structured demand for labour [doc 3]. The main reason why workers are available for low-paid jobs is the shortage of high-paid jobs, stemming both from industrial developments and worker pressure to create secure employment sectors. But the position of individuals also derives from the social or family structure which influences their aspirations and opportunities. This is well illustrated by the job aspirations of women, the expected standard of living of young people and the restricted opportunities for immigrant or black workers. While acknowledging this, Craig *et al.* maintain that a worker's social, sexual or racial position does not explain the structure of the labour market independently from the supply side. Consequently they suggest that these inequalities could 'conceivably be removed by the appropriate policy' (p. 90).

These inequalities, however, have been largely resilient to the numerous policies enacted to overcome them. In some instances it can be argued that labour market policies (such as many of those outlined in Ch. 4) implicitly accept and adopt human capital theory as their underlying rationale. Examples of the failure of anti-discrimination policy (such as the Equal Pay Act and the Race Relations Act) are legion. Even policies of positive discrimination (such as the quota scheme for disabled people) obstinately fail to serve their purpose. The line between introducing compensatory policies to offset discrimination and policies which aim to overcome personal inadequacy often becomes blurred in their administration.

More importantly, institutions such as the family have created roles for men and women which directly affect their employment opportunities. Free of domestic labour, male labour is preferable to employers. Female labour is available at lower wages because domestic responsibilities limit their availability and flexibility both geographically and in time. The implications for policy of this one example of institutional barriers to employment are profound. It can be argued that anti-discrimination policy in the labour market alone will be insufficient to remove them unless combined with other measures of redistribution and child-care provision – often more familiar areas in the struggle for social policy provision. Such changes in family and other social institutions could have an important effect on the supply of labour and on expectations of reward and self-value.

Chapter two
PATTERNS OF EMPLOYMENT

INTRODUCTION

In recent years certain changes have occurred in patterns of employment and unemployment which have led to an increase in the number of vulnerable workers in the labour force – in terms of their pay, their bargaining strength, their conditions of work and their access to work itself. Many of these patterns reflect socially and politically determined phenomena both inside and outside the labour market. Some of the most notable changes to have occurred over the last two decades have been the growth in the service sector, the growth of female employment, the growth in part-time employment and, more recently, the growth of unemployment. There have been other changes such as the decrease in overtime working and the large increase in short-time working but these have generally been a reflection of growing unemployment and, to a lesser extent, a result of trade union gains for better working conditions. The nature and implications of some of these changes will be outlined in this chapter except for unemployment, which will be dealt with separately in Chapter three.

The composition of the economically active* population of approximately twenty six million people is shown in Table 2.1 by employment status, sex, and marital status of the women.

SECTOR CHANGES

Most modern economies have shown a shift in employment from industry to the service sector. This is partly due to aspirations for

---

* The terms 'economically active' and 'working population' are used here in their traditional (albeit very unsatisfactory) sense of referring to those in or seeking waged labour.

Table 2.1. Economically active persons aged 16 and over by employment status, sex and, for women, marital status, Great Britain 1981

Employment status	Men (%)	Married women (%)	Other women (%)	All persons economically active (%)
In employment	90.1	93.2	87.3	90.5
Employees	78.0	87.1	83.8	81.2
Full-time	74.7	39.5	66.7	64.5
Part-time	2.3	46.8	16.0	15.7
Self-employed	11.1	5.4	2.4	8.4
No reply	1.0	0.7	1.1	0.9
Unemployed	9.9	6.8	12.7	9.5
Seeking work	9.4	6.3	11.6	8.9
Waiting to start work	0.2	0.2	0.4	0.2
Temporarily sick or on holiday	0.3	0.3	0.7	0.4
All economically active	100	100	100	100

Source: *Labour Force Survey, 1981* OPCS

better social welfare which could be paid for as industrial efficiency increased and partly due to the expansion of banking, finance and insurance. Another reason may be that in times of recession, service sector employment can be readily expanded without capital investment. Since 1961 the increase in the service sector in the United Kingdom has been higher than in the USA, West Germany, France, Italy or Japan (Bacon and Eltis 1978). In 1979 the growth in service sector employment began to reverse but the fall was moderate in relation to that in other sectors. Whereas in 1960 manufacturing had held 40% of total employment, this had dropped by the end of 1981 to 28%.

The 1981 *Labour Force Survey* shows the distribution of employees according to the Standard Industrial Classification as illustrated in Table 2.2. These do not include the self-employed who, when taken into account, increase the proportion of people in construction and distribution and decrease the proportion in manufacturing.

Within the different sectors there are differences with regard to the changes in male and female employment. During 1981, male employment in manufacturing dropped by 7.6% as against 8.6% of female employment. However, in services, male employment

Table 2.2. Persons aged 16 and over in employment by industry, Great Britain

Industry division	Employees (%)
0 Agriculture, forestry and fishing	1.5
1 Energy and water supply industry	3.6
2 Extraction of minerals and ores, other than fuels, manufacture of metals, mineral products and chemicals	4.4
3 Metal goods, engineering and vehicle industries	13.7
4 Other manufacturing industries	11.9
5 Construction	5.4
6 Distribution, hotels and catering, repairs	17.2
7 Transport and communications	6.5
8 Banking, finance and insurance, business services and leasing	7.5
9 Other services	27.1
No reply/Inadequately described/working outside UK	1.2
All industries	100

Source: *Labour Force Survey, 1981*, OPCS.

dropped by 2.6% as against 2.1% of female employment (MSC, 1982d). There is clearly an interrelationship between the growth of the service sector, of female employment and of part-time work. Most part-time work is in the service sector. Most employed women are in the service sector and the majority of part-time jobs are filled by women.

FEMALE EMPLOYMENT

Over 40% of people in paid employment are women. At the turn of the century only 29% of the labour force were women, the proportion increasing slowly until the 1960s when the increase reached its present level. The increase was concentrated among married women and women over the age of thirty-five. It was not an increase of *working* women as such but one of officially recognised economic activity undertaken by women. Housework and child care are not (and have never been in this century) acknowledged forms of economic activity. The view that they are part of the more 'normal' female role is partly responsible for many women, especially married women, failing to register as unemployed. For instance, according to the OPCS monitor *Labour Force Survey*, 40.9% of married women and 24.8% of other women failed to register as unemployed compared to 9.7% of men (*Labour Force Survey* 1981: 18). The expansion of the female labour force is almost all to be found in the growth of part-time jobs. Women's paid employment is usually structured around their domestic work and child-care responsibilities. This has undoubtedly led to the growth of part-time employment. There are important differences with regard to married and non-married women. Economic activity rates of the latter decline fairly steadily with age while married women show a fall in waged economic activity rates between the ages of 25 and 34, increasing again in later years and then declining substantially after 60 years (Elliot *et al.* 1981). Explanations for these patterns will be explored further in Chapter five.

Women workers generally tend to work in low status, poorly paid jobs. Much of this is due to the part-time nature of their work. There is a legal distinction between those who work less than 16 hours a week and those who work more which creates disadvantages for the former. According to the *Labour Force Survey* 1.3% of men work less than 16 hours a week compared to 21.8% of married women and 9.9% of other women. Working less than 8 hours brings even greater disadvantages and here too the sexual differences are considerable: 0.6% for men, 6.6% for married women and 5.1% for other women (*OPCS Monitor* 1981: 17).

Despite a growing number of people of working age, both male and female employed populations have begun to decline. This has been more marked for females, with the employed population falling by nearly a quarter of a million in the first half of 1981 (MSC 1982d). This is despite the increase in part-time employment and may indicate that women more easily lose or leave their paid jobs in periods of recession.

Although women are now participating in employment to a far greater extent then they were 20 years ago, there is a marked difference between their occupations and male occupations (Hakim 1978). Throughout the 1970s, one quarter of all jobs were typically female, the remainder typically male. This 'horizontal' occupational segregation was matched by 'vertical' occupational segregation, i.e. people doing more skilled, responsible and better paid jobs within the same job categories. But there is some evidence of a decline in the latter between 1973 and 1977 whereafter the decline reversed, suggesting that the recession may be affecting the gains made by women in the labour force (Hakim 1981).

Table 2.3 illustrates the extent of vertical segregation between males and females in paid employment.

The expansion of women's paid employment occurred in poorly unionised sectors of the labour market, i.e. distribution, hotels and catering. The greatest concentration of women workers is currently in these sectors and in other service sectors. Much of the evidence regarding the segregation and distribution of women's employment reinforces the earlier contention that patterns of employment reflect socially and politically determined decisions in the labour market which in turn lead to disadvantage and inequality.

PART-TIME WORK

The growth of part-time employment reflects an ongoing and what appears to be a permanent change in the composition of the labour forces of most EEC countries. There are many ways of defining part-time work. One is the ILO definition of it being 'regular voluntary work carried out during working hours distinctly shorter than normal'. At the other extreme from this very generalised catch-all definition is the practice of adopting the legal hourly definition. In Britain the government's definition is 30 hours or less per week, which is the one adopted by virtually all government

Table 2.3. Occupation of persons aged 16 and over in employment by sex and, for women, marital status, Great Britain 1981

Occupation	All persons (%)	Men (%)	Women All (%)	Women Married (%)	Women Non-married (%)
Managerial and professional	27	30	22	22	21
Clerical and related	16	6	30	28	36
Other non-manual occupations	7	6	10	9	10
Craft and similar occupations including foremen in processing production, repairing, etc.	18	27	5	5	5
General labourers	2	2	0	0	0
Other manual occupations	31	29	33	36	27
All occupations (thousands)	23,290	13,962	9,328	6,208	3,120

Source: *Labour Force Survey 1981*, OPCS May 1982.

surveys. However, there is another implicit definition which relates to the protection offered to part-time workers. In 1977 the Employment Protection Act extended to some part-timers the same employment rights as full-time workers (Hurstfield 1978: 56). At that time, people working 16 or more hours per week, or who had worked between 8 and 16 hours per week in the same job for at least five years, were given rights such as redundancy payments, unfair dismissal compensation, written contracts, maternity rights and maternity leave with reinstatement. The Act in effect created two classes of part-time work: the protected and the unprotected. The rationale for this was to exclude employees who have so tenuous a link with their employer that the latter should not be expected to have the same obligations towards them. In the years immediately following the Act there has been a steady decline in the proportion of female part-time workers working more than 16 hours with a corresponding increase in the proportion working less than 8 hours and between 8 and 16 hours a week.

Both in absolute numbers and in proportions of the labour force part-time work has grown in most EEC countries in recent years (Mallier and Rosser 1980). In 1975 there were 10.9 million part-time workers in the European Community as a whole representing 9.4% of the total employed labour force, 1.9% of male and 23.6% of female employment (Robinson 1979). By 1977 this had increased to 2.6% of male and 26.4% of female employment (Mallier and Rosser 1980). In all countries there is a strong predominance of women in part-time employment, in particular married women. There is also a divergence in most countries in the age patterns of men and women working part-time, with men tending to be concentrated in the over-55s while 75.7% of women working part-time are concentrated in the middle age ranges of 24–54. In all three factors, namely the size of the part-time labour force and the sex and age ratios, Britain shows an extreme pattern in relation to most other EEC members. In 1975 Britain's part-time labour force was 16.9% of all employment, 2.2% of male and 40.9% of female employment, as compared to 9.4%, 1.9% and 23.6% in the EEC as a whole. Married women accounted for 88.3% in Britain as compared to 85.1% in the EEC. Male part-timers aged over 55 constituted 81.9% of the total as compared to 46.8% in the EEC (Robinson 1979). There is another aspect in which Britain stands out which may be related to its employment protection legislation. In all EEC countries the proportion of people working fewer than 10 hours a week was 8.4%, whereas in Britain it was 12.7%.

It seems clear that while part-time work is increasing generally in the industrialised countries of Europe, this trend is particularly marked in Britain. More and more recognition is being given to this phenomenon (MSC 1982d; Clark 1982; Robinson 1979; Mallier and Rosser 1980). Increasingly questions are being asked about the quality of the work and the working conditions under which it is being undertaken (Hurstfield 1978, 1980; Sedley 1980; Leicester 1982). Some of the explanations put forward for this increase are the following: that it is due to fundamental changes in the industrial structure; that part-time work has now become a source of cheap labour; that the secondary sector to which they belong as marginal workers has expanded; that part-time work is a response to trade union demands for a reduction in the working week. There may be some truth in all of these explanations.

The expansion of the service sector has already been noted. Mallier and Rosser note that part-time employment has always been less common in manufacturing than in service industries and suggest that, because of this bias, the inter-industry structural change itself caused a substantial part of the increase in part-time employment. Presumably since women have been less predominant in manufacturing, this would also account for their bias in part-time work along with their own socially generated needs. However, Mallier and Rosser do not accept that an increase in the supply of part-time labour, i.e. an increase in the number of women wanting part-time work, would in itself have increased the availability of such jobs. Other structural changes which may have affected part-time work are the decline in manual work and the increase in non-manual work due to mechanisation and automation which have offered more opportunities for part-time work (Mallier and Rosser 1980).

A number of factors in employment generally and within part-time work specifically have combined to make part-time work more attractive to employers, partly because of its low cost. According to the *New Earnings Survey 1981*, 64% of part-time female manual workers were in professional and scientific services or miscellaneous services while 77% of part-time female non-manual workers were in the distributive trades, professional and scientific services and miscellaneous services. More than three-quarters of these manual workers and the non-manual workers in the distributive trades earned less than £1.80 an hour and a half earned less than £1.60 an hour. Even so, these figures underestimate the true extent of low-paid part-time workers since the *New Earnings Survey* bases its sample on national insurance numbers. In a reply to a parliamentary question in the House of Commons in May 1980, the government estimated that one-third of all part-time workers had earnings below the level of taxation and national insurance contributions. This means that about 1.5 million part-time workers, 80% of whom are women, fall outside the national insurance system (Pond and MacLennan 1981). The implications of this are that the NES estimates of the wages of part-time workers are too low. More significantly, by having a lower earnings limit, the national insurance system depresses wages by providing an incentive to employers to keep wages below the level at which both they and their employees will pay insurance contributions. This may have been offset slightly in 1975 when the employer's contribution changed from a flat rate to a percentage of earnings. The tax system may have encouraged the supply of cheap part-time workers by making it more advantageous for a family to replace the male's highly taxed overtime with the female's low paid part-time wage which might be untaxed and ineligible for insurance contributions. In the short term this arrangement may suit families by removing the unsociable hours of overtime and providing an untaxed source of income. In the long run, however, exclusion from national insurance and the poor working conditions of many part-time jobs may outweigh the advantages.

A further way in which part-time labour has become a low-cost means of employment has already been mentioned and that is its exclusion from protective legislation. In addition to this it is often easier to exclude part-timers from some of the fringe benefits which full-time workers receive such as sickness benefit, holiday entitlement and pension rights and there is evidence that they are denied these (Hurstfield 1978; Lonsdale 1980; Leicester 1982; Mallier and Rosser 1980). Mallier and Rosser suggest that changes in policy such as the removal of Selective Employment Tax in 1972 encouraged the growth of part-time employment too by removing the incentive which that tax contained to employ full-timers.

Given the advantages of part-time work in terms of cost for employers and in terms of flexibility for married women with children, it is no longer sufficient to perceive such work as marginal. It seems unlikely that part-time workers will disappear or that they will be replaced by presently unemployed full-time workers if or when the economy picks up. They are too profitable for some and too essential for others: namely employers and families with children and/or low incomes. As such they are part of an expanding secondary sector with its current role of providing a plentiful reserve of low-paid workers. The real question for policy makers in the future will concern the conditions of that work. Ironically, one of the factors aiding the acceleration of part-time employment may well have been trade union demands for a shorter working week and reduced overtime and feminist demands for employment which is more appropriate to the needs of people with child-care responsibilities (EOC 1981 a and b; Coote and Campbell 1982). In assessing the pitfalls of exploitative part-time work, its real value as an alternative employment-form should not be lost. Ways of losing the bath water while saving the baby might include legislation ensuring parity between full and part-time workers and widening opportunities for part-time work such that it becomes more available for men and is not restricted to low-paid unskilled work often in small non-unionised firms.

Chapter three
THE UNEQUAL BURDEN OF UNEMPLOYMENT

INTRODUCTION

When considering the extent and costs of unemployment as well as the responses to it in terms of policy, two important issues need to be taken into account:
1. The factual position regarding the number of jobs available, the number of people out of jobs and what these seemingly irrefutable statistics leave out.
2. The beliefs people have about how many jobs are available, why people are unemployed and what their social security benefits are.

Unemployment has been increasing rapidly since the mid-1970s. This increase has occurred concurrently with a growing acceptance that a society with four or five million unemployed is inevitable and inexorable. Adrian Sinfield puts it this way: 'From the deepening gloom has emerged a consensus that the days of "full employment" are not only over; they are now . . . a part of social history' [doc 4]. In rejecting this view, he goes on to say that 'our complacent failure to recognise the need to maintain the struggle to achieve full employment has left us far too vulnerable to the cries for its abandonment' (Sinfield 1981: 4). However, despite this, there is an increasing concern that people on the dole should not be there or are simply scrounging on the rest of us. So we need to look at why these seemingly contradictory attitudes or beliefs occur. But first the actual state of affairs [doc 5].

DEFINING UNEMPLOYMENT

The compilation of data and statistics on employment and labour matters began about 100 years ago and can be said to have been a response both to the needs of capitalism and to calls for social welfare. Today, information on unemployment is only one of many such statistics including earnings, hours of work, prices, output, industrial injuries and more. Statistics, however, require definitions and nowhere more so than in the area of unemployment. The official figures for unemployment usually tell us more by what they leave out than by what they include. Two misleading concepts are evident in labour statistics. These are the definition of employment as being paid labour and the concept of economically active and inactive people. Both exclude the large and important areas of domestic labour and caring labour. The latter refers to those members of the population, mainly women, in full-time but unpaid jobs of caring for children and dependent adults about whom increasing evidence is emerging (Finch and Groves 1980; 1983; EOC 1982a).

These exclusions need to be taken into account in any consideration of the monthly publication by the Department of Employment of the numbers of unemployed people. Likewise at various other times during the year when it publishes the number of unemployed by industry, occupation, geographical area, age and duration. As well as administrative records such as registration for work or benefit, statistics on unemployment can also be obtained from labour force surveys. Such surveys have the advantage of including people who may not be in the administrative count. Until October 1982 the official count covered people who were actually registered as unemployed, i.e. those who were fit and able to work, since receipt of benefit was subject to signing on for work. It therefore excluded anyone not registering, such as those ineligible for benefit, those who had lost hope of getting work and those who did not perceive themselves to be either unemployed or even entitled to paid work, such as housewives. After October 1982 registration of the unemployed claiming benefit was made voluntary following a recommendation by the Rayner Report, *Payment of Benefits to Unemployed People*, which proposed major changes to the employment service. Since that time the monthly count has been based on claimants of benefit. A discussion of the coverage and concepts of unemployment can be found in the document section [doc 6].

There have been some suggestions that we could use an alternative basis for indicating unemployment to registration or eligibility to benefits. One is the suggestion that we grade unemployment, in order to illustrate the full dimensions of the problems, into categories such as registered jobless, long-term unemployed (i.e. more than 6 months), youth unemployment, black or immigrant youth unemployment, those estimated to be discouraged from looking for work and who are, therefore, outside the labour market, and so on. (Merritt 1982: 15–16)

This kind of approach might avoid losing those people who are excluded deliberately from the count and people who exclude themselves for a variety of reasons. The former includes adult students, workers who have been temporarily stopped or who are on short-time work, certain early retired workers and young people on training schemes. The latter includes women paying the married women's insurance contribution, women who do not perceive themselves to be legitimately entitled to work, married or cohabiting women who are not entitled to claim supplementary benefit, the long-term unemployed who have lost faith in getting work and black people who face racial discrimination both in seeking work and in claiming benefit. There is also evidence that in periods of high unemployment, certain groups define themselves as economically inactive (Sinfield 1981: 11–12). Recent studies have indicated that women are less likely to go out to work when their husbands are unemployed (*Lloyds Bank Economic Bulletin* 1982). Marginal workers who might be employed in 'good times' are prone to being defined as unemployable when the level of demand for labour is low. Field has documented some of the arguments put forward for not counting such workers on the grounds that they are unemployable but argues that they will be counted as part of the labour force when in work. As the demand for labour changes, so does their status as eligible for work (Field 1977: 3–5).

Various calculations, therefore, suggest that official unemployment is considerably lower than actual unemployment. For some time the number of people officially unemployed has been over three million. However, the Manpower Services Commission (MSC) has estimated that the correct number of people unemployed is 25% greater than the official figures if it includes those on special employment measures, the unregistered and elderly workers no longer seeking work (*Financial Times*, 4.2.82). There is other evidence too that the figure may be even greater. The number of unemployed persons recorded in the 1971 census was 75% greater than the official figure for the month of the census (Irvine and Evans 1979: 229). A number of surveys suggest that specific groups in the population have a lower tendency to register. The *General Household Survey* has regularly estimated that about half the number of women seeking work do not register, in particular married women (Dex 1978: 137; Sinfield 1981: 11, 84). The 1971 census showed that the majority of unemployed black people were not registered as unemployed (Runnymede Trust and Radical Statistics Race Group 1980: 67).

One useful source of data on unemployment is the *Labour Force Survey* which is carried out on a sample of households every two years on similar lines in all EEC countries. Recent surveys in the UK have shown that about half a million people were not registered but were identified as unemployed. Although a similar number of registrants were found who were not actively seeking work they were predominantly female and likely to be discouraged from seeking work. This coincides with the sex breakdown of *General Household Survey* estimates of unregistered unemployed. In 1971 it was thought that 230,000 women and 80,000 men were unregistered as unemployed. By 1981, these figures had increased to 270,000 women and 130,000 men (*Employment Gazette*. June 1983: 267).

THE EXTENT AND DISTRIBUTION OF UNEMPLOYMENT

The present period of stagnation in the western economies has brought about unprecedentedly high levels of unemployment. These have been aggravated in particular by the use of new technology in production and by multinational companies transferring production to low labour cost countries. Old skills have been destroyed in the process and a pool of labour has been released, some of which has been absorbed into the growing service sector. Both processes have increased the size of the new social groups which are being drawn into the system of waged labour, to the extent that the traditional concept of the working class as male, white and manual is no longer accurate. The new class of workers today contains a large and important, if hidden, element of disadvantaged groups, of which the majority are women.

Vulnerable and marginal in work and accepting low rates of pay, women none the less suffer disproportionately when it comes to unemployment. According to Friend and Metcalfe, when women can be exploited more effectively than men they are recruited into jobs, when in competition with men they are expelled from jobs (Friend and Metcalfe 1981: 63). This applies equally to racial minorities, disabled workers and young workers.

Unemployment is officially recorded as over three million and it seems unlikely that this figure will drop for some time. Seventy-one per cent are male and twenty-nine per cent female. Forty-one per cent are less than 25 years of age, with 3% being school-leavers; 12% are over 54 years of age, (*Employment Gazette*, March 1984).

Work and inequality

The proportion over 54 years of age no longer includes those men who from April 1983 were exempted from registering as unemployed. If it did the proportion would almost double. Seventy-two per cent are from manual work, 28% from non-manual work. However, there are marked differences in the previous occupational status of men and women. Fifty-six per cent of registered unemployed women have previously been in non-manual work as against only 18% of men. This again calls into question some of our stereotypes of who the working class is. About 4% are recorded as being ethnic minority group workers although the proportions in the South-East and the West Midlands are higher: 7.6% and 8.5% respectively. Forty-three per cent have been unemployed for up to six months, 33% for over a year (*Employment Gazette*, June 1982).

Despite the importance of the overall figure and how it is constituted, it is in another respect misleading. It gives the impression of what has been referred to as a stagnant pool of labour which is redundant to an economy in which demand is low. To some extent this has lately become a more accurate impression since one-third of all unemployed people have been out of work for more than a year and the median length out of work is 6 months or more (in contrast to the mid-1970s when 50% of the unemployed left the register within a month). Just as important as figures of how many people are unemployed at any one time is information regarding the flow of unemployment, i.e. the number of people joining and leaving the register. Many who join the register leave again very quickly; for example, in April 1982, 334,000 joined the register and 323,000 left it (*Employment Gazette*, June 1982). This is not to say that some do not join it again fairly soon and there is evidence of a tendency for specific groups to move on and off the register. These are those in jobs where turnover is high and conditions of work poor. But their incidence also seems to be related to class, race, age and sex, reinforcing the notion referred to above of the existence of a large disadvantaged sub-group in the working class (Pond 1980; Metcalfe 1980). Unemployment is clearly unequally shared in the population. Instead of each member of the workforce experiencing unemployment every 6 years (due to an annual figure of 4 million unemployed out a labour force of 24 million), 3% of the labour force account for 70% of unemployment weeks (Metcalfe 1980). This 3% tends to consist of low-paid workers: unskilled manual workers, for instance, who would fit this category are six times more likely to become unemployed than non-manual workers (Smith 1980). Both in addition to this group and within it, there is evidence that unemployment (long and short-term) is concentrated in groups who are already disadvantaged in various ways: older workers, young people, ethnic minorities, the disabled and, of course, women. A much higher proportion of people under 24 and over 60 are unemployed than in any other age group (MSC 1980: 10). For instance, in April 1983 the unemployment rate for men of all ages was 16.5% whereas it was 20% for those aged 60 and over, and 25% for those men under 20 (*Employment Gazette* 1984).

According to the Department of Employment, registered unemployment between February 1979 and February 1980 among black workers showed an increase nearly five times greater than that of the total unemployed population (*Employment Gazette* 1980a: 245). There is also evidence that the disabled suffer far higher rates of unemployment than the general population (Lonsdale 1981). Women are in a more complex position. As already noted, accurate indications of female unemployment are difficult to obtain because their situation is confounded by their status as domestic or caring labourers. Although their participation in waged labour has increased, there was a sharp rise in female unemployment in the late 1970s, when it increased twice as much as male unemployment (Elliot *et al.* 1981: 122).

There exists, therefore, a large reserve of surplus labour, much of which is vulnerable because of social position, which is reflected in a racially, sexually and age-determined division of labour. These groups are disproportionately susceptible to either long-term unemployment or to employment under poor working conditions which is low-paid, inconvenient and poorly protected in times of rising unemployment.

THE COST OF UNEMPLOYMENT

Unemployment is expensive. There is no doubt that its cost in human terms is very great both to the individuals who personally bear it and to the communities which face disintegration from the slow erosion of jobs in their area. The cost of unemployment to the Exchequer is also great, as is its cost to the national economy. However, as already indicated there is more to the latter than a simple bookkeeping exercise. If unemployment is a mechanism which among other things decreases the power of workers by devaluing the only thing they have to sell, then its fiscal and economic costs may be less than the gains in power and control for employers and owners. So the costs and benefits which one is evaluating shift to include the realm of struggle for control in the workplace.

Looking at one side of the balance sheet, unemployment has given rise to costs in a number of different ways. First, since people who are unemployed do not produce goods and services, the level of national output is below that which it could be if they were. The Manpower Services Commission (MSC) has estimated that a level of unemployment of 2.5 million represents £10.7 billion of foregone production, i.e. 6.6% of the Gross Domestic Product (MSC 1981a: 7). Given that unemployment is officially above 3 million this figure should be closer to £14.8 billion and given the MSC's own estimate that true unemployment is higher than the official figure, it would be even more.

Secondly, in addition to lost production, unemployment imposes financial costs on the government. Again the MSC has quantified the main costs involved, by taking into account transfer payments such as unemployment benefit, supplementary benefit and housing payments, and revenue foregone by way of income tax, national insurance contributions and indirect taxes. When the level of unemployment was only 1.34 million, the cost involved in these reached £4 billion.

The MSC and the Institute for Fiscal Studies estimated that in 1981–82 each unemployed person cost the Treasury approximately £4,500, making an aggregate cost of £13 billion. Neither of the above calculations include the costs incurred by the MSC itself in creating special employment programmes (as against training schemes which it might provide in any event in the attempt to match supply and demand for labour in a changing economy).

Thirdly, the MSC has estimated some of the financial costs for different people of being out of work. Using gross weekly earnings set at three-quarters of the national average, they calculate the percentage of income for people becoming unemployed in April 1980. Table 3.1 illustrates income out of work as a proportion of income in work for certain representative family types:

These calculations assume a full take-up of various benefits when out of work such as child benefit, rent/rate rebates, free school meals and welfare milk. If these are not claimed then income out of work will be lower. However, account is not taken of work expenses which are saved such as travel, or work gains which are lost such as electricity, heating, etc.

Turning to the other side of the balance sheet, if one starts from the assumption that unemployment is part of a greater struggle for

Table 3.1. Income in and out of work for certain family types

Family types	Income out of work as a percentage of income in work (%)
Single female	63
Single male	43
Married male and wife	57
Married male, wife and two children	74
Married male, wife and four children	87

Source: *Review of Services for the Unemployed*, MSC, (1981a) p. 8

control in the workplace, then the first and second costs may be of less concern for employers because of the advantage gained over a workforce growing in power, and the third cost may be one of the means of reasserting control over labour. The conditions and terms of employment reflect a balance of power between the buyers and sellers of labour, e.g. the seller's power decreases if his/her labour can be substituted for another's or if competition for jobs is high; the buyer's power decreases if labour is well unionised or scarce. (This is generally true but the balance of power may vary in different labour markets where control over work and working conditions may be at different stages.)

Increasing unemployment generally can lead to a lowering of worker resistance, the introduction of new techniques of production (which in turn lessen the power of employees even further) and the implementation of wage cuts. However, one needs to explain why certain unions manage to negotiate good wage increases in times of high unemployment. Firstly, it could be argued that although the wage increase is high, it does not reflect an increase in power and control over work. Some writers argue that unemployment is used as a mechanism to adjust the workforce to new methods of production which in the long run effectively weaken their control over work (Glasner *et al.* 1981). Higher rewards to workers in work does not necessarily contradict this. A second explanation may lie in the notion that more than one labour market exists and that the processes which occur in them are very different. The different labour markets themselves may be a response to the increasing availability for work of certain vulnerable groups such as women, migrant labour and young workers (Rubery 1978). Once in existence they have the effect or perform the role of dividing the labour force and ensuring a supply of labour for unskilled jobs. They supply skilled workers in different ways, workers who are bound by security and privileges and a sense of commitment to their company or firm unlike their secondary sector fellow-workers who are bound by fear and insecurity. The MSC often acts as broker between the two sectors in supplying skills training when skilled labour is needed.

It may be argued that, with the large increase in unemployment, categories other than the low-paid, unskilled and vulnerable worker increasingly account for the unemployed total. This is probably not occurring, for a number of reasons. First is the 'trade down' effect noted by Daniels whereby younger, fitter and more skilled people who lose their jobs accept jobs at lower occupational and wage levels, further exacerbating the position for less skilled workers (Daniel 1981b: 497; Moylan and Davies 1981: 31). Secondly, people are defined as older at a younger age; as unskilled higher up the occupational scale; and as unfit when in better physical condition than before. The latter is a complex phenomenon discussed in detail below. Generally though, there is still evidence that men who become unemployed are disproportionately concentrated among lower earners (Davies *et al*. 1982: 238).

The costs of unemployment to the individual are high both in terms of personal health and personal pocket. Contrary to popular belief, very few people have large, generous redundancy payments on which to fall back. Only one in four people become unemployed because of redundancy in the first place. Less then one in ten men get redundancy payments of more than £500 and one in twenty get more than £2,000 (Daniel 1981). Even £2,000 is very little for a family with the prospect of a breadwinner facing a prolonged period of unemployment. Like many provisions of the welfare state, those who are articulate and informed (and often less in need) can usually find their way around both service and cash provision ending up with a more generous deal. This no doubt applies to redundancy provision as well.

This chapter began by proposing that we need to consider not only how many jobs are available but what the public believes about how many jobs are available. These two things are linked. They are inextricably linked when a government is attempting to cut back its spending on social security and one way in which it can do this is by creating a climate of belief that more people are receiving social security than need be. It is probably not an accident that public concern at the abuse of social security benefits for the unemployed gained momentum in 1976–77 when the then government was faced with major public expenditure cutbacks and had a resurgence again in 1980–81 when public expenditure was being cut even further.

The concern with scrounging has always centred on the low paid because it is at these levels of income that wages come closest to benefit levels (as Table 3.1 indicated). While low wages are often close to benefit levels and sometimes might be less one can interpret this in two ways with regard to unemployment. One way is to say that most unemployment results not from a shortfall in the demand for labour but from benefit levels which are too high and provided too easily by the state. The other is to say that there is too low a demand for labour. This creates unemployment, obviously, but it also permits employers to pay low wages. Low wages are, therefore, the problem, not over-generous benefits (Deacon 1978). Given the very low rates of benefit this is a more likely explanation.

UNEMPLOYMENT AND SOCIAL SECURITY

In the post-war period two systems of benefit developed, to a large extent independently of one another and without reference to the system of taxation. The level of national insurance benefits was allowed to fall below that of supplementary benefits, particularly when the earnings-related supplement to unemployment benefit was abolished but also because supplementary benefit claimants automatically received rent/rate rebates which unemployment benefit claimants had to claim separately. However, in November 1983 this changed, with near parity being introduced in the basic rates.

In addition to this, the tax threshold, from being 137.5% of the supplementary benefit level in 1965 (when supplementary benefit replaced national assistance), had dropped to below the supplementary benefit level in 1979–80, when it was 96.9%. From July 1982, however, the Department of Inland Revenue began taxing all benefits, including unemployment benefit and supplementary benefit. This does not affect those out of work for the full tax year because benefits are less than the personal allowance or tax threshold for a full year. It does, however, affect those intermittently unemployed during the year. The benefit paid will not be any less in these circumstances but the money will be reclaimed the following year. In 1980 the government cut benefits by 5% instead of immediately introducing the taxation of benefits. The intention was stated to be one of restoring the 5% in 1982 when the taxing of benefits began. However, it was only restored in 1983. The cost of restoring the cut is estimated to be £60 million in contrast to the

£650 million envisaged from taxing the unemployed.

In 1978 the Department of Health and Social Security embarked on a cohort study of unemployed men. Its main purpose was to examine the adequacy of benefits for the unemployed and their effects on financial incentives to work. In the study weekly income during the first 3 months of unemployment was compared with that received in the last job of the 2,000 men interviewed. Two types of comparison were used: (*a*) the benefit-earnings ratio, i.e. the difference between unemployment benefits and earnings (taking into account the different value of an extra 5% to high and low earners); and (*b*) the family income replacement ratio, i.e. comparing the total of all sources of regular income. Table 3.2 gives their findings.

Table 3.2.   Benefit/Earnings ratio and Family Income Replacement ratio

	B/E ratio	*FIR ratio*
0	3	1
Under 25%	10	7
25% but under 50%	33	27
50% but under 80%	39	40
80% but under 100%	10	16
100% and over	6	9
All	100	100

Source: Davies *et al.*, *Employment Gazette*, June 1982.

The men with high family income replacement ratios, i.e. over 80% of income in work, tended to have dependent wives and children and to be generally very low paid. Nearly 50% had gross earnings in their last job of under £50 per week. But 15% had become eligible for occupational pensions which contributed to their high ratios. Only 6% of the men received unemployment benefits exceeding their previous earnings. Taking occupational pensions and other sources of income into account, 9% had a higher income out of work than in work. The cohort study considered the argument that the availability of means-tested benefits in work ensures that people are better off in employment than out of work. They found evidence of a very low take-up of in-work benefits among all the men but more so among the high ratio men. In the latter group, of those entitled, only 16% received housing rebates, only 12% received Family Income Supplement and 39% received free school meals. More disturbingly, failure to claim means tested benefits increased with the number of children present in the family. Low wages and low take-up of in-work benefits seem, therefore, to be the main causes of high income replacement ratios (Davies *et al.* 1982). Most of the above should be evidence that benefits are not very high, although this is a relative notion and they are obviously higher in relation to lower wages.

The Department of Health and Social Security (DHSS) has estimated that detected fraud accounted for 1p of every £32 paid out in 1976 (HMSO 1977). The total amount of fraud seems to be around the £2 million mark annually. Approximately ten times as much is lost in tax evasion every year. In addition, the Inland Revenue Staff Federation has calculated that accountants help clients to underassess their income by about £45 million a year, consequently avoiding £15 million in taxes. It is quite clear that while dole scrounging exists, tax scrounging both legal and illegal is far greater. Yet the degree of public concern for the first is out of all proportion to reality and is virtually non-existent for the second.

The active anti-scrounger campaign was begun in July 1976 by a Conservative MP who gave 196 cases of alleged fraud to the then Minister for Social Security to investigate. Seventeen of the 196 were found to contain fraud. After another 4 months an additional 441 cases were examined out of which 22 contained fraud. Alan Deacon has analysed the newspaper responses at the time and found that while the initial allegations were widely reported, the later findings were virtually ignored. He also draws attention to the London correspondent of the *Wall Street Journal* who in the same year claimed that Britain had become a 'nation of tax fiddlers'. This did not receive coverage in the daily press (Deacon 1978).

In attempting to explain this, firstly, there is clearly an element of either careless press reporting or press reporting which is ideologically biased. Secondly, there is the issue of taxation and low wages. Tax thresholds have fallen so low in Britain that the poorest workers are paying tax. Taken together with falling living standards this is bound to cause resentment because poor people through their taxes are subsidising other poor people. Thirdly, as Deacon suggests, the belief in scroungers performs 'the useful and supportive role of a reassuring social myth, externalising and objectifying widespread confusion and frustration by holding out the prospect of a simple and immediate remedy if only it could be tried' (Deacon 1978).

The effects of such public concern over dole scrounging is that it encourages those administering the benefits to do so harshly. Michael Hill calls this 'the psychological climate in which officials operate'. However, the 'psychological climate' creates actual obstacles. These include random checks on the identity of claimants, increases in manpower for detecting abuse, the issuing of 'fraud awareness' packages to all local officers and other devices like these. Unemployment benefit is surrounded by ambiguity. 'Help for the unemployed is hedged around with more constraints and limitations than for most other claimants' (Sinfield 1981: 113). Consequently, although there are more pensioners receiving social security, more time and staff are taken up with administering benefits to the unemployed. Presumably these costs are considered worthwhile in terms of the longer-term savings of discouraging people from claiming, and in legitimising lowering the rate of benefit.

Unemployment itself as well as the climate in which unemployed people claim benefit has severe effects on health and well-being. Public lack of sympathy for the unemployed and public suspicion about their being unemployed voluntarily not only provides a climate in which the level of benefits can be kept down but effectively demoralises those losing work. The unemployed are subject to the prevailing ideological framework no less than everyone else and they may internalise a particularly damaging set of values which diminishes the economic realities they face. This effectively prevents militancy and fosters feelings of inadequacy. Taken together with severe financial hardship and the 'loss of a working role and the time frame that a working day provides' (Merritt 1982: 87) the unemployed face a battering with which few people could be expected to cope. According to a MORI survey, unemployed people do not tend to adopt militant political positions (*New Statesman* 27 March 1981). Instead, they seem to respond to their situation by looking for individual solutions to their problems or by a variety of sectarian responses, e.g. separatist groups outside mainstream politics.

Some writers have suggested that one of the ways in which the unemployed deal with their situation is to attribute it to a physical or psychological disability (Fagin 1979/80: 58). Hill *et al.* found that of the unemployed they interviewed in three cities, 22%, 27% and 28% reported being disabled whether registered or not. However, they felt that disability was a good predictor of unemployment since there was a significant association between weeks of sickness absence while at work and reported disability when out of work (Hill *et al*. 1973: 43. The attribution of unemployment to disability causes may, therefore, be based on fact (despite only a few receiving medical treatment). Since there is evidence of more ill health among the country's lower socio-economic groups – who are also more vulnerable to unemployment – this is not surprising. Disability, however, may also make it more difficult to return to work, as evidenced by a number of men in Hill *et al*.'s study. They conclude that the disabled were a markedly disadvantaged class as a whole.

Many forms of work including employment are viewed as 'normal' and provide legitimate forms of activity in society. Some forms of work provide intrinsic satisfaction and others provide recognition and large economic rewards. A great deal of paid and unpaid work, however, involves drudgery and alienation on the part of the worker from his/her labour. Since the unemployed derive mainly from the ranks of those who have experienced this, it is important to understand why unemployment is so demoralising physically and mentally. Three reasons could be postulated. Firstly, all forms of work, in particular employment and child care, provide some structure (usually in time) which could be argued to be crucial to most people in managing their lives. Secondly, the more alienated someone is from their labour the more likely they are to be linked to others in similar circumstances. Severing this contact and these links could be extremely disturbing. Thirdly, however poorly paid, most wages are higher than most benefits paid. The loss of a 'legitimated' economic reward will both jeopardise self-esteem and, perhaps more importantly, lower living standards. As already indicated, unemployment falls disproportionately on those with less power, less money, poorer housing, worse nutrition and worse health to start with. Those at risk are put at even greater risk.

The loss of structure, comradeship or money arises in a number of situations similar to job loss. For instance, those nearing retirement face all three, as do young people leaving school. One of the most serious ways in which these phenomena can affect individuals is in their physical and mental well-being. There is a growing body of evidence to suggest that unemployment creates ill health for those out of work as well as for those in work who feel vulnerable to unemployment (Popay 1981a, 1981b). With regard to the latter, the Office of Health Economics (OHE) recently reported that claims for sickness benefit have fallen sharply as the numbers of unemployed have risen. They suggest that people are more prepared to tolerate minor episodes of ill health when jobs are scarce.

However, since more trivial ailments were found to have become an important cause of absence, it seems more likely that serious conditions are being ignored because they can be managed in the short term. The danger in this is that these conditions can well prove more harmful and time-consuming to repair if not dealt with immediately. This may already be evidenced in the finding that there has been an increase in the number of very long-term spells of incapacity (OHE 1981). The cost to the Exchequer in sickness and invalidity benefits in 1979 was £1.5 billion but the OHE estimates its true cost in lost production to have been £5.5 billion, compared to government expenditure in that year on the NHS of £7.8 billion (OHE 1981).

Over the last few years, a number of large studies have been conducted in the USA and fewer, more recently, in the UK into the effects of unemployment on a number of social indicators including health (The Black Report 1980; Brenner 1980, Fagin 1981; Hayes and Nutman 1981; Popay 1981a, 1981b). But it is only recently that unemployment as a cause of ill health, stress and even death has received the attention of either academic research or the media. This may be part of the general lack of concern and often hostility towards the unemployed, especially because physical and mental ill health can be perceived as excuses for not working. But it is also partly due to the inconclusiveness of much of the evidence relating to single or even multiple causes of stress, ill health or death (Greenwood 1981). One of the best known studies has been that of Professor Harvey Brenner who suggested that a number of pathological reactions can result from unemployment, as can death (Brenner 1980). The major problem with this kind of research is that statistical associations such as those found by Brenner do not necessarily prove either a causal factor or in which direction the causal relationship is going. What they do illustrate, and this may be their importance and value, is that greater investigation is worthwhile, especially given the seriousness of the matter under discussion. Like many issues which social policy making must face, there is a danger in delaying action until definitive research findings are produced. This is not to argue that research should be abandoned but that indicative findings are very often all that policy makers have to go on with. The processes of policy making and research are both dynamic and feed in on one another, nowhere more so than in the field of unemployment where the problem must be both met and understood.

POLICY MEASURES

Does unemployment help maintain industrial discipline in a capitalist society? Is it caused in the first place by trade union wage demands which are beyond the capacity of industry to meet? Or is it due to decreases in consumer expenditure, exports and investments; in other words a decrease in aggregate demand? Policy measures ultimately rest on explanations such as these about what causes or creates increasing unemployment [doc 7]. Some writers have argued that the logic of a capitalist economy together with increasing automation will require Britain's levels of unemployment to increase (Jordan 1982). The nature of the capitalist mode of production, it is argued, precludes a smooth and peaceful transition from stagnation to growth (Friend and Metcalfe 1981). Not only are high levels of unemployment used to control wage bargaining but a flexible labour force can be said to be necessary to the cyclical course of capitalism. The main policy options to overcome or decrease unemployment, therefore, are located in building up trade union membership and continuing to struggle for different working conditions. This approach is indirect in that it does not immediately take on board the needs of the unemployed themselves. Policies are essentially focused on the workplace, anticipating that the indirect effect of stronger unions or more worker control would be to protect jobs. More recent initiatives have included not just wage bargaining but the development of new industrial priorities and alternative objectives in production (Elliot 1977; CAITS 1978). A different set of explanations and remedies for unemployment focus on the 'voluntary' nature of unemployment. Some writers have argued that benefits reduce the cost of unemployment for the individual who accordingly reduces his/her efforts to get a new job and refuses to take on jobs below a certain wage. Therefore unemployment increases and wages rise. Others suggest that unemployment benefits encourage workers to search for new jobs and employers who would otherwise keep workers on in good and bad times, profit by more lay-offs in slack periods. More popular is the view that excessive wage demands by over-powerful unions create unemployment. Remedies deriving from these kinds of explanations include policies of restrictive legislation on trade unions to curb their powers, such as the 1982 legislation; measures to keep wages down, again evidenced in the public sector pay disputes of 1982; and a combination of policies which attempt to create jobs while keeping their costs down. The Young Workers Scheme and the split jobs scheme announced in July 1982 are good examples of the latter. In addition, since unemployment is seen to result from worker greed and high levels of benefit, a punitive administration of unemployment benefits is seen as justifiable as well as necessary to encourage a quick return to work at reasonable wage rates.

Within social policy a more common tradition (which still prevails to a large extent both theoretically and in practice) has been to relate unemployment among individuals to the under-use of resources and a deficiency in aggregate demand which in turn may be seen to arise out of structural changes in the economy and in the labour market. Many writers have argued more optimistically (and still do) that the goal of full employment is still possible and that active employment policies must be developed which both increase demand and ensure that the heaviest costs of mass unemployment are not borne by the weakest in society (Sinfield 1981; Showler and Sinfield 1981; Field 1977). The view that a flexible reserve of labour is necessary for the expansions and contractions of capitalism is implicitly rejected in that full employment is seen to be feasible in and compatible with the type of economic system which Britain currently has. The concern of these writers and policy makers has been with policies related to improved systems of social security, to other forms of provision for the unemployed, e.g. unemployment centres, to job creation and job sharing.

Four sets of policy measures relating to unemployment will be outlined in more detail in the following chapters. These are:
1. Maintaining the incomes of those out of work;
2. Creating special employment measures;
3. Sharing existing jobs; and
4. Tackling inequalities at work of which the prevalence of unemployment among certain groups is one instance.

Chapter four
POLICIES FOR EMPLOYMENT

INTRODUCTION

Policies related to employment include a very wide range of activities from creating jobs, protecting jobs and assisting in matching up the supply and demand for jobs on the one hand, to training people for work (especially for shortages in skilled work) on the other. Social security policy was traditionally also linked to employment policy in that the availability of income maintenance was seen to provide an incentive for people to register for work and their registering for work provided proof of their right to receive benefits. It was, therefore, also seen as the coercive end of policies for employment. Ending the requirement that unemployed people register with the employment service as a condition of receiving benefit was also linked to important employment issues, one of which was the size of the unemployed population. Voluntary registration served two purposes. It reduced the number of unemployed and achieved reductions in administrative staff (MSC 1982a: 12). However, the more effective employment and 'manpower' policies are, the less reliance there would be on social security benefits. It could be argued that the failure of employment and 'manpower' policy to ensure an adequate supply of jobs will lead to an unnecessary and expensive reliance on social security.

MAINTAINING THE INCOMES OF THOSE OUT OF WORK

Underlying Britain's system of social security is a distinction between long-term claimants of benefit and those who claim benefit for a short period of time. Within unemployment benefit, the benefit can only be claimed for 12 months in any one period of interruption of employment. Thereafter the right to benefit is exhausted and the individual or family falls onto the second system of support, supplementary benefits. In 1979, 62% of the unemployed in the United Kingdom were not eligible for unemployment benefit as against 52% in the USA and 49% in West Germany (Hart 1982). Within the supplementary benefits system as well, a distinction is made between long and short-term claimants (other than the unemployed, e.g. the sick, elderly or disabled claimants) with the former receiving a higher rate of benefit. It is a higher rate, however, from which the long-term unemployed are excluded. The distinction in both systems is based on the notion of 'deserving' and 'undeserving' claimants which in turn relates to the view that some unemployment if not most is voluntary. Attitudes towards unemployment in Britain have been influenced at various times by the belief that benefits act as a disincentive to work. It has been shown already that punitive attitudes seem to coincide with periods of high unemployment. These public attitudes have their counterparts in the opinions of both politicians and economists (Deacon 1976, 1978; Benjamin and Kochin 1979a,b; Atkinson 1981).

However, the 'voluntary' nature of unemployment has been refuted by others for not taking into account factors such as the imperfect mobility of labour, the acceptance by many workers who are most vulnerable to unemployment of low-paid work and the difficulties of applying a concept like voluntary unemployment in practice at an aggregate level rather than theoretically at an individual level (Worswick 1976; Pond 1980; Field 1977a). Despite this, certain measures have been taken which indicate that there is still concern that benefits can be substantially abused. In the middle of 1981, at a time of extremely high unemployment, an additional 1,050 staff were appointed to detect social security fraud and abuse. Their work was to concentrate largely on supplementary benefit claimants and the extra detection was claimed to have cut off the benefits of 53,500 unemployed workers (Weir 1981b). In early 1982 an experimental scheme was started to test a person's eligibility for work at the unemployment benefit office instead of a Jobcentre. The MSC itself acknowledged that while the central aim of the employment service was to find jobs for people, it also enabled a check to be kept on claimants' willingness to work. This appeared to be regardless of high levels of unemployment (MSC 1981a: 17).

The policing of benefits is not new. Neither is the use of training as a sanction against malingering. Deacon records the conflict over Beveridge's recommendation for indefinite insurance benefit in recognition of the involuntary nature of most unemployment and to

avoid means-tested benefits. In order to introduce this it was suggested that attendance at a work training centre be required for
those claimants appearing to settle down indefinitely on benefit.
The intention of these centres was twofold: to encourage good
working habits and to improve the chances of getting work. Opposition to work centres and to linking benefit eligibility with work
or training led to the rejection of the latter and of indefinite benefits
at the time (Deacon 1981b). The coercive nature of the benefit system has not been resolved and regularly emerges as a controversial
issue. For instance, in June 1982 the Employment Secretary attempted to withold supplementary benefit from 16-year-olds who
refused training scheme places. Although these plans were abandoned after pressure from the Confederation of British Industry
(CBI) and the Trades Union Congress (TUC), it was made clear
that the government did not believe that young people should receive income maintenance in their own right when unemployed.

There are seventeen Re-establishment Centres which are usually
used for people with poor work records or who have been unemployed for long periods of time. The work undertaken at the centre
is usually manual and people are referred by the Unemployment
Review Officer (URO), one of whose main tasks is to investigate
those in receipt of benefits. Attendance is voluntary but the URO
has the power to direct a claimant to attend as a condition of continuing to receive benefit. While only a small proportion attend
compulsorily, this power exists none the less.

SPECIAL EMPLOYMENT MEASURES

In recognition of the negative consequences of unemployment outlined in Chapter three, a variety of special employment measures
have been instituted by government and operated and administered
through the Manpower Services Commission [doc 8]. The purpose
and objectives of these measures are to be found on two levels. On
a socio-economic level they aim to (a) counteract cyclical move-
ments in unemployment; (b) alleviate the effects of structural unemployment; (c) redistribute unemployment; and (d) relieve the
effects of the recession on particular groups in society. On a personal level they aim to (a) maintain job motivation and skills; (b)
prevent individuals from sinking into chronic unemployment; and
(c) protect vulnerable groups in the labour market.

It is questionable to what extent the Manpower Services Commission, as an arm of the state, can act independently of the econ-

omic system. The constraints on social policy resulting from the workings of the economic system are very evident in the work of the MSC and the role it sometimes perceives for itself. For instance, in its strategy for unemployment it states (MSC 1981a):

The commission can do nothing about demand deficient unemployment. It cannot compensate for the inadequacy of the job generation process or for deficiencies in the British or the world economies. The Commission can, however, play a considerable part in helping unemployed people back into work by reducing frictional or mismatch unemployment through employment and training services and by providing work experience or temporary work for unemployed people.

None the less, it also talks in terms of job creation through its Job Release Scheme (JRS) and its scheme to avert redundancies. The main thrust of its work, however, is clearly on a personal level and is oriented towards individuals and groups. It is difficult to avoid the implication of this: that the individual's attitudes and behaviour are seen to be playing a substantial role in their unemployment. In much of the MSC's work there is an uneasy compromise between recognising the realities of a stagnating and contracting economy on the one hand and, on the other hand, implementing social policies which often reduce economic questions to personal ones.

Since 1973 there have been five major divisions in the MSC: (*a*) Employment Service Division; (*b*) Special Programmes Division; (*c*) Training Services Division; (*d*) Manpower Intelligence and Planning Division; and (*e*) Corporate Services Division. Since (*d*) is concerned primarily with intelligence and information gathering for the rest and since (*e*) is largely concerned with planning and administering the MSC itself and is, therefore, implicit in much of what is written, this section will concern itself with the first three divisions, although in 1983 the Training Services Division and the Special Programmes Division were subsequently merged [doc 9].

The Employment Service Division employs about 13,000 people, although this will be reduced considerably in 1984. It represents 56% of the Commission's total staff component in these three divisions. Apart from its size, the Employment Service is the linchpin of the public employment service. Its main purpose is to 'assemble and to make available information about vacancies and people looking for work so as to help the labour market work more efficiently'. The MSC always points out that similar services are provided out of public funds by all major industrialised countries.

The Special Programmes Division, by contrast, only employs about 2,000 staff or approximately 9% of all staff in the three divisions. This division was established on 1 April 1978. It arose out of a series of initiatives by both government and MSC and was essentially a response to the high unemployment of the mid 1970s. The two groups who were the focus of attention were (*a*) young people who were being hardest hit by unemployment, especially young black people, (*b*) long-term unemployed adults whose numbers were growing, and disabled people. The most well known of these initiatives was the Job Creation Programme launched towards the end of 1975, but then phased out.

The Training Services Division comes somewhere between the two in terms of staff size. It employs about 8,000 staff or 35% of staff in the three divisions. The MSC has long believed that the primary responsibility for industrial training rests with employers. It recognises that in other European countries 'the state assumes the responsibility for a broad based vocational training, both of young people and adults, and productive enterprises are then expected to refine and upgrade the skills so learned according to their own needs' (MSC 1978b: 5). However, it sees its own role somewhat differently and says 'the role of public finance in training must be to support the efforts of industry and commerce, either where these efforts are manifestly failing or most prominently where they fail to cover the needs of individuals'. This is essentially a reactive and residual role as against the initiating and 'institutional' role adopted by some other countries. The merger of training services and special programmes reflects the emphasis being placed on training and work preparation for the young unemployed. It would also appear to have an administrative purpose as there is a degree of overlap in some of the programmes.

The Manpower Services Commission is not the only body concerned with creating more jobs although it certainly plays the largest role and is the most significant in social policy terms. Policy makers have three main options regarding the shortage of jobs. They can increase the demand for labour by creating permanent and/or temporary employment opportunities. They can reduce the supply of labour by promoting later entry to and/or earlier exit from the labour force. They can arrange for jobs to be shared. Since 1973 when the MSC came into being, various varieties of the first two policies have been adopted both by the MSC and by the Department of Employment. It is only recently that jobsharing has come under serious discussion. Policies attempting to increase employment opportunities include predominantly the Youth Opportunities Programmes (YOPs) and Youth Training Schemes (YTS), Community Industry (CI), Community Enterprise Programme (CEP), Community Programmes (CP) – although all of these have a strong training element – and the Young Workers Scheme (YWS). The majority of these types of programmes indirectly increase the demand for labour by making labour more attractive rather than by creating more real jobs. One of the ways of making labour more attractive is by developing skills; another is by subsidising labour. Among the former are the Training Opportunities Schemes (TOPS), the Training for Skills Programme (TSP), Unified Vocational Preparation (UVP), Direct Training Services (DTS), and the Open Tech Programme (OTP). Policies attempting to reduce the supply of labour include the Job Release Scheme (JRS) or any forms of early retirement. Training which delays the entry of people into the labour market could also be considered part of these policies.

Since the Youth Opportunities Scheme, Community Industry and the Unified Vocational Programme are all directed specifically at young people, they will be dealt with in some detail in Chapter six. The Job Release Scheme and early retirement policies likewise will be dealt with in detail in Chapter seven on older workers. There is also an additional range of schemes for the disabled which will be covered in Chapter eight.

The Young Workers Scheme

The YWS is directly designed to encourage employers to take on more young people at lower rates of pay which in the government's view reflect their lack of training and relative inexperience. Employers can claim a weekly subsidy in respect of each employee whose gross average earnings are less than £40 a week or a smaller subsidy for employees whose gross average earnings are less than £45.00 a week for a period of 12 months. This only applies to workers who are under eighteen and in their first year of employment. The jobs must be full-time and permanent, which in practice means more than 35 hours a week and more than 8 weeks. Training is not a condition of the scheme. The scheme has received criticism on a number of levels, particularly in encouraging cheap labour. Employers do not have to create new jobs and there are no safeguards that older workers will not be replaced by younger, cheaper workers (Low Pay Unit 1982: 12–13). The gross wage is all-inclusive and there is, therefore, no possibility of it being increased by overtime, commission, bonuses, productivity payments, merit payments, travelling or large-town allowances (DE 1982).

The Community Enterprise Programme

The CEP replaced a scheme known as the Special Temporary Employment Programme (STEP) to become one of the main measures to help the long-term unemployed find work. It is available for those who have been unemployed for more than a year or for more than 6 months in the case of 18–24 year-olds. CEP is administered by the Employment Service Division as are the Community Programmes. Unlike its predecessor, STEP, it is not restricted to assisted areas and lasts for three years rather than one. It provides temporary work on projects associated with environmental improvement and energy conservation which will benefit the community (MSC 1982b). Twenty-five per cent of CEP entrants are from Scotland. There has been a steady increase in the proportion of male entrants and a corresponding decline in female entrants since 1978 (when STEP began) although over 75% of all entrants have always been male. The rationale behind CEP is to break the demoralising effect of long-term unemployment and to provide a recent reference to aid a return to work. Given the enormous numbers eligible for CEP (over 1 million), the increase in places has not been sufficient to match the increase in the number of long-term unemployed.

Community Programmes

These programmes (CP) were announced in Parliament in the middle of 1982. The scheme was designed to give work experience to 200,000 people, mostly part-time and for up to one year. Local authorities, voluntary bodies and private industry were to be sponsors of projects. Those long-term unemployed eligible for CEP are also eligible for CP. Again, the projects are intended to be for the benefit of the community. The scheme has given rise to misgivings among unions who fear that they will encourage cheap labour and the National Council for Voluntary Organisations which fears that too little money is available for too many jobs. However, the programmes did not take off very successfully – only 1.7% of the 130,000 funded places had been filled by the end of 1982.

The Temporary Short-Time Working Compensation Scheme

This scheme was introduced a number of years before any of the above schemes. Employers who agreed to withdraw an impending redundancy of ten or more workers were refunded 75% of normal wages when these workers were put on short time. Employers were also reimbursed for their national insurance contributions. Originally this was for a period of 6 months but it was subsequently changed so that 50% of normal earnings were paid for a period of 9 months. In the first year of its operation, 93,000 jobs were saved (MSC 1981a). Job subsidies such as these have been criticised because the jobs that are saved (or created in the case of recruitment subsidies) are often only saved at a hidden cost of unemployment or short-time work elsewhere in the economy. A more serious long-term criticism is that subsidising firms which are weak and declining hinders the structural adaptations needed in the economy, at the same time penalising efficient and growing firms (Burton 1977). Obviously this kind of effect needs to be measured against the advantages of reducing unemployment if, indeed, subsidies do alleviate the costs of and reduce unemployment.

The New Enterprise Programme

This is part of the TOPS programme: it began in 1977 and was expanded a few years later in response to demand, according to the MSC. It aims to assist individuals who wish to launch businesses which have a potential for large growth. Another scheme, the Small Business Course (SBC), is aimed at smaller ventures. In 1981–82 120 people attended New Enterprise courses and 461 attended Small Business Courses. The MSC estimates that since their inception they have led to the creation of almost 800 businesses lasting more than a year employing 3,500 people. Three additional schemes provide a weekly allowance for a year intended to provide some security while new businesses are being established. The Enterprise Allowance Scheme (EAS) provides this when unemployment and supplementary benefit are no longer payable (MSC 1982b: 220). Both the NEP and the EAS are planned to be extended over the next few years.

The Training Opportunities Scheme

TOPS, unlike many of the others, has been in operation since 1972.

The original declared aim of the scheme was to provide training 'to enable the adult population to change their occupations quickly in the face of increasing industrial change; and generally to promote the idea of adult retraining'. Government Training Centres, now known as Skillcentres, educational institutions and employers' premises were intended to be used for this purpose. Originally the scheme was intended as a counter cyclical measure, training people when the economy was on a downturn so that they could fulfil industry's needs on the upturn (MSC 1978b).

TOPS is an expensive form of provision because it involves full-time, off-the-job training which requires income support for trainees. The gross cost of TOPS in 1981–82 was £242.7 million. Since 75% of people applying for TOPS are unemployed, however, there is a saving on benefits paid out. In addition, the EEC through its Social Fund and through the European Coal and Steel Community contributed £18.5 million towards retraining in Britain. Despite this, future provision under TOPS is in question. People completing TOPS courses have fallen steadily since 1978–79. The cutbacks are allegedly due to low placement rates, now at 35%. This is particularly marked for Skillcentre trainees. This is important given the large number of trainees at Skillcentres, i.e. 23,211 as compared to 30,311 in educational institutions and 7,253 in employers' establishments (MSC 1982a, 1982b). Under a third of TOPS trainees are women.

Second to cost, another issue of concern in TOPS is the type of training provided and its appropriateness to the needs of the economy. It has, therefore, been cut back and, in terms of skill training, appears to be being replaced by lower level skill training for unemployed young people. TOPS provision is, however, being extended at some levels, namely the technician level in the field of electronics and microelectronics and in programming and systems analysis. It is being reduced in certain skills training, namely automobile repair and mechanical engineering. This represents some recognition of the introduction of new technology and the decline in demand for many manual skills or changes in technology which affect them. A formidable problem lies in the existence of many Skillcentres with fixed capital equipment and trained instructors which need to be altered to make new provision. There are 68 Skillcentres and 24 annexes to them. A review of Skillcentre training was set in motion early in 1982 (MSC 1982a, 1982b). The problems of rationalising the system are illustrated in the example of a centre in the West Midlands opened in 1972 for general engineering trainees whose skills were then in demand. With the decline in this demand the centre was closed in March 1981. However, it could not easily be relet and the MSC continues to pay £112,000 a year in rent, for which sum it is liable until 1993 – an example of a very expensive cutback and the problems of rationalisation (*Guardian* 4 Feb. 1982). Training in colleges and other institutions is to continue taking into account Open Tech initiatives.

The Open Tech Programme

OTP is intended to provide training, retraining and updating of technician and supervisory levels of skill. This is to be undertaken collaboratively with existing training and qualifying bodies in order to use existing resources cost-effectively. A task group was established to recommend criteria for selecting an initial programme of projects and a plan of action. The group anticipated that the programme should cover 50,000 workers a year. However, only £1 million was allocated for the programme initially. This rose to £8 million after two years. Since the TOPS programmes cost £242 million for 60,000 trainees, this was an unrealistically low figure despite a plan for employers and local authorities to contribute in money, premises, equipment and labour (MSC 1982a, 1982b). However, in principle, the Open Tech Programme aimed to free courses of study and training 'from the constraints that prevent their effective availability' (MSC 1981c). The 'Open' aspect refers to any approach which makes a course or syllabus accessible or more readily available, by overcoming constraints such as time, place, class, size, learning methods, entry criteria and costs. The 'Tech' aspect refers to the need for properly qualified and updated technical support staff. As an open learning system, it is primarily centred on the needs and circumstances of students rather than the needs of the educational establishment. Again this is seen as a counter cyclical approach to intervene during the recession 'to help prevent the widespread re-appearance, when the economic upturn takes place, of the persistent shortages' of skills (MSC 1981c).

The Training For Skills Programme

TSP covers both apprenticeships and adult training and retraining. It provides training for 35,000 people each year, including funding for apprentices faced with redundancy. Like TOPS, TSP is moving towards developments in new technology. It runs three schemes designed to train people in computer skills. These provide training in computer programming for unemployed school-leavers, grants to employers who send staff on approved courses in programming and systems analysis, and grants to students to attend computer science sandwich courses.

Direct Training Services

DTS provide training within industry and include the following services and numbers of individuals: (*a*) training of firms' employees on sponsored courses in Skillcentres (4,550 people); (*b*) training of firms' employees at their place of work by mobile instructors (5,600 people); (*c*) training of firms' supervisors in international trade procedures (9,600 people); (*d*) training of firms' instructors at instructor training colleges (550 people). The number of people trained has declined substantially from the time of the scheme's inception which is likely to be due to industry's reluctance to invest in training in difficult periods.

Generally and despite the programme outlined above, Britain has been slow to adopt and promote vigorous manpower policies (Sinfield 1981: 97). Its spending on labour market programmes has been lower than that of Sweden, Germany, Canada and Japan and has been about the same as that of the USA (Showler and Sinfield 1981: 197–8). There has been a consistent struggle between long-term aims and short-term political expediencies. This was nowhere better exemplified than in the extension of special programmes whereby the cost of devoting time, money and energy to the longer-term goals of employment services and training services aimed at full employment were diverted to temporary expediencies.

The allocation of expenditure will follow a similar pattern, declining in both employment services and certain training schemes and doubling in special programmes despite the often heavy costs of the latter (MSC 1982a). This increase is undoubtedly related to concern over school-leavers who are unemployed and the consequent disruption and social unrest which is feared. Consequently, certain training services have been seen as more easily expendable in the short term than special or training programmes for school-leavers and the young unemployed.

EMPLOYMENT SERVICES

Although in its review of services for the unemployed the MSC states categorically that it can do nothing about 'demand deficient unemployment' or the inadequacy of the job generation process, its annual report published in the same year, 1981, states that 'one of the Commission's aims is to contribute to efforts to raise employment and reduce unemployment'. The principal means of fulfilling this aim is the placing service of the Employment Service Division (ESD). However, despite the increasing demand for its services on account of rising unemployment, nearly 2,000 ESD staff have been cut back, many of whom work in Jobcentres and employment offices. Given the links which exist between the employment service and social security it is interesting in this context to place these cuts in staff against the extra 1,050 staff put on social security abuse work over the same period of time (*New Society* 11 June 1981). The cut-backs envisaged in the ESD will be even greater given the government's decision to end the requirement that unemployed people register with the employment service as a condition of receiving benefit. The decision was based on a recommendation by the Rayner Scrutiny team, one of whose proposals was the following:

Registration for employment at a Jobcentre should no longer be a condition of entitlement to benefit. Responsibility for questioning whether a claimant is available for work should be transferred to Unemployment Benefit Offices and Unemployment Review Officers with an initial test when a claim is first made and stricter availability criteria. The number of UROs should be increased by 300, and they should adapt their work to local conditions and have close links with Jobcentres.

The MSC did not envisage that voluntary registration would affect the use of the employment service by either employers or jobseekers because of the use made of the service as one of the most important job-finding mechanisms. The Rayner team recommended also that Jobcentres should do less by way of matching people to jobs and rather leave vacancies to be filled through the self-service section of the Jobcentre. However, due to pressures on staff, Jobcentres had already been asking people to record their own details on self-registration forms.

There are a total of 787 Jobcentres. Expenditure on the employment service was £224 million in 1981–82. The volume of business in Jobcentres and employment offices for 1981–82 was as follows: over 6 million people registered for work (of whom over 5 million were unemployed); just under 2 million vacancies were notified and 1.5 million placements were made. As unemployment increases, so too will the work of Jobcentres.

Within the ESD is a separately organised and managed specialist service for the jobseeker at the level of the professional and executive. It is known as PER or Professional and Executive Recruitment. Employers are charged for recruitment but public funds meet other costs. If someone enrols with PER, he or she is 'sent some information about how best to plan and carry out their job search and about additional services which PER can provide'. These include advisory interviews, self-presentation courses and job search seminars. The Secretary of State recommended that PER be run in the future completely on private funding, but this was rejected by the MSC in its Corporate Plan. The need for economies has led to the computerised matching system in PER being replaced by a weekly jobs magazine called *Executive Post* which is sent to all enrolled jobseekers. The MSC suggest this accounted for an all-round increase in business seen by PER. PER's volume of business is far smaller than that of the Jobcentres. Five and a half per cent of the Jobcentre total enrol with PER, 0.7% the amount of vacancies are notified and 0.4% of placements are made. PER is now running at a deficit despite having been in surplus for many years.

In addition to providing information and placing services, the employment service is the starting point for a range of other services. It recruits for YOP, TOPS and CEP. Its other major function is the resettlement service for people with disabilities.

SHARING EXISTING JOBS

In its *Corporate Plan 1982–86*, the MSC raised the question of the longer-term distribution of work and employment and the possibilities of worksharing and early retirement as some of the 'new approaches to dealing with unemployment' (MSC 1982a). For some time the fall in the demand for labour has been reflected in a decline in overtime working and an increase in short-time working. In manufacturing, overtime dropped from an average of 15–16 million hours a week between 1977 and mid-1979 to 10 million hours a week by September 1980. Likewise, short-time working increased from 0.75 million hours lost per week in 1979 to 5 million lost by September 1980 (MSC 1981b: 8). None the less, British workers, especially manual workers, tend to work longer hours with more overtime than most other EEC workers. It is important to consider working time generally before considering worksharing as a solution to high unemployment.

Since Britain's entry to the EEC, manual workers' hours of work including overtime have increased and are now the longest in the EEC. The average weekly hours they work are 43.2 compared to 41.4 in Germany, 40.4 in France, 34.8 in Belgium and 33 in Denmark (Labour Research Department 1981). One of the reasons for this is the extent of overtime worked in Britain. Britain is the only country without any legislation restricting overtime in Western Europe. In the Netherlands, Italy and Ireland, for instance, such legislation has existed for over 45 years. Real wages in Britain too, are not only below all other EEC countries but have increased more slowly.

There is widespread recognition that hours of overtime are correlated with low pay and that overtime is a method of ensuring a decent wage for many male manual workers. By excluding overtime pay from the calculation of low wages, the Low Pay Unit has found that the number of low-paid men increases by 50% to one-fifth of the adult male workforce (Pond 1981). The Trades Union Congress, while normally favouring collective bargaining as the appropriate means of dealing with working time, is considering whether legal limits should be set to hours of work (TUC 1981). Legislation to reduce overtime, however, without dealing with wage rates would 'catapult an increasing number of low-paid manual workers below the poverty line' (Pond 1981). While recognising the problem of low wage rates, the fundamental concern of the TUC seems to lie with the erosion of collective bargaining by legislation.

More recently the issue of overtime working has become linked to unemployment. Faced with prospects of redundancies many unions see overtime bans or short-time work as a means of saving jobs which would otherwise become lost. A number of issues arise in doing this. One is the effect of cutting the levels of earnings of existing workers, especially when they are low paid. Another is whether the level of overtime was due to a shortage of particular skills in the first place. Another is what would happen to output in a shorter week.

Reduced overtime is only one of a variety of methods of worksharing, albeit an important one – particularly in view of its high levels in Britain. Other worksharing schemes include a shorter basic working week, a shorter working year and increased holidays, a shorter working life with earlier retirement and more educational and training leave, less shiftwork and more part-time work or actual jobsharing. One of the main problems confronting all of these is their relationship to earnings. It is clear that the unions see them as a means of improving working conditions and are, therefore, unlikely to accept any such measures if they involve a real cut in wages. It is equally clear that they will not be acceptable to employers if they increase labour costs. Employers might accept some worksharing at the cost of others, e.g. a shorter week but an increase in shiftwork which by making more intensive use of capital equipment will offset any increased labour costs (Taylor 1978).

The Department of Employment estimated in 1978 that a reduction in the basic working week from 40 to 35 hours would cut unemployment by between 100,000 and 500,000. If weekly earnings were maintained, total labour costs would increase by between 6–8%. Similarly, increasing holiday entitlements by a week would produce between 25,000 and 100,000 jobs at an increased labour cost of 2%. On the other hand, if overtime hours and pay were given up, unemployment would be reduced without any increase in labour costs (*Employment Gazette* 1978). However, there are difficulties in costing changes in working time. There is some evidence from two studies of the effects of shorter working time on employment, wages, labour costs and output that shorter working time does not necessarily lead to either increased recruitment or increased costs (White 1980, 1981). Recruitment and job creation were found to occur at a very high level of reduced working time but generally little effect was found. While there was evidence of increased productivity, it was not clear whether this was due to the shorter working week, the parallel introduction of shiftwork, or more efficient managerial practices. The companies studied introduced shorter working time for both external and internal reasons. Shorter working time was sometimes seen as the means of achieving higher productivity and/or the means of giving better working conditions, not only as a response to union demands or competitors' practices (White 1981: 67). Consequently, there was little indication of increased costs arising from working time.

In July 1982, the government introduced a controversial policy of paying firms to split existing full-time jobs into two part-time jobs from January 1983. A grant is paid to employers during the first year in which the splitting of a job results in an unemployed person being recruited. A net saving in public expenditure was anticipated from the saving in unemployment benefits. The scheme would, therefore, increase the number of part-time jobs and decrease the number of unemployed. Britain at present has the largest part-time labour force in the EEC, of which the large majority consists of women. The growth of part-time work has been a major feature in British employment since the 1960s, as outlined in Chapter two. Between 1961 and 1980 a large fall in full-time employment (mainly of males and in manufacturing) was matched by an equivalent increase in part-time employment (mainly of females and in the service sector). The sectors showing the fastest growth in total employment have also showed the fastest growth in part-time employment (MSC 1982c). Now nearly one quarter of the labour force works part-time. It seems clear that part-time work is not a marginal phenomenon but is, as the MSC and others argue., a major growth area in employment (Clark 1982). The reasons for this are likely to be found in the financial and other incentives existing for employing workers on a part-time basis. Many are not covered by the Employment Protection Act 1975, part-time work may be a means of avoiding the Equal Pay Act, and national insurance contributions are not required for those below a certain wage. The job-splitting scheme supported by the government requires a minimum of 15 hours work a week by each of the incumbents. They will not, therefore, be covered by the Employment Protection Act. The Equal Opportunities Commission expressed concern over features such as this. They make a clear distinction between jobsharing which is seen as a means of increasing women's employment opportunities and worksharing which is spreading a reduced volume of work and is potentially exploitative (EOC 1981a, 1981b). Without wishing to reject jobsharing they clearly are concerned that job splitting is primarily aimed at creating less advantageous jobs rather than lifting constraints on women (EOC 1982c) [doc 10].

There are certain problems with part-time work which make it questionable whether its extension is a suitable solution to unemployment. As already indicated, many studies have shown that the pay, working conditions and employment protection rights of part-timers are considerably worse than for the rest of the workforce (Hurstfield 1978, 1980). Many part-time workers are in small firms where their rights may be even further weakened. These may be just the firms most likely to take up the new grant.

It seems, therefore, that in practice the policy of worksharing can mean a number of different things and can be introduced in a number of different ways, some more advantageous than others. Shorter working time does not always result in worksharing. Within shorter working time, some forms of it can lead to better working conditions for workers, e.g. reduced overtime and a shorter working week. Other forms of it, however, can lead to worse conditions of work such as increases in shiftwork with all its attendant bad effects on health and part-time work with its poorer protection. Perhaps the only conclusion to be drawn is that worksharing and shorter working time cover a multitude of differing working arrangements, not all of which will absorb unemployed workers into the labour force.

Part three
SOCIAL POLICY AND VULNERABLE GROUPS

Chapter five
WORK AND THE FAMILY

INTRODUCTION

As discussed in Chapter three, it is particularly important to consider how official statistics are interpreted in order to put them into proper perspective when considering the part played by women in the labour force. For example, their exclusion from the social security system led many women not to register for work when unemployed (when registration was a condition for receiving benefit), seriously distorting the figures of female unemployment and, therefore, of estimates of the female waged labour force. In any event the historical definition of women as dependants has tended to blur their dual role of worker in the home and paid worker outside the home. This has been exacerbated by the confusing use of the term 'economically active'. In official statistics economically inactive people are those never in employment or not seeking it, including the retired, students, permanently sick and housewives engaged in unpaid domestic duties (Irvine and Evans 1979). This has the effect of rendering an enormous amount of unwaged work officially invisible. Women themselves may contribute to this process by returning 'housewife' on censuses and surveys even if employed casually or part-time. As noted in Chapter two, the term 'economically active' will still be used here in order to use the available data but the reader should remember that it is only a partial statistic.

SOME FEATURES OF WOMEN'S EMPLOYMENT

Since the Second World War the proportion of women aged 15 to 59 in the labour force has increased substantially, in particular the proportion of married women. In the early 1950s only 25% of married women in this age group were 'economically active', in contrast to over 60% in the early 1980s. The increase in married women over 45, whose childbearing years are presumably over, who work or wish to work outside the home is even greater. These increases contrast sharply with the more steady participation rates of men and unmarried women which hovered between 90–96% and 72–76% respectively (Lewis 1983). However, in the 1970s there were increases in unemployment for both men and women. During this time female unemployment increased fivefold and male unemployment twofold. Much of the former may not have been 'real' in that it reflected an increase in registration and an increase in unemployed female school-leavers who had a higher propensity to register (Lindley 1980). There is some evidence that the large majority of women who participate in the labour force are married before their late twenties and typically interrupt their working lives to have children. Consequently, there are differences in the patterns of economic activity rates of married and single women according to age, as evidenced in Table 5.1.

Table 5.1 Economic activity rates by age, sex and marital status Great Britain 1981

Age	Men	Married women	Other women
16–19	69	48	64
20–24	90	56	82
25–34	97	51	76
35–49	97	68	77
50–59	92	58	66
60–64	70	23	24
65 and over	11	5	3
All aged 16 and over	78	49	44

Source: *Labour Force Survey 1981*, OPCS 1983.

While the increase in economic activity rates has been common to all women of all ages since the Second World War, there has tended to be less participation by married women at all times and in all ages below 60. The participation in employment of women over 60 has declined in recent years to less than it was just after the War. This may be due to their status as both old and female – two groups often seen as having less claim to a dwindling supply of jobs. Just as noticeable is the decline in activity among women of childbearing age. About 60% of married women under sixty years of age have dependent children. This clearly has had an effect on their ability to work with only 39% being economically active as against 63% of married women with no dependent children. The differences are even more pronounced in the early years with 16% of those with children and 84% without children being economically active in ages 20 to 24, and 23% with children and 82% without children being economically active in ages 25 to 29. These are the ages when women are more likely to have pre-school children, which makes employment even more difficult. Two factors operate when the number of dependent children increases which may have the effect of forcing women back to work. More children cause a squeeze on family income, especially with regard to the rising costs associated with older children. But older children often effectively substitute for their mother's domestic labour and can aid in child care for their younger brothers and sisters (Elliot *et al.* 1981).

The life cycle pattern of labour force participation by women can generally be explained by that which determines their life cycle itself, namely the bearing and rearing of children. There is a need to look further, however, for explanations of their increased participation in the labour force in the post-war period as well as their overgenerous share of unemployment. Lower fertility, the provision of child-care facilities, labour-saving domestic technology, an increase in female education and rising real earnings have all helped to bring about an increase in female employment (Elias 1980). Their secondary status in a segmented labour market and their easy 'disposability' when not needed in the labour force, however, have also led to women's greater susceptibility to unemployment. At certain points these explanations overlap in providing a coherent picture of women and the work they do. However, in order to understand more fully the position of women in the labour market we need to consider the sexual division of labour and women's rising consciousness of this division.

THE SEXUAL DIVISION OF LABOUR

Women's experience of work is very different to that of men and the difference is due to a sexual division of labour both at work and in the family. This refers to the tasks undertaken by men and women in society. It is strongly associated with an ideology that all women must give precedence to their homes and families over work and the world outside, even if husband and home are still only goals to be achieved in the future. This has been referred to as the 'primacy of the housewife role in women's lives today' (Oakley 1976).

Consequently, women are in somewhat of a deviant position if they take on waged labour, which in turn legitimises the unequal status of women in the labour force with its concomitants of low pay, part-time work, little or no fringe benefits and poor working conditions. The 'primacy of the housewife role' forces many women into homeworking. It makes women entering the labour market 'migrants from the domestic domain' (Porter 1982). It undoubtedly encourages the invisibility of female workers. In other words, women's employment patterns are largely determined by their position in society as unpaid domestic labour. The majority of social policies sustain and perpetuate an ideology which gives to women prime responsibility for providing domestic services and to men prime responsibility for providing family income. However, since the wages of a great many working-class men are inadequate to support a family, their wives are often required to provide additional income for the home. Those who can overcome the practical problems of child care and the psychological barriers of deviancy and marginality join the full-time labour force. The others take on part-time work, casual work or homeworking. Within social policy certain policies have helped perpetuate the sexual division of labour, most notably in social security and taxation policy.

Social security

For many years the British social security system has embodied a number of assumptions about the role of women in society and the economic relationships between men and women, especially between husbands and wives. It has defined men as waged breadwinners and women as dependent housewives. This has occurred in both tiers of social security, i.e. in the national insurance system and the supplementary benefits system. The national insurance system discriminates against women indirectly in a number of ways. Much of this has to do with the contributory principle on which it is based (i.e. a benefit system based on paying contributions into a fund and on contribution tests to determine eligibility to their claim from that fund at certain times)*. Contributions are usually

---

*Entitlement to benefit is assessed according to a contributor's 'earnings factor' for the contribution year. For example, to claim unemployment benefit, a contributor must have paid or been credited with contributions totalling fifty times the lower earnings limit within the year. Higher-paid employees will meet this requirement in a shorter time than low-paid employees (Elliot *et al.* 1981: 164).

Work and inequality

linked to paid work. Women have been excluded fully from national insurance in their own right unless they are in paid work. Even then, they have been partly excluded while paying a disproportionate share of national insurance by being given the 'choice' of paying a reduced rate contribution which made them ineligible to claim most benefits. This reduced rate contribution was abandoned in 1978 (under the Social Security Pensions Act of 1975) but women paying it prior to that time could still opt to continue doing so.

The contribution principle excludes certain people automatically such as those who have never worked, e.g. people disabled from an early age and women who have not engaged in paid labour, and those who earn below a certain limit, e.g. many part-time workers. Some women are, therefore, also excluded from the system on account of the types of jobs they do and ironically, on account of the low rewards they receive for them. Women are excluded if they are full-time housewives doing unpaid domestic labour. They are excluded if they are earning wages below the limit which entitles them to contribute and claim (the lower earnings limit). They are also excluded if they are low-paid workers intermittently employed who have failed to build up enough contributions within a specified time. Despite having paid into the system, they may find themselves unable to claim because of the harshness of the entitlement test. The test favours higher paid employees who will more quickly have built up enough credits (because of the proportional nature of the contribution) to claim benefit. Women are also excluded because of the official definition of their jobs. Many women undertake jobs which to all intents and purposes bring them a wage but which are defined as self-employment, e.g. contract work such as cleaning or typing and even homeworking and, therefore, exclude them from claiming.

The national insurance system has failed to cover many people, both male and female and, even when it does, it often fails to do so adequately. The second tier of social security, the supplementary benefits system, functions, therefore, to fill the gaps left by national insurance. Conceived originally to be no more than a small fall-back arrangement for a minority of people, it has now grown enormously. Much of this is due to the harshness and strictness of the entitlement tests of national insurance. For instance, nearly a half of all registered unemployed people are dependent on supplementary benefits. As unemployment rises the proportion of claimants reliant on supplementary benefits will also increase due to the growth in

66

the number of long-term unemployed who have exhausted their entitlement to national insurance. The basic condition for receipt of supplementary benefit is that the person is not in full-time work, has an income below the basic scale rates and has less than a certain amount in savings. Certain things are disregarded in calculating income, e.g. the first few pounds of the individual's and his/her spouse's earnings, earnings of dependent children, and educational grants.

Although it is a safety net system, certain people are also directly excluded from claiming supplementary benefits, e.g. newly arrived immigrants to the country. Others exclude themselves because of the stigma of claiming. The largest group excluded from the system is married women or women cohabiting with a male. The reason for this is the classification of wives and female cohabitees as dependants. It has already been shown that the concept of female dependency bears little relationship to the reality of female participation in the labour force. None the less, a married woman who is sick or unemployed has no automatic right to apply for supplementary benefit while her husband in similar circumstances may.

In situations where women are claiming supplementary benefits, the DHSS will first make every effort to obtain maintenance payments for her from a man who is called her 'liable relative'. A liable relative officer will attempt to establish the whereabouts of the man upon whom she is dependent by reason of marriage or paternity. Within the system it is rare for a woman to be independently defined. However, in 1978 the EEC Commission issued a limited and loosely worded directive that member states should treat male and female claimants equally and that arrangements should be made to rectify any anomalies by the end of 1984. In Britain this was implemented no sooner than necessary. From November 1983 women have been entitled to call themselves head of their household thus enabling them to claim social security benefits on the same basis as men (*Guardian* 18 Aug. 1982). Housewives, however, are still excluded (Land 1980a). The other numerous exceptions, exclusions and conditions attached to the directive have cast doubts on its capacity to bring about real change (Rights of Women 1983).

Other benefits, more recent in origin, which are unrelated to either national insurance or supplementary benefit have also been based on the assumption that women work inside the home rather than in paid employment. These are Child Benefit, Non-Contributory Invalidity Pension (NCIP), Invalid Care Allowance (ICA) and Family Income Supplement (FIS). Child benefit, introduced in

1975, (see Land 1977b) represents the merger of child tax reliefs and family allowances, both of which had been in existence for a long period of time. It is available to anyone who is responsible for a dependent child. Unlike, and in stark contrast to, the others, it is usually payable to the mother of the child and can only be paid to her husband with the woman's signed consent. If the parents are cohabiting only the mother may claim. A major gain for poorer families (against whom child tax allowances had discriminated by being worth less in value) and a gain for women who were *de facto* caring for their children, it none the less still reinforces the role of female as 'carer'.

Other benefits which place married women's primary responsibilities in the home are the ICA and the NCIP. The ICA is paid to anyone who gives up paid employment to look after a severely disabled relative who is getting an attendance allowance, *except for a married or cohabiting woman*. The NCIP is paid to anyone who is incapable of paid work on the basis of sickness or disability but who is not part of the national insurance system or who has failed the contributory tests. Married or cohabiting women, however, had to undergo a household duties test first to ensure that they are truly incapable of carrying out their unpaid tasks in the home. When introducing housewives' NCIP, the Department of Health and Social Security argued that married women regarded caring for their home and family as their main occupation, in the same way that other people regarded their paid employment. More than a few women were affected by this. Within two and-a-half years, 86,512 applications for housewives' NCIP had been made, less than half of which were successful (Glendinning 1980). According to Land this was the first time the concept of 'household duties' had been written into social security legislation, suggesting that assumptions about the sexual division of labour are not as pervasive as they used to be and must now be made explicit (Land 1980a). The implications of this kind of labour will be discussed further in the following section.

A final benefit which, until recently, adversely affected women was FIS. This was a benefit introduced to support employees and the self-employed who were bringing up children on a low wage. It is paid to full-time workers earning less than a specified amount. FIS was introduced as an alternative to a national minimum wage, as a state subsidy to low paying employers. Until the EEC directive a mother on a low wage supporting an unemployed husband or cohabitee was not eligible to claim FIS while a man on a low wage could do so. The mother would be doubly disadvantaged because FIS acts as a passport to a range of other means-tested benefits such as free dental treatment, free prescriptions and free school meals. The assumptions underlying this unequal treatment were again those which perceive women as having primary responsibility in the home with paid work being secondary to this. As long as the social security system continues to be based on these assumptions, women's opportunities and income will be limited not only in the labour market but outside it as well.

Taxation

The tax system both reflects and shapes social roles. Like the social security system it embodies assumptions about men and women and presumes certain responsibilities and needs on the part of each. The marriage relationship has always been important in determining taxation. Since the introduction of income tax nearly 200 years ago, husband and wife have been taxed as one unit. On marriage a woman's property became her husband's as did earned and unearned income. Although the Married Women's Property Acts passed around the turn of this century gave women the right to control their own property and income, it did not affect the principle of 'aggregation' which is still in force today (Land 1977a). It is found in the Income and Corporation Taxes Act 1970, which states that the income of a married woman living with her husband shall 'be deemed for income tax purposes to be his income and not to be her income' (Elliot *et al.* 1981: 196; Lister 1980). The principle of aggregation can be overcome by applying for the earnings of husband and wife to be taxed separately but the man then loses his more generous Married Man's Allowance (MMA) for a Single Person's Allowance (SPA), the implications of which will be dealt with below. This option, introduced by the Finance Act 1971, was taken up by very few people since it is of benefit only to those in higher income brackets.

Taxation is clearly an instrument of social policy. This is particularly evident in two fundamental features of the British tax system which concern women. The first is the aggregation of the income of husbands and wives into one unit. The second is the MMA. The issue of aggregation is a complex one. It is clearly inappropriate to classify all married women as dependants and it is clearly discriminatory to aggregate only in the name of the husband, giving him economic power in the home. However, there is a case to be made for assessing tax liability fairly. There is some consensus among groups of different political persuasions such as the Meade Committee and the Conservative Party Committee on Women and Tax that earned income should be individually taxed. Disaggregation of earned income is clearly a trend in most OECD countries (Lister 1980). Disaggregation of unearned income, however, is more difficult because it would encourage the division of income in wealthy households in order to reduce their tax bill and this would mean a considerable loss of revenue for the state.

Tax allowances are sums of money which are not taxed in order to take into account certain financial responsibilities. They effectively set the threshold at which someone begins to pay tax. The MMA was introduced in 1918. When graduated rates of tax were introduced in 1909, married couples became liable for more tax than if they simply lived together. This, together with the recognition of the wife as a dependant, constituted the origins of the MMA (Land 1977a). Today all married men are entitled to the MMA regardless of whether their wives are in paid employment or not. For those men whose wives do work, an additional allowance, the wife's earned income allowance, is set against his tax. There is now a growing body of opinion that the MMA is inequitable as a form of provision for dependants because of the growth of females in the labour force and because of the advantages to childless married couples (Tunnard 1978; EOC 1979; Lister 1980). The abolition of the MMA would bring a substantial sum of increased revenue to the state, estimated to be in the region of £8–9 billion (Elliot *et al.* 1981: 215). This sum could double the rate of child benefit, thus achieving one of its original aims of supporting dependants – this time true dependants, namely children.

The MMA is only one, albeit the most significant, of many tax allowances which discriminate against women and which implicitly or explicitly regard them as fulfilling the dual role of dependant and homemaker/housekeeper. Other tax allowances are the Additional Personal Allowance (APA) and the Dependent Relative Allowance (DRA). The APA is designed to assist single parents but it is also available for a married man with children and an incapacitated wife. A married woman in a similar situation is ineligible. The APA further discriminates in favour of marriage as it is awarded on top of the MMA, thus placing the married man in a more advantageous position than the single parent (Elliot *et al.* 1981). The DRA is also sex-specific but in a somewhat unusual way. Widowed or separated mothers are defined as dependants for whom the DRA may be claimed but not fathers, regardless of age or infirmity. It is also paid to the husband of a married couple even if the wife is the actual person caring for the dependent relative. As Elliot *et al*. state, 'the dependency allowances as a whole convey an impression of the assumed structure of the family and the role played by women in particular (Elliot *et al*. 1981: 203).

DOMESTIC LABOUR

The existence of a sexual division of labour reinforced by social policy measures has been further explained by some writers by an analysis of the role which domestic labour plays under capitalism. It has been argued that the continual social reproduction of the capacity of men and women to work is a necessary condition of all human societies. Under capitalism this occurs in three ways: first, by the wage with which goods and services can be bought for consumption; secondly by domestic labour which, like the food, clothes and recreation bought by the wage, replenishes the capacity to work; and thirdly, by the welfare state which provides services like health and housing to aid men and women to work harder and better. Domestic labour, pre-eminently undertaken by women, provides daily sustenance and care for workers. It also rears the next generation of workers by providing the major form of child bearing and rearing (Gough 1979: 44–8). Women are identified as being responsible for this part of the reproduction of the labour force not only by biologically creating it, but by maintaining and socialising it as well.

The question arises of to what extent domestic work as we know it is a requirement of capitalism and whether it is another form of labour which can be classed as productive alongside wage labour. Different positions have been taken regarding this. On the one hand has been the argument that housewives engaged in unpaid domestic labour are just another form of labour and, since they are involved in producing and creating profits, they are an exploited group as is the working class as a whole. The concept of class is thus retained as integral to the analysis. On the other hand is the argument that domestic work is private and that the household has a set of economic and labour relations particular to the family. Therefore, the concept of gender becomes more crucial to the analysis (for details of the debate surrounding this issue see Seccombe 1974; Gardiner 1975; Coulson *et al*. 1975; Himmelweit and Mohun 1977; Molyneux 1979; Holland 1980; Wajcman 1981) [doc

11]. While recognising the importance of some of these issues, it is not the purpose of this book to engage in the debate. Our concern is rather with the implementation of certain social policies which impinge on women's unpaid labour within the home and an analysis of how these affect their choices with regard to employment outside the home.

'CARING' LABOUR

As might be expected, the majority of children live at home with their parents and are cared for by their mothers. In addition to this the majority of old and handicapped people are cared for at home. There is increasing evidence that the people who care for them are women. An EOC study in 1978 found that three times as many women as men were looking after elderly or handicapped relatives (EOC 1980). A later survey of mentally ill people living at home found that twice as many women as men were caring for them on a day-to-day basis (Lonsdale *et al*. 1980). Hunt's survey of elderly people at home found that relatives who visited and were visited by these old people tended more often to be female. More daughters and daughters-in-law visited and were visited than sons and sons-in-law. Similarly, more sisters and sisters-in-law visited and were visited than brothers and brothers-in-law (Hunt 1978). The care of both children and other dependants can be extremely arduous work. The burden is especially great because the demands of all groups, children, elderly and handicapped, tend to be continuous. Women and mothers, therefore, tend to work very long hours. In addition to being on call 24 hours a day the year round, mothers appear to be spending on average about double the average paid working week on housework and child care (Oakley 1974; Hughes *et al*. 1980). The proportion of time spent on domestic work and child care decreases slightly among women in employment. The extent to which their husbands participate in domestic work and child care is about one-third that of their wives and this does not change very much when wives are employed (Elliot *et al*. 1981: 146). Very similar evidence emerges regarding the care of elderly or handicapped people. One study found that almost half the carers in their survey (of whom the majority were women) spent between 4 and 10 hours a day on activities which directly related to caring for the handicapped dependant, excluding household tasks. Again wives spent fourteen times as much time on caring activities than husbands and four times as much time on simply being with the dependant (EOC 1982b).

There is a large body of evidence that the costs of a household increase substantially with the presence of either children or handicapped members of the family (Baldwin 1977; Layard *et al.* 1978; Piachaud 1979; Burghes 1980; Coussins and Coote 1981; Durward 1981). Ironically, at a time when many women might need to go out to work to supplement the family income, they will be least likely to be able to do so. In many cases, mothers and/or carers may have to give up an already existing job that is paid or move into part-time work in order to look after dependants. Hunt found that among the women in her sample who gave up work below the age of 39, the majority (71%) did so on marriage, with the second largest group doing so to have a baby. Among women between the ages of 40 and 50 the need to look after sick and infirm relatives was second only to ill health as a reason for giving up work (Hunt 1978). In addition to the interesting finding that husbands also fall into the 'dependant' category, the burden of caring for the young, sick and elderly dependants was found to fall mainly on women.

The question of who should bear the burden of caring for dependent members of the family is clearly an issue of social policy. If the state decides to take on this task it will provide nurseries and pre-school care for children and various forms of provision for the elderly and handicapped. The latter could be institutionalised care; it could be a range of home-care services such as home helps, meals-on-wheels, adaptations and appliances to aid daily living and so on. If the state decides not to take on this task, given the present social arrangements, it will be undertaken by the family, by voluntary effort or not at all. What is current British social policy in respect of dependants? For some time policy making has hovered in between the two approaches and through incrementalism has ended up with a 'mixed economy' of welfare which does not meet all needs and which has tended towards the private rather than the public. This has increasingly been the case since 1979 when public expenditure has drawn back at least from these areas. Much of this is due to a policy of community care which has been variously interpreted by different administrations. The idea of community care has regularly been a policy option in the field of mental health, where it has been taken to mean a policy of reorientation away from institutional care in the community (Personal Social Services and Central Health Services Councils 1978). Whether care in the community was to be care by the family or care by the local authority services was never spelled out. As a result of cutbacks in public

73

expenditure which included local authority spending, however, the reality of care in the community has come to be family care which in turn has meant female care (Finch and Groves 1980, 1983) [doc 12]. Originally an implicit consequence of financial restraint, community care has now become an explicit aim of current government policy. A handbook of guidelines for health and personal social services stresses the 'vigorous tradition of voluntary and community service' in Britain and suggests that most people needing help or care 'look first to family and friends' (DHSS 1981).

Community care which is care by women at home is a low-cost solution for the state but it does involve costs for the families concerned. The research of Breslau *et al.* in the United States goes some way to suggesting that the burden will be even greater on the earning potential of low income families than on other families (Breslau *et al.* 1982). Nissel and Bonnerjea have calculated the opportunity costs to women of being unable to take up full-time employment in the occupation of their choice because of the need to care for a handicapped elderly relative in the home. They have also calculated the actual cost of caring in terms of the cost of substitute care. These give us some idea of the savings made by the state and the costs borne by women, of certain forms of community care policies. Earnings forgone by wives wishing to resume previous occupations averaged £87.00 a week. Earnings forgone by wives forced into part-time work averaged £37.00 a week. The cost of substitute care measured at the market rate for home and domestic helpers and hospital ward orderlies, based on 3.5 hours a day, averaged £47.50 a week (Nissel and Bonnerjea 1982: 51–6). Given the government's calculation that the numbers of people over seventy-five will increase substantially to over 3 million by 1990, the savings to be made by encouraging women to care for the elderly will be very great. The government has also calculated that by 1990 there will be 3.6 million children under five, suggesting that the rising birth rate is a trend which will continue (DHSS 1981). These increases in dependent members of the population have coincided with a reduction in the provision of local authority services for them by directly abolishing or reducing services, delaying provision, reducing eligibility or introducing charges (Durward *et al.* 1980; EOC 1982b).

CHILD CARE AND HOMEWORKING

The position with regard to pre-school provision has long been one of insufficiency. This is reflected in the low employment rates for women with pre-school children. Only 18% of women with children aged 0–2 were in employment in the mid-1970s compared to 43% in France, 33% in West Germany and 58% in Sweden. Only 31% of women with children aged three to school age were in employment in Britain compared to 44% in France and 64% in Sweden (Hughes *et al.* 1980).

Hughes *et al.* list seven types of pre-school services in England and Wales which go to make up the complicated pattern of provision. In total these provide 298 places per 1,000 children aged under five. Forty-six per cent are provided by the state sector, 54% by the voluntary or private sectors. Nearly 1.25 million children use these services, some part-time. They do not include unregistered child minders or private schools. None the less, on the information available, it is clear that provision is far from adequate with 70% of under-fives not being catered for. Even when there is provision it is often part-time which has serious implications for mothers wishing to work and may contribute to forcing them into part-time work. Many children are cared for in a number of different ways during the course of a week. The scarcity of arrangements has probably also led to an increase in unregistered childminding although its true extent is very difficult to gauge (Coulter 1981). Childminding, largely undertaken by women, is another low-cost solution to child care which coincides with some of the views about community care outlined above. A number of studies have begun to document the pay and working conditions of childminders. In 1975 the National Union of Public Employees produced a charter to improve the very poor conditions of service for childminders. Ironically, it may be low-paid families where the mother works to supplement a meagre family income who are then only able to afford low rates of pay to a childminder who herself may be working to supplement a low income. As Coulter notes, the low rates of pay 'encourage a higher turnover of minders which has disturbing implications for the continuity of care . . . and means that efforts to train minders in better childcare practice can have little long term effect' (Coulter 1981). Her survey of over 800 childminders across the United Kingdom found evidence of full-time childminders who were earning very low incomes for working an average 42-hour week. As with other homeworking, there were few fringe benefits such as holiday and sickness pay and additional expenses such as heating and wear and tear in the home. Most significantly, 85% of the minders did such work in order to look after their own children or other dependants who were old or disabled. There was an obvious need to combine paid employment and their own child care. The true 'self-help' nature of childminding is revealed in the informal subsidy many childminders operate for low-paid families. Despite this, many childminders felt they were in low-status inferior work which may well be a reflection of society's ambivalence towards motherhood and child rearing. Extolling it in theory and ideology, it is nonetheless recognised for the difficult, tedious task it sometimes is and for its secondary status to paid work in the world outside the home.

One of the ways of 'solving' problems of child care (and other dependants) for a large number of women has been working at home. One estimate is that between 200,000 and 400,000 people work in or from their homes for an employer who provides the work and then markets and sells the finished product (Hakim 1980). Most homework is not undertaken out of choice but is needed, however poorly paid, because of an unequal division of labour in the home. Almost all homeworkers are women. In her study of homeworkers in England, Hakim found that a strong commitment to their child-care responsibilities was the main reason for working at home. She also found a feeling of sacrifice on the part of the women she interviewed. However, other factors contributed to the choice of homework such as ill health, financial difficulties and language problems among immigrant women. The flexibility of homework was helpful for child care as well as for complementing husbands with irregular work patterns such as shiftwork (Hakim 1980).

The significance of homework lies in its hidden costs and hazards for women and its often exploitative and low rates of pay. Despite this, the earnings provided by homeworking are often a significant and important part of family income. Between 25,000 and 30,000 homeworkers are covered by wages councils and receive some minimal protection. However, illegal underpayment persists, often because of ignorance of their rights on the part of homeworkers or fear that they will lose what little they have. In a sample of homeworkers in one industry covered by a wages council, over 90% had not heard of the wages council or their right to a minimum rate of pay (ACAS 1978; Crine 1981a). Most of the homeworkers putting buttons on cards in this study said they were working for more than 20 hours a week for less than £8.60. In her study Hakim found rates of pay for those engaged in manufacturing work to be from 25 pence to £1.50 an hour. Rates for sewing and similar work were even lower. The rates did not appear to vary according to work done or levels of experience but to the employer concerned. Payment in manufacturing homework appears to be almost always on a piecework basis.

Most studies of homeworkers indicate that their earnings are vital to the family income. There is often a correlation between accepting low rates of pay and the need to work to supplement the family income (Hope *et al.* 1976, Crine 1979; Hakim 1980). An important finding is that homeworkers tend to perceive that they are in a different labour market to other workers, giving some credence to the view that the labour market is segmented. For some homeworkers, their earnings help overcome fluctuations in their husband's earnings due, for example, to a loss in overtime. In addition to low rates of pay, homeworkers face a number of additional expenses which other workers do not. Because they are working at home, they face the costs of heating, lighting, electricity for machines used and the supply of tools and machines where these are needed. For those collecting and delivering their own work there are the costs of travel or postage. These costs are very rarely reimbursed. There are inconveniences to working at home such as space taken up and the noise of machines. When these extend to large quantities of dust or chemicals in the air, inconveniences become hazards. When machines, dust and fumes are present there is often a need for additional ventilation of the kind that few homes can provide. While homeworkers are covered by the 1974 Health and Safety at Work Act, little can be done to ensure that health and safety standards are not contravened at home, particularly when homeworkers are vulnerable and fearful of losing their job and the extra money it provides.

WOMEN'S EARNINGS

Women's earnings remain significantly below those of men and have done so for some time. Much of this is due to the factors outlined above. They have increased only slightly since 1970. The male/female earnings gap decreased more substantially between 1974 and 1976 but this decrease did not persist beyond then. The reason for this was the implementation of the Equal Pay Act 1970 which came into force in December 1975. Women's earnings have generally reached approximately two-thirds of men's earnings. It is striking that there has been virtually no change in the male/female ratio since 1913, when it was 53% (Routh 1980). The greatest gap has been shown to be in the private non-manual sector which possibly reflects the fact that many low-paid women in the private sector, such as shop assistants, are classified as non-manual. There also appears to be differential provision in the fringe benefits received by women as a whole. This may well be due to the different types of jobs done by women and their shorter length of service within jobs – at least with regard to fringe benefits such as company cars, pension schemes, sick pay and holiday entitlements (Elliot *et al.* 1981). This would be an indirect result of women being over-represented in part-time work and in small-scale establishments which in turn would be due to the sexual division of labour.

Job segregation is probably the most dominant influence with regard to the male/female earnings gap, together with the growth of part-time work. However, although part-time work has increased there is still evidence that full-time female employees earn less than men. Table 5.2 indicates the proportion of men and women at the lower end of the earnings scale.

Table 5.2. Percentage of full-time working men and women earning less than certain amounts, Great Britain 1981

Earning less than (£ p.w)	Male (%)	Female (%)
50	0.4	5.1
60	1.1	15.3
70	3.4	30.7
80	7.9	46.8
90	15.0	59.8
100*	24.0	70.0

* From this point the male proportion starts to increase rapidly.

Source: *New Earnings Survey*, Part A 1981, Table 1.

The perception of women's family responsibilities limits some women's availability to work the same hours as men. This has become entrenched in legislation which aims to limit the number of weekly hours a woman may work and the amount of shiftwork and night work they may do, in addition to other health and safety measures. Consequently part of the reason for the difference in the wages of men and women is related to how their pay is made up. Most notably overtime affects the differential. This has led to calls for the extra protection afforded women to be abolished since it acts as a barrier to equal opportunity. In response to this, however, there have been calls to extend the protective laws to all workers irrespective of sex on health and safety grounds alone (see Coussins 1979 for a summary of these arguments). There is a far higher incidence of overtime working for men and this would seem to be a reason why they work longer hours. In addition, overtime payments contribute about four times as much to male earnings as to female earnings. It is becoming increasingly recognised that the wages differential has to be understood by reference to men and women's different relationship to working time. One writer notes that it is conventional wisdom among trade union negotiators that 'male workers will often view campaigns for a shorter working week as an indirect wage rise (because they seem to increase opportunities for overtime) whereas for women it means real time off' (Campbell 1982).

Job segregation in the labour market means men and women doing different kinds of work and, therefore, not in competition with one another. It is necessary to distinguish between vertical and horizontal segregation. The latter exists when men and women are most commonly working in different occupations. The former exists when men are most commonly in higher-grade (more skilled or better paid) jobs and women in lower-grade jobs within the same categories of work. Trends in job segregation are crucial to an assessment of how social policy has affected the low level of women's pay. Within social policy, two pieces of legislation have attempted to lift women out of low paid work, the Equal Pay Act and the Sex Discrimination Act. It is increasingly becoming evident that as instruments of social policy neither has been able to deal with the effects of job segregation in maintaining male/female differentials (Hakim 1981; Snell *et al.* 1981; Glucklich and Snell 1982). This appears to be largely because the separation of men and women's jobs prevents equal pay comparisons and the introduction of new grading schemes depresses the grading of women's jobs. In other words, horizontal and vertical segregation have removed certain jobs from the reaches of legislation.

Throughout the 1970s the general sex structure of jobs remained constant with a quarter of all jobs being typically female and three-quarters being typically male. However, taking into account the proportion of women in the labour force, there has been a decline in job segregation since 1901, particularly with regard to vertical segregation. In order to assess the impact of legislation, Hakim has looked at the decline over the years 1973–77. She found a decline four times greater than might have been expected from past trends, and greater than over any other four-year period. However, the situation almost completely reversed in the following period, from 1977–79, eliminating virtually all the gains of the preceding four years. The explanation she proposes for this finding is other trends in the labour market, most notably the fall in activity rates of married women, the increased share of female employment and the rising birthrate. All of these are likely to affect women's work aspirations and expectations and attitudes to women working (Hakim 1981). Others are also starting to look at employment practices which by increasing job segregation make possible non-compliance with the legislation (Glucklich and Snell 1982).

Between 70% and 75% of all employees who fall within the scope of wages councils are women. This means they are in those industries where workers traditionally have not been protected by competent (or any) trade unions and consequently have been low paid. Although the wages councils set statutory minimum wages these are usually very low and illegal underpayment is widespread. The rationale for low rates was to provide an incentive for the development of collective bargaining to negotiate higher rates. In the light of this it is interesting to note that where the actual earnings of female workers in these industries exceed the minima, they do so on average by only 25% in contrast to 100% for males (MacLennan 1980). This may suggest a perceived legitimacy on the part of employers, even in low-paying industries, regarding increases in male wages which does not prevail when it comes to female wages. This perceived legitimacy is reflected in another phenomenon which has been explored by Land and others, *the family wage* (Land 1980b). The notion of a family wage is the idea that an adult man ought to earn enough to support a wife and dependent children. It is part of the standard practice of trade unions to take into account the family wage in drawing up pay claims. It has been extended beyond being an instrument of collective bargaining to constitute the official definition of the family for purposes of setting levels of benefit, of defining the poverty line and so on. The implications of a 'family wage' are many. It is an inaccurate representation of what most families are. Many male wage earners do not have dependants and many breadwinners are female. Not all wives are economically dependent and the idea of a family wage is likely to have a profound effect on equal pay, perpetuating the view that women's earnings are extras rather than essentials to the household budget. It therefore undermines the ability to negotiate equal pay between men and women (Barrett and McIntosh 1980)and, more seriously in the view of some, gives organised labour a vested interest in keeping women at home and in a dependent position. It perpetuates the view that men have a right to the best-paid jobs (Land 1980b).

LEGISLATION AND POLICY

In 1970 Parliament passed the Equal Pay Act, establishing a five-year gap between its enactment and its coming into force in 1975. In 1975 the Sex Discrimination Act was passed incorporating the Equal Pay Act, and the Equal Opportunities Commission (EOC) was established with the task of implementing both. Two other pieces of legislation in the same year promised to improve the position of women. The Social Security (Pensions) Act introduced a new state pension scheme which, for the first time, included provisions for women who had been out of waged work for certain periods because of their 'home responsibilities'. The Employment Protection Act gave women rights to paid maternity leave and to getting their jobs back after such leave, although these have now been amended by the Employment Act 1980. But from 1975 substantial legislative provision has recognised the dual role of home-keeper and worker which most women have to adopt. Despite this statutory protection and the existence of laws to enforce equal opportunity, women still earn less than men. The anti-discrimination legislation has largely failed in its goal of bringing about better working conditions and pay and combating discrimination.

The Equal Pay Act covers contractual matters relating to employment whereas the Sex Discrimination Act covers recruitment policies, promotion, dismissals, redundancies, fringe benefits and other aspects of employment that are non-contractual. Under the Equal Pay Act a woman must be paid the same rate of pay as a man if she is doing work that is the same or similar to his. The legislation did not adopt the International Labour Organisation Convention of 1951 which required member states to adopt equal pay for work *of equal value*. Because of the difficulties involved in assessing the relative value of work the Act settled on dealing only with the same type of work. This means the legislation can only be applied when men and women are doing the same job, which occupational segregation at the same time prevents. Wage structures which systematically ensure that women's work is low paid are legal as long as no man enters those segregated workforces. There is some evidence that the five-year gap between the law being passed and coming into force was used by some employers to ensure that women and men were not doing the same work (quoted in Coote and Campbell 1982: 108). In their study of the implementation of equal pay in twenty-six firms, Snell *et al.* found very few cases of women doing the same or similar work to men (Snell *et al.* 1981).

If a women believes that she is being discriminated against contractually, i.e. in wage rates, overtime or fringe benefits, for instance, or in terms of the Sex Discrimination Act, she can take the case to an industrial tribunal and if necessary to an Employment Appeals Tribunal. In both cases she has to prove that the discrimination has occurred and must provide evidence to this effect. There has been a sharp decline in the number of applications made under these two Acts since 1976. In 1976, 1,742 applications were made under the Equal Pay Act and 243 under the Sex Discrimination Act. By 1980 these figures had fallen dramatically to 91 and 181 respectively (Scorer and Sedley 1983: 22). The EOC does not have a duty to assist applicants and indeed, has limited funds and staffing to do so. Between 1975 and 1980, however, it gave financial and legal assistance to about 200 industrial tribunal cases. There is evidence that a number of applicants face a variety of pressures which cause them to withdraw or to settle for less than they feel to be just (Gregory 1982) [doc 13]. In July 1983 the European Court of Justice ruled that the British equal pay legislation needed to be amended to conform with an EEC equal pay directive. One of the requirements was that the principle of equal pay for work of equal value had to be embodied in the legislation. An amendment was introduced which went some way towards meeting this [doc 14]. The burden of proof was shifted back to the employer but was a different standard of proof to the existing one.

By and large the legislation rests on the assumption that the problem is one of lack of equal opportunities. It accepts the operation of the market mechanism and sees the role of policy as one of making adjustments where necessary to ensure the smooth working of a fundamentally free labour market. It does not begin to touch the division of labour between men and women at work or between men and women in the allocation of domestic duties.

The overriding determinant of women's position in the labour market has been suggested to be the sexual division of labour. This has led to a higher incidence of part-time work among women, less training among women, less overtime worked by women and a segregation of women into industries and establishments which are relatively low paid, less skilled, less secure and with poorer working conditions. There is a predominance of women in this secondary sector of the labour market which both reinforces the sexual division of labour and acts as a source of reserve labour which can be drawn upon by employers at will.

Chapter six
TRAINING THE YOUNG FOR WORK

The preceding chapter illustrated in a number of ways the vulnerability of women in the labour market in terms of their pay and conditions, their susceptibility to unemployment and their lack of employment protection. They are not alone in this, however. The composition of the labour force has been changing since the 1960s. Women and young people now form a sizeable and larger portion of the labour market than previously (Sorrentino 1981: 187–91). Both groups have fewer skills and less experience than older males. For different reasons both groups have a weaker attachment to their jobs. There is a greater incidence of voluntary and involuntary job changing among younger people. They are more prone to dismissal for disciplinary reasons such as poor timekeeping. Young people also leave jobs voluntarily due to dissatisfaction with pay and working conditions as well as a desire to explore the new world of work which they face. They may have fewer financial or household commitments, although not all are teenagers living at home and many contribute to the income of poor households. Female workers, by contrast, may change jobs for precisely the opposite reason, i.e. because of the nature of their household responsibilities. Despite their increase in numbers in the labour market, both groups remain underemployed and marginal workers in the secondary labour market. Both groups pose competition for one another in that they often pursue the same jobs at the same lower wage than an older male would command. There is some evidence that, given a choice of recruits, many employers prefer to recruit women or to operate an internal labour market by upgrading existing employees (which could adversely affect both women and younger workers) (MSC 1978a: 40).

It has been argued that early experience in the labour market exerts a strong influence both on subsequent attitudes to work and on subsequent job opportunities (Casson 1979). What in the past may have been seen as a short period of adjustment and experimentation on the part of young people entering the labour market for the first time has now become a period of prolonged unemployment accompanied by despondency and a sense of grievance. It was ostensibly to avoid this and in recognition of the importance of early experience that there has been an employment service oriented towards young people since early this century. Initially the Labour Exchanges, established in 1909, made provision for both adults and juveniles. This overlapped with provisions in the education services, creating an 'administrative duality' of services which was to persist until 1974 (Showler 1976: 63–71). The conflict over whether the bridge from school to work required an educational or an employment service has not really been resolved. It remains in existing policy more as a reflection of the transitionary nature of the issue.

INDUSTRIAL TRAINING

By 1910 local authorities had the power to provide an employment service for all those up to the age of seventeen. At the same time central government's Board of Trade provided a juvenile advisory service through its Labour Exchanges. After some fluctuation between the two, the Employment and Training Act 1948 established a Central Youth Employment Executive consisting of officials from the Ministries of both Labour and Education in an attempt to resolve the duality. The vast majority of local education authorities became responsible for the service. This led to an emphasis on vocational guidance in schools rather than placements in industry (Showler 1976: 64–6). However, it did not resolve the issue of what the relationship was or should be between formal education and industrial training. During the 1950s and 1960s the British economy did not show the same growth rates as its European counterparts. In addition, there were persistent shortages of skilled labour. This shifted attention from vocational guidance and youth employment to a concern with skill training and a perceived underinvestment in training for industry. Up until 1964 skill training, unlike education, was almost completely a private and non-governmental affair although further and higher education may have contained elements of skill training. Industry and commerce either provided direct training or attempted to avoid such costs by recruiting skilled workers trained elsewhere. Rather than providing or financing industrial training the state preferred to persuade and influence individual firms to do so (Ziderman 1978: 38). Training was concentrated on craft apprenticeships for male school-leavers. Little provision was made for adults, females and less skilled people (MSC 1980d).

Growing criticisms of the system of industrial training led ultimately to the passing of the Industrial Training Act in 1964. The Act had three main objectives. It wished to increase and improve industrial training and it wished to share the cost of training more equally between firms. The mechanism through which these were to take place was to be the Industrial Training Board (ITB). The ITBs were tripartite bodies consisting of members representing management, union and education, in each branch of industry. They had wide powers to improve the quality of training and the supply of skilled labour. A Central Training Council co-ordinated the work of the ITBs. Within five years, twenty-seven ITBs covering 15 million employees (or three-fifths of the labour force) had been established. They operated a levy-grant system to spread the cost of training. A rate of a percentage of the payroll was levied on all firms within the jurisdiction of each ITB to cover the costs of training. This money was then reimbursed by way of grants to those firms who were investing in training. Money, therefore, was redistributed from firms offering little or no training to those that were, although it also led to greater equality in provision (Ziderman 1978: 47). Through this legislation the state had moved into a position of regulating training without directly providing or financing it. The proportion of employment outside this system began to increase, however, due to the decline in manufacturing and the increase in the service sector which tended not to be covered by the ITB system, e.g. local and central government, banking, insurance, shipping. In 1972 a review of these arrangements took place (Department of Employment 1972b) which gave rise to the Employment and Training Act the following year. The review was extremely critical of the levy-grant system and the high rates levied by some boards. It recommended phasing out the levy and allowing some firms to apply for exemption from payment if they were meeting their own training needs. But it also made recommendations which would lead to the financing of training shifting from industry to the Exchequer. The 1973 Act did not take up this option of more direct state intervention (except for the administrative costs of the ITBs). Instead it established a new body, the Manpower Services Commission, to co-ordinate ITBs, in effect replacing the Central

Training Council. An upper limit was set on the levy and small firms were exempted from paying it. The essential nature of the 1964 Act remained unchanged. However, over the following five years the Exchequer's contribution to influencing training within industry increased almost tenfold (MSC 1980d: 11). In addition, the MSC pursued a more active role in identifying training needs and establishing a variety of training instruments for both adults and young people.

In particular, concern had already been expressed about the growing number of young people. In 1970 the employment or careers service for the young had come under scrutiny. The National Youth Employment Council (established in 1948) set up a working party to consider the structure and the target group of the service. The issue was whether there should be a primarily educational service for people up to the age of twenty-two (based on the view that the needs of new entrants to the labour market were special) or whether there should be an employment service for all people. Under the Employment and Training Act 1973 it became mandatory upon local education authorities to provide a guidance and placement service for all school, further and higher education students. This was to be the retitled Careers Service, with a more flexible approach based on the point of entry into the labour market rather than on age. Ninety per cent of school-leavers register with the Careers Service which acts as an important channel to employment programmes. It is, however, more concerned with guidance than with placements with the exception of the scheme known as Community Industry (CI).

An unusual and singular policy development occurred in 1972 when this scheme was established. It aimed at job creation, undertaking projects related to the needs of the community. Recruits had to be under eighteen years of age and referred through the Careers Service. They had to be unemployed, have a record of instability in employment, or be socially and personally disadvantaged. At the cost of £21 million (1981/2 prices) it provides 7,000 places for young people. Those involved tend to be male (two-thirds) and work in teams of eight to ten. Local authorities provide the premises, the National Association of Youth Clubs runs the scheme and employs the adult staff involved in it (MSC 1982b: 15).

The MSC continues to finance and support a number of training programmes, some of which were considered in Chapter four. For young people these include Community Industry, Unified Vocational Preparation, Youth Opportunities Programmes and more recently the Youth Training Scheme. However, since 1980 government has stressed the need for voluntary arrangements in training. A year after coming into office and consistent with its overall approach to social policy, the Conservative government made it clear that they wished to extend the voluntary sector, keeping only a few statutory boards if necessary, and to centralise any remaining training provision. The MSC was involved in a process of consultation with regard to which of the statutory boards should remain, although this took place in the extremely short time period of six months. It also occurred within the context of a declared policy of abandoning statutory training provision. Despite this, the Commission strongly recommended that the government defer the implementation of its decision to stop funding ITBs. It claimed that 'left to themselves, companies are unlikely to invest substantial resources in training unless they are reasonably confident that they will reap significant benefits from the output of the trained workers' (MSC 1981d: 3). The truth of this is evident, given the effect of the recession and the reluctance of firms to involve themselves in the costs of training. Nonetheless, the Employment and Training Act 1981 was passed, allowing the Minister to wind down ITBs without reference to anyone, including the MSC. Within a year sixteen ITBs had been closed, entailing a further redirection of government funds into non-ITB sectors. One of the results of this approach has been a proliferation of temporary training measures.

YOUNG PEOPLE IN THE LABOUR MARKET

About 800,000–900,000 young people leave school in Britain every year. Only a quarter of these go on to full-time general education, the remainder are available for employment (*Employment Gazette*, June 1983). Many school-leavers do find work but an increasing proportion either remain unemployed or enter a temporary programme of training or work experience such as the Youth Opportunities Programme (YOP). There is generally a higher rate of unemployment among young people who are unqualified. There is also a tendency for this unemployment to last longer. Britain has lagged behind many European countries in providing further education or apprenticeship programmes for young school-leavers despite the history of statutory intervention outlined above. Just over a half of British school-leavers go into some form of general or vocational education or apprenticeship training in contrast to 95% in Belgium, 90% in West Germany, 80% in France, and 73% in the

Netherlands (MSC 1980d: 27) which may explain Britain's skill shortage. The comparison with West Germany is particularly apposite given certain similarities in the two countries regarding population, size, population density, age distribution, and working population by economic sector.

Concern about employment opportunities and conditions of work for young people have been continuing issues in policy. Young people form a distinctive group in the labour market. They are concentrated in certain industries and occupations and have a very high rate of unemployment. The latter is often explained by the former in that the industries in which they are concentrated are vulnerable to lay-offs or to recessions generally (i.e. construction and distribution for boys, distribution, clothing and footwear for girls). It may also be easier for firms faced with a need to reduce labour costs to adopt a policy of reducing their recruitment rather than laying-off workers, in which case younger workers are likely to suffer disproportionately. This may be offset by the lower wages which have traditionally been paid to young workers, although research indicates that such an effect of youth wages on employment is not significant (Makeham 1980a) [doc 15].

WAGES OF YOUNG WORKERS

There are traditional arrangements in Britain for lower wages to be paid to younger workers. The average earnings of young people relative to those of adults are low and have been so for many years. However, the average earnings of boys relative to men have grown slowly but substantially in much of the post-war period. The average earnings of girls relative to adults and relative to boys have remained about the same. In 1969 girls' earnings were 69.2% that of boys and 66.6% that of women. Ten years later they were only 71.9% and 67.3% respectively. In 1969 boys' earnings were 46.9% of men but by 1979 they had increased to 56.2% (Wells 1983). Girls' earnings increased quite substantially in 1973 and 1974 relative to adults and boys but declined again in 1975. This may have been caused by the raising of the school-leaving age, the effect of which later dissipated. Young people's wages have not increased substantially in recent years as youth unemployment has increased. It seems likely that the earlier increases were due to raising the school-leaving age, lowering the age of majority, the return of many 18–20 year-olds to work as National Service was phased out, and so on. If the average earnings of young people increase with age, then these factors would have an effect by increasing the proportion of 'older' young workers (worth more to employers as a result of their additional year's schooling) and changing the definition of adulthood.

While only average relative earnings have been considered so far, there is greater variation for instance within craft apprentice rates, which range from £24 a week to £64 a week and from 33% of adult rates to 56%. But most basic rates for those starting out from school are below £50 a week whether they are for apprentices, unskilled workers or junior clerks (Incomes Data Services 1981). Generally, craft apprenticeships command a starting rate which is higher than that for unskilled work. In engineering and building, starting rates are below £40 per week. It therefore seems generally true that it will be worth while for an employer to take on a young person if their productivity is about half that of an adult. More often than not their productivity and effectiveness on the job will be worth a great deal more.

Britain's statutory minimum wage system, operating in selected industries through the wages council system which sets legally enforceable minimum wages, reflects the tradition of paying lower wages to younger workers. The main industries covered by this form of statutory machinery are catering and retailing, both well known for their disproportionately large numbers of young people, as are hairdressing and laundries. These industries cover almost 2.5 million workers altogether (Crine 1980: 14). In the majority of industries covered, the adult rate of pay is awarded at 18 years. The three wages councils covering the largest groups of workers, 1.5 million in all, only pay the adult rate at 19 years. The hairdressing wages council only sets the adult rate at 20 years but until the 1982/3 settlement it was set at 22 years. It is probably no accident that these councils are responsible for extremely high proportions of young workers, particularly hairdressing. They are also notable for awarding fewer holidays than other councils, again hairdressing in particular. Hairdressing is a substantial industry consisting of 140,000 workers and is the lowest paying industry recorded in the *New Earnings Survey* undertaken by the Department of Employment (Crine 1981b; Crine 1982). Despite this, every year a quarter of all hairdressing employers are found to be illegally paying below the minimum rates. This may particularly affect younger workers who in their newness to the labour market are likely to have less knowledge of its workings. These low wages and the lack of apprenticeship schemes have made Britain's young workers a source of cheap labour rather than an investment for the future of industry.

UNEMPLOYMENT

Many factors affect rates of unemployment among young people, just as they do among women. Most governments face pressure to keep down rates of unemployment (particularly if they are politically contentious) and operate policies which directly have this effect, such as providing training schemes which reduce the number of young people officially regarded as out of work. Such policies can reduce political controversy but do not always solve unemployment. One factor affecting rates of unemployment has to do with claiming benefits. Many employers tend to recruit in September which has meant school-leavers signing on for supplementary benefits in the preceding months and, therefore, registering as unemployed. This changed in 1981 when a rule was established whereby only those who left school before their Easter exams could claim supplementary benefit. If they left school after writing their exams, they were deemed to be on summer holidays. The disincentive this creates to take the exam is all the more interesting in the light of claims that British industry needs better qualified workers. A further change reduced all numbers on the unemployment register by no longer requiring benefit claimants to register for work before being eligible for benefit.

Despite this, registered unemployment among young people has remained extremely high. This is not a phenomenon peculiar to Britain and has become a matter of increasing concern in a number of Western European countries. Part of it is due to high overall unemployment; part of it is due to high birth rates in the early 1960s for which little planning and provision was made, but much of it is due to the particular vulnerability of young people in relation to work. Recruitment has declined as a response to low demand, many jobs are closed to young people and, if not, they are having to compete with experienced adults. Consequently, the majority of 16 year-old school-leavers are either unemployed or on a temporary youth training scheme. Table 6.1 illustrates how many under-18 year-olds are either in work, signing on, or participating in a government training scheme.

About half of those who are not in employment are in a government sponsored scheme, indicating the extent to which such

Table 6.1. Employment status of those under 18 years of age, Great Britain (thousands)

September	Total in labour force	Employed	Unemployed or on a Government sponsored scheme
1980	1155.9	745.8 (64%)	410.1 (36%)
1981	1135.3	606.4 (53%)	528.9 (47%)
1982	1111.5	527.1 (47%)	584.4 (53%)
1983	1102.0	523.5 (47%)	578.5 (53%)
1984	1091.4	523.1 (48%)	568.3 (52%)

Source: *Youth Task Group Report*, MSC, 1982.

schemes are lowering the official rate of youth unemployment.

There is some evidence that unemployment is even greater than the table indicates. In 1974 the Community Relations Commission published a report based on interviews with unemployed young people across England. The survey found unemployment among young black people to be substantially higher than among their white counterparts. More than 40% of the full sample were not registered at the time of interview and 25% had never registered. In particular there appeared to be cynicism and distrust on the part of young blacks about the employment services. None the less, the report recommended strengthening and improving the Careers Service as a means of improving the situation (Community Relations Commission 1974). The issue of non-registration was seen to be extremely important because it reflected on the careers and employment service, although it has been reported that non-registration among adults is equally high (Roberts *et al*. 1981). Although subsequent research has been less conclusive about non-registration, the Department of Employment decided in 1978 to fund certain outreach posts within the local authority Careers Services. This was based largely on the recommendation of the MSC (MSC 1978a). The outreach workers were intended to be a more informal means of seeking out unemployed people and in particular of contacting non-registrants.

A later survey by the Commission for Racial Equality of 1,000 16 to 20 year-olds in inner city areas found that teenagers of Afro-Caribbean origin were far more likely to be unemployed than their white or Asian counterparts. Together with Asians, they were also less likely to get jobs than equally qualified young white people (Hirsch 1983: 11).

A pervasive explanation for increases in youth unemployment has been that young workers are pricing themselves out of jobs [doc 15]. It is suggested that employers cannot afford to take on younger workers because their wages are too high in relation to experienced adults. This argument is not too different from the general one that uncompetitive wage claims contribute to increasing unemployment overall. A detailed analysis of the wages of young people in relation to youth unemployment undertaken by the Department of Employment, however, failed to find any evidence for this. The increases in relative youth wages in the post-war period were not found to bear a relationship to levels of youth unemployment (Makeham 1980a). Given the static pattern of relative girls' wages referred to earlier, we should expect unemployment among young girls to have been less than that found among young boys. This has not been so. A further analysis by the Department of Employment updating Makeham's work has reiterated his findings that no clear link can be found between the earnings and levels of unemployment of either young males or young females.

Despite the clear absence of evidence that high wages are putting young people out of work, policies have been enacted which are directed at 'pricing young people back into jobs'. The Young Workers Scheme referred to in Chapter four represents a fairly unambiguous scheme for encouraging the employment of young people at low wages. Employers are paid a subsidy for keeping the gross pay of each young worker below a specified amount. A written response in the House of Commons revealed that very few new jobs were created by the scheme in its first year of operation. Ninety per cent of the jobs subsidized by the scheme were found to have been in existence despite the subsidy. While the scheme continues to operate, youth unemployment continues to rise. Its effect on reducing young people's wages seems more obvious than its effect on reducing young people's unemployment [doc 16].

A second pervasive explanation for youth unemployment has been in terms of the quality of young people on offer to employers. Young people are perceived as being untrained and ill-equipped to meet the needs that industry and their potential employers require. This was not the conclusion reached by Makeham at the Department of Employment. He suggested that:

Those conditions which produce high overall unemployment produce high youth unemployment. The most important reason why youth unemployment is higher in one town than another is that the local economy is more depressed and overall unemployment is higher. When changes in the whole economy take place the unemployment rises and falls, youth unemployment also rises and falls, but to a much greater extent . . . The implication is that if significant changes in youth unemployment are to be made, policies which affect the whole economy are essential. (Makeham 1980a: 65)

More recently, however, policy has focused on the vocational and training needs of young people. Some have interpreted this as a temporary response to a potentially disruptive situation of very high rates of unemployment. Others have seen it as the beginning of a national strategy for industrial training. Few believe any longer that schemes like the Youth Training Scheme create any more real jobs. For the individuals involved, their attraction is at best the experience offered, the possibility of gaining a skill and at worst, simply occupying empty time.

TRAINING AS POLICY: YOP

An account of the development of policy along these lines should start with a report, *Young People and Work*, published in 1977. From the outset the report's view of youth unemployment was that it merited special attention because young people represented an investment in the national workforce. It subsequently commissioned research which resulted in interviews with 3,550 young people, 1,100 employers and information on the experiences and attitudes to training of 7,000 young people. Many of the report's findings confirmed an already acknowledged picture of young people's behaviour in the labour market. They changed jobs frequently, their patterns of employment had changed little over time, they received little formal training on entering work and they wished for more assistance in starting work. One of the most important findings was that over half of those who were unemployed had left school without any qualifications while the majority of the rest had low-calibre CSE qualifications. Although not as severe this pattern of little education applied to all the young people, not just those who were unemployed (MSC 1978a).

The Youth Opportunities Programme (YOP) scheme got off the ground in April 1978. It did not intend to provide opportunities for all unemployed 16–18 year-olds. Its original target was to provide for 187,000 unemployed young people by August 1979. These were to be those unemployed for more than six weeks at the time when the cycle of youth unemployment was lowest, in particular school-leavers. The overall aim of YOP was 'to offer unemployed 16–18 year-olds opportunities of training and work experience that will improve their prospects of obtaining a satisfactory permanent job at the earliest possible moment and will provide a real and constructive *alternative to unemployment*' [author's emphasis] (MSC 1979b: 9). The programme offered different types of work-preparation courses and work experience. The former lasted from between 2 and 3 weeks to 13 weeks. The latter lasted from 6 to 12 months. Sixteen per cent of YOP entrants undertook work preparation courses of which there were three: employment induction courses, short training courses and remedial courses. Eighty-four per cent undertook work experience courses of which there were four types. Work experience on Employers' premises (WEEP) had to provide young people with experience of a variety of different types of work and not just one single job. They were able at the same time to attend further education courses. The opportunities were not intended to serve as a replacement for the normal recruitment of employees, but a survey of sponsors by the MSC itself indicated that YOP people were replacing permanent staff right from the inception of the programme (MSC 1979b: 19). Project-based work experience offered a variety of practical experience on specific projects under adult supervision but unlike WEEP was mainly in the public sector and had to involve outdoor environmental improvements. Training workshops would make and sell products or provide services. Community service, which later amalgamated with the project-based experience to form 'Community Projects', offered work experience within health, welfare, social or education services.

The original YOP scheme had a very clear purpose. This was to give young people some expertise in looking for work and for performing well in interviews. It was not considered feasible or sensible to provide opportunities for all unemployed 16–18 year-olds but was aimed at those who had been unemployed for some weeks. It was clearly seen as being a solution, albeit partial and temporary, to youth unemployment, the cause of which could be put down to inexperience or ineptitude at job searching. Twenty-eight Area Boards were formed to oversee the preparation of area plans. The boards typically had representatives of employers, trade unions, voluntary organisations, local authorities and the education service. Principal Careers Officers had right of attendance on the board although they were not members (MSC 1980a). Certain rules applied to YOP: no person was eligible until they had been out of work for six weeks. This was to ensure that young people had made every effort to get work. No one leaving school or college was eligible until 1 September. This was also to ensure that young people tried to get jobs for themselves in a period when there was substantial employer recruitment anyway. Whatever their age or the particular scheme they were on, all YOP participants got the same allowance. This was intended to keep the programme simple to run but also to prevent certain programmes attracting recruits for monetary considerations. The payment was free of tax and national insurance contributions. Travel expenses over a certain amount were also paid.

Originally one half of YOP entrants had no qualifications, 25% had CSE (below grade 1) qualifications and 26% had higher qualifications. This distribution then altered considerably, suggesting that YOP moved away from catering for those most in need of training and education.

Those participating in the WEEP (Work Experience on Employers' Premises) scheme tended to be better qualified than other YOP recruits. This had the effect of making them more likely to replace full-time workers and more likely to be taken into permanent employment by their sponsoring employers. The latter was certainly evidenced by research evaluating YOP schemes. Three evaluative surveys undertaken to assess the employment status of ex-YOP participants found a steady decline in employment over time, although this was less evident in WEEP schemes. Within the overall decrease in the proportion who were employed, some groups did worse than others. These were black youths, those youths with no qualifications, and those who had had a long period of unemployment prior to their YOP scheme (Dawes *et al*. 1982: 12–13).

There have been and are many criticisms of the YOP scheme. The early aims of the programme implied that it was aimed at what was a temporary and marginal problem in the labour market. It therefore made sense to help a smallish group perform better at job search and job interviews. It implicitly accepted the view that young people needed to invest some of their own 'human capital' in acquiring the skills which would make them more attractive units of labour to sell in the market place. When the problem of youth unemployment increased beyond expectations and became manifest, as many felt, in the street riots of 1980 and 1981, expectations of what YOP could actually do changed. The fear gradually developed also that 'a programme which had been put together and built up to a large size very quickly, to deal with what was seen as a temporary and marginal problem might become a permanent part of our education and training institutions without proper consideration of its content and quality' (Youthaid 1981). The danger that this had already happened was recognised by the Secretary of State for Employment as well when he announced an expansion of YOP to the House of Commons and, more importantly, 'the development of YOP in the wider context of improving preparation for and training in work of *all* young people, and not just the unemployed'. This statement was indicative of the significant shift that has taken shape in the Youth Training Scheme.

By the time of this statement in November 1980, more than 0.5 million young people had voluntarily gone on a YOP scheme because they found it preferable to the alternative of unemployment and another 0.5 million and more had taken it up by March 1982. This in itself is important in reflecting the desires and expectations of young people for training and employment. The first problem was the steady decline in the proportion of people on YOP work experience schemes who were subsequently employed or in education and training six months after leaving the programme. In 1978, 78% were employed or in education or training. By June 1980 this had dropped to 45% (MSC 1981e: 7). The second problem was the limited real experience gained. The bulk of YOP was made up of WEEP and the majority of WEEP was concentrated in small, often non-unionised firms usually in distribution or services. The experience gained was often of unskilled work where little training was involved (Youthaid 1981: 4). The third problem was in overall terms extremely important. Research undertaken by the MSC itself indicated that about 30% of WEEP placements were substituting for permanent jobs, predominantly by replacing the recruitment of ordinary employees but also by replacing adult workers (MSC 1981e: 9). Unions who expressed concern over this did not necessarily reject YOP but called for more adequate monitoring of schemes like WEEP. In order to get young people into jobs as quickly as possible the quality of YOP schemes was constrained. YOP's credibility all round fell steadily, young people lost confidence in its ability to provide them with lasting employment, and places on YOP began to decline as unemployment grew.

THE 'NEW DEAL' YOP

In November 1980 the Secretary of State for Employment announced a £250 million set of proposals which he defined as 'nothing less than a new deal for the young unemployed' (*Guardian* 22 Nov. 1980). The package aimed to provide 180,000 work-experience places for 16 and 17 year-olds in addition to the then existing 260,000. In addition, 1,000 extra places would be provided in CI and 200 extra Careers Service posts created. The expansion was to occur in firms already co-operating in YOP. A YOP place was to be guaranteed for every school-leaver within a year and in an even shorter period of time for every 16 and 17 year-old. The burden this would place on the YOP scheme gave rise to fears that corners would be cut and standards would decline even further on programmes like WEEP. Serious monitoring would have to decline. At the same time steps were being taken to dismantle the ITBs, as outlined above. Within six months of this announcement, the MSC put out a consultative document, *A New Training Initiative*, endorsed by the Secretaries of State for Employment, Education, Scotland and Wales. The starting point of the document was the need to invent, invest and exploit new technologies (predominantly in fields such as microelectronics, biotechnology, advanced chemicals, new materials, computer applications, energy systems and communications systems). In order to do this a need was perceived for a better and differently skilled workforce. The document acknowledged that Britain traditionally had taken a short-term view of skill training rather than seeing it as an investment for the future. It contrasted the fact that only 50% of Britain's young people are trained further after school, compared with 81% of French and 93% of West German youth (MSC 1981f).

From the start it seemed evident that the consultative document intended to build up a five-year experimental programme which had been in operation since 1976 – the Unified Vocational Preparation (UVP) programme. This scheme provided financial support to firms offering school-leavers who entered their employment a programme of induction training, planned work experience and further education. The programme was small, dealing with only 3,500 young people, but was reported to be successful. The consultative document's three main aims were to develop skill training, to guarantee education, training or planned work experience for all under-18 year-olds and to provide wider opportunities for adults to acquire, increase or update their skills and knowledge. The document's main thrust, however, was towards youth training. It was surprisingly complacent about YOP, saying that it had demonstrated that 'work can be the mainspring for motivating many young people towards learning'. In relation to the cost of the scheme, the document saw a three-way advantage and, therefore, a three-way means of financing it, through employers, government and trainees. It recognised the public benefits to be derived from the scheme and the need for a contribution from the Exchequer. It also suggested that trainees needed to understand the personal benefits that might accrue to them through investment in training and that they could share the burden of cost by accepting lower rates of pay. The payment to YOP participants had already been frozen at its 1980 level.

In December 1981 the MSC published *New Training Initiative: An Agenda for Action* – a report based on a consideration of the 1,000 written submissions received in response to the consultative document. In the standard traditions of social policy making, the public was consulted, its views scrutinised and a programme of action devised on the basis of a consensus of opinion. The new *Agenda* reported overwhelming support for the three objectives. In addition most responses to the consultative document were reported as believing a comprehensive training strategy to be a 'crucial and integral part of Britain's overall strategy for economic recovery and sustained growth' (MSC 1981g). This is important given the scepticism with which the many youth training schemes have been viewed.

The argument from many quarters was that while traineeships (of 6 or 12 months) were important and necessary for industry, there was no guarantee that all the jobs necessary would be available for all the trainees as they completed their periods of training. Again, those who commented on the consultative document were in no doubt about the need for public intervention. The MSC felt that market forces alone would not produce the quality or quantity required of training because of the financial constraints facing employers and their uncertainty about the return on such investments. They therefore recommended devising a means of funding which included substantial state support in recognition of both the public and private benefits of training. The three objectives of the consultative document were retained. More immediately, the *Agenda* recommended expanding and developing the YOP scheme into a programme providing up to a year's training for *all* young people not in work or full-time education. The target of 100,000 places in the year immediately following the report was planned. Again the UVP programme was quoted as a model arrangement. Although prompt action was envisaged, an additional proposal was for the establishment of a high-level task group to include representatives from the CBI, the TUC, education and others. This was to produce a report on guidelines for the structure, scope and content of a general scheme, the allocation of costs between the employer and the state, the timetable for introducing the scheme and the income of participants. The emphasis was on rapid and immediate improvement based on consultation and negotiation. On the same day that the *Agenda for Action* was published, a government White Paper *A New Training Initiative: A Programme for Action* was also published. Its author was a new Secretary of State for Employment more committed to the role of market forces in the economy than his predecessor had been. (Interestingly, this was followed by a replacement within the MSC itself of its chairperson by a political nominee, without the normal processes of consultation with unions and employers.) The White Paper set out a ten-point plan which in essence established an ambitious new Youth Training Scheme (YTS) guaranteeing a full year's foundation training for all those leaving school at the minimum age without a job.

Although the YOP allowance was increased slightly (to maintain a differential from supplementary benefits) the White Paper put forward certain very contentious proposals regarding benefits and training allowances on the YTS. It envisaged an allowance for 16 year-olds to reflect the 'learning role' of the scheme. Unlike YOP, this was intended to cover travel expenses. In addition, 16 year-olds on the scheme would not be eligible for supplementary benefits in the year following their leaving school. This compulsory element in the new YTS was very critically received and ultimately abandoned by the government. The training allowance, too, became more generous than the level originally proposed. The new scheme was intended to build on but effectively replace YOP and UVP. Effectively it was an exercise in co-ordination. More fundamentally, it represented a continuation of the shift from training under the auspices of further education institutions and ITBs (in which trade unions and professional educators had substantial influence) to training sponsored by employers. The sum of £1 billion was allocated to YTS in its first year (compared to the cost of YOP of about £400 million). Participation in the scheme was voluntary on the part of employers and trainees and both sets of participants were subject to public relations exercises advertising the scheme. Two types of places were available in the scheme. One, known as Mode A, was employer based – the MSC subsidises an employer to provide training schemes for young trainees. In Mode B places were organised by the MSC itself. YTS was dependent on there being sufficient Mode A places, but clearly in a voluntary scheme which none the less 'guarantees' places, a fall-back arrangement had to exist to honour both the guarantee and its voluntary nature. Such a two-tier arrangement, however, jeopardises the equality of opportunity which the scheme promises [doc 17].

YTS was backed by both the TUC and the CBI. Some individual unions, however, were more restrained in their participation. Remembering the problems associated with YOP, there were calls for more careful monitoring of the scheme in terms of its quality and its potential to replace full-time jobs. However, it was a vocational preparation programme modelled on the UVP. It involved a shift to large employers in both the private and public sectors. A great deal more was being demanded of employers. An advisory group on content and standards was established to undertake detailed work on the schemes and to assist the Youth Training Board which was to oversee and monitor the schemes. The MSC stressed that the scheme was not just a measure to reduce unemployment but was primarily a vocational training programme (MSC Special Programme News, July 1982). It none the less reduced the register of unemployed people substantially, as did YOP.

The introduction of YTS coincides with a number of events which suggest that it is more than simply a vocational scheme to train young people to become the labour needed for British industry. Recommendations for a new training initiative came in the wake of extremely high and serious levels of youth unemployment. It also coincided with a decline in the ability of YOP trainees to find jobs or to be placed in jobs by the employment service, and a series of street riots in which the participation of young people was prominent. Youth training can, therefore, be seen to have a strategic value in diverting attention away from unemployment and in keeping young people busy and off the streets. More surprisingly, the YTS was introduced at the same time as the statutory training scheme outlined earlier was abolished. Instead of using the ITBs for a renewed drive in youth training, a largely voluntary system has replaced them in which cash payments are provided as incentives to employers to participate in the scheme. The ITBs, established in 1964, were set up precisely because employers were reluctant to invest in skill training. It remains to be seen whether they are any more enthusiastic about doing so now, but they have so far not been over-eager to provide the large numbers of places required. None the less, the move back to the privatisation of industrial training continues, with the state taking a residual role in relation to young people and employment.

Chapter seven

FROM WORK TO OLD AGE

INTRODUCTION

In recent years biological age has become increasingly important in determining one's social and economic position. Old age has become demarcated by a count of years rather than by how an individual feels or wishes to act. This social definition of old age is specified in particular by the enforced transition from paid labour to retirement. One of the reasons people take up employment is not only to secure current financial security but also to cushion their future lives. Retirement is a phenomenon peculiar to industrial societies. Retirement at age sixty-five for men and sixty for women is the general rule, a fixed retirement age having been first introduced in Britain in 1859. It has come to signify in a rather artificial way the dividing line between employment and productivity on the one hand and leisure and dependency on the other. This distinction is imposed on older workers either by a mixture of custom and policy or by law in the case of compulsory retirement, regardless of their abilities. A number of policy decisions have determined who is allowed to be productive in our society as well as how the fruits of that productivity should be allocated in the form of pensions. Decisions about the age of retirement are not based primarily on people's capacities and choice, but on the demand for labour and on the costs of pensions [doc 18].

The general perception of the role of older workers in the labour force has changed quite considerably since the 1950s and 1960s. Labour shortages during the post-war period led to an increased demand for labour and a manpower policy which encouraged the participation in employment of certain groups. Within this category was the older worker who was encouraged to postpone retirement. For instance, the 1951 Budget argued that the retirement age should be increased to meet the labour shortage and ensure a balance between the productive and non-productive population (Walker 1982a: 62). The 1950s and the 1960s were years of economic growth, prosperity and labour shortages. At the same time there was also a demographic increase in the number of older people, who were living longer and often in a fitter condition.

These changes were characteristic of both the United Kingdom and the United States. In the 1950s when unemployment was at an all-time low there was a surge of interest in older workers both in research and in policy. In Britain a National Advisory Committee on the Employment of Older Men and Women (the Watkinson Committee) was established in 1951. It led to a number of publicity and recruitment campaigns aimed at promoting more opportunities for older workers. The detrimental effects of retirement were publicised, as were the advantages of older workers. In the United States some years later but still riding on the crest of a prosperous economy and vigorous labour market, protective legislation was passed aimed at older workers.

However, in a very short space of time the economic arguments about employing older people began to disappear. The growth of unemployment generally and especially the increase in rates of unemployment for school-leavers completely reversed the labour shortages of the post-war period. In consequence policies were framed to reduce the size of the labour market. The desire to dispose of older workers from the labour market for economic reasons led to the construction of policies of early retirement and redundancy. This did not occur to the same extent in the United States, although it too had a surplus of labour. This was possibly due to their legislation which proscribes discrimination against older workers. In the United Kingdom there were unsuccessful attempts to introduce more solid anti-discriminatory legislation in 1973 and 1974 in the form of outlawing age limits to jobs and introducing quotas. As unemployment increased, it proved more difficult to keep such policies on the political agenda even though the effect of flexible retirement on the size of the supply of labour is uncertain (Walker 1982a: 70). It is more likely to have a significant impact in reducing the pension bill. As the number of economically active people declines, the financial costs of social security rise. Older workers are often caught in the cross-fire between rising unemployment (and their vulnerability to it) and the desire by most governments to keep the costs of pensions down. More often than not older workers pay for this predicament by receiving inadequate pensions.

THE OLDER WORKER

Approximately 36% of the labour force are aged between 45 and 64 years. In all age groups the proportion of males and non-married females still active in the labour force has declined steadily since the mid-1970s. There has been an even greater decline in the older age ranges prior to official retirement age in the case of males. Participation in employment has declined very little after the age of sixty-five by contrast, although there has been a long-term decline this century as far as those over sixty-five are concerned. The activity rates of older married women have increased and are higher for all women beyond the retirement age of sixty than the rates for men beyond the retirement age of sixty-five.

Workers who are fifty-five years and older make up approximately 17% of the economically active population. As already indicated, this proportion has declined steadily over the 1970s and into the 1980s. The increasing tendency for men to retire earlier may be due to specific policies such as the Job Release Scheme (discussed below) combined with factors such as the increase in unemployment among older workers who then face diminishing prospects of getting back into work (Fogarty 1980: 10–11). There is evidence that many older people who would like to continue working are compelled to leave for reasons such as redundancy or compulsory retirement and then have to give up looking for work through lack of success (Hunt 1978: 67; Parker 1980, 1981; Fogarty 1975: 23). Part of the burden of unemployment is being increasingly borne by older workers. The unemployment rates of males aged fifty-five and over have consistently been higher than for other males except in recent times with the growth of youth unemployment. The unemployment rate for economically active men aged 55–59 is 16% and for men 60 and over it is 20%, in contrast to 12% for men between the ages 35–54 (*Employment Gazette* March 1984). After April 1983 some men over 60 were no longer obliged to sign on at an unemployment office. This reduced their officially recorded rate of unemployment by more than a half to 8%. It is also well established that once unemployed, it is the older person who is more likely to suffer prolonged unemployment and to exhaust entitlement to unemployment benefit (Colledge and Bartholomew 1980; Makeham 1980b: 11). Becoming discouraged, they are then more likely to drop out of the labour force altogether.

Unemployment is not the only negative experience facing older workers. Age/earnings profiles show a pattern of earnings which increase to a peak long before retirement age for most males. (Female earnings remain constant for longer, peaking at a later age for non-manual workers, which reflects the different nature of their participation in the labour force.) Manual workers reach their peak earnings in their thirties, professional and technical workers and middle-level managers in their forties, while top managers and some professionals continue increasing their earnings into their fifties (Fogarty 1975: 95). With regard to manual workers, this is probably a reflection of how their pay packet is generally made up. Older manual workers work less overtime and on average receive lower payments on PBR (payment by results) and shift systems – which could reflect declining abilities, declining opportunities, fewer financial commitments or the choice of more leisure (Makeham 1980b: 12). Whereas younger workers usually experience an increase in earnings when changing jobs, older workers experience a decrease in earnings and downward mobility, particularly when over 55 and 65 years of age (Daniel 1974). Since they also experience more difficulty in finding jobs and have less mobility, they may be hindered in making advantageous job moves which could maintain or increase the value of their earnings. Whatever the reason, many older workers are concentrated in particular industries and occupations. This especially applies to men over 65 and women over 60 who are concentrated in low-paying industries such as agriculture and distributive services. Older men and women are also concentrated in specific occupational groups which tend to be low-paying, i.e. predominantly in unskilled manual jobs but also, for men, in junior non-manual jobs (Parker 1980; Atkinson *et al.* 1982; Byrne *et al.* 1983). Part-time employment is also characteristic of those industries and occupations which may attract older workers, especially those over retirement age. Older workers who are unemployed show a greater tendency to apply for jobs and to take jobs at a lower skill level than previously (Daniel 1974).

It is important to ascertain more precisely the reasons for older workers' susceptibility to unemployment and low wages. Their labour market experience can be judged in terms of lower productivity on the part of older workers, employer discrimination against older workers, their attachment to the labour force, the amount of education and training they possess or the institutional barriers they face. (Makeham 1980b: 19; 1981).

THE PRODUCTIVITY OF OLDER WORKERS

The measurement of productivity is fraught with difficulty and varies according to how such research is undertaken as well as how its findings are interpreted. In addition, the variation found in different types of work may be more important than trying to make a general judgement on the productivity of older workers. Should we be looking at laboratory data on general abilities such as memory and dexterity or should we be looking at performances in actual work situations? In the former we neglect the older individual whose long experience on the job has overcome any possible biological decline. In the latter we may not be able to generalise about 'older workers' because of the variation that will occur according to the type of work involved. In both cases we ignore the heterogeneity that exists in all age groups. An additional problem in measuring productivity is the change that occurs from one generation to the next with regard to the productive task as a whole. The next generation of older people is likely to be better educated and healthier (relative to existing occupational class differences) and, therefore, more capable of performing well, and at the same time the laborious nature of work is steadily being reduced. However, automation may require speed, concentration and quick reactions rather than the experience and reliability for which older workers may be known. Measures of productivity must constantly be changing and are usually too specific to be generalised according to age.

Because of the difficulties of measuring productivity, older workers can be considered in relation to various other facets of employment such as physical and mental ability, absenteeism, accidents and adaptability on the job (Makeham 1980b: 19). There is a great deal of evidence that the incidence of chronic sickness and disability increases with age and that breakdowns in health are highest in the years before retirement. The incidence of dental problems, visual defects and hearing impairments also increases with age. All illnesses or impairments can affect the energy of individuals and their capacity to meet the obligations they face. Perhaps more importantly, they can affect individuals' perceptions of themselves and their self-esteem which may further affect their ability to perform certain roles. The stress created by impending retirement or redundancy may contribute to a decline in health. Although health and work ability may decline generally with age, they are also subject to considerable individual and occupational variation.

As far as absenteeism is concerned, certified sickness absence increases for men over 60 but decreases for women over 60. Uncertified sickness, voluntary absence and lateness vary inversely with age. Older workers have been found to be absent less frequently but when they are absent it may be for longer periods of time. Generally, however, there is a marked difference between sickness absence and casual absence (Makeham 1980b: 20). Evidence produced by the Watkinson Committee did not support the view that older workers sustain more accidents; neither does DHSS data on injury benefit. Accident rates are more likely to be correlated with risks of exposure. With regard to adaptability, there is some evidence that older workers are more rigid and traditional. However, older workers have also demonstrated that a retraining investment in them yields as much as it does for younger workers (Reubens 1970: 96).

With regard to performance in actual work situations, the US Bureau of Labor Statistics made comparisons of performances by workers in different age groups and found a decline in output in age group 55–65 but with considerable individual variation. Because of this problem in using statistical averages, some writers suggest we should pay more attention to functional age. The key feature of this is the focus on the ability rather than the pathology of the older worker. Special attention is paid to those conditions which make for (or against) successful adaptation to work tasks, e.g. ignoring statistical averages and searching for variables that could explain the heterogeneity of job performance within age groups. Recognition is given to the 'job-specific' dimension and to the possibility that experience and retraining frequently compensate for a decline in ability. It is recognised, however, that these declines do not occur within the individual at the same rate for each different function, and that for some functions the decline may be only slight or irrelevant in relation to job-performance criteria (Sheppard 1976: 296).

If one approaches older workers on this functional basis, then solutions to problems of work lead to a different set of policy options. These include redesigning the nature of the task as well as the technology or equipment and developing special training principles and techniques for assisting older workers to adapt. Job redesign is important as regards improving the work environment and productivity generally [doc 19].

Between 1964 and 1970 the OECD undertook a series of studies on training and job design for older workers. Some of the features of jobs likely to be unfavourable to older workers (particularly in routine and manual grades) but which could be selected for job redesign were listed. They included those where there was inadequate lighting, close visual or intense auditory activity, narrow tolerances of accuracy, and design features causing prolonged stooping, bending or stretching. They also included features relating to the organisation of work which could be altered, e.g. requirements for short-term memory, short bursts of extremely heavy work or continuous heavy work, and so on (Griew 1964). Despite the relative ease with which many of the changes could be made, in the eight countries studied the OECD found few examples where the redesign of ordinary operative jobs had been seriously considered and action taken. This was particularly so in Britain where firms tended to suggest that the best solution was to transfer older workers to other work. Undoubtedly in periods of recession the effect of this would be to transfer them out of the labour force altogether.

Retraining too has developed an importance beyond older workers since professional and skill obsolescence has become part of our rapidly changing society. Recurrent education and training is particularly important for older workers because the qualifications they possess are more likely to be obsolete because they were obtained long ago. They are also least likely to be located in new or expanding industries and crafts. Despite this, older workers tend to be underrepresented in national manpower training programmes even though they have higher completion rates than younger trainees. Training programmes have tended to neglect the older worker and the need for adult retraining, concentrating rather on young people. Where there has been a focus on adult training it has often concentrated on married women returning to the labour market or unemployed people whatever their age (MSC 1980d). None the less some provision has been made for adult retraining, as described in Chapter four, even though the share of older workers has remained limited. The question often facing policy makers is what share of training expenditure and effort should go on older workers, given the pressure of youth unemployment. Implicitly, as the previous chapter indicated, policy has either favoured youth training schemes or reverted to them whenever youth unemployment increases. But it has gone further and has actively encouraged older workers to leave the labour market early. This has occurred in two ways: directly through the Job Release Scheme and indirectly through the policy contained in the Redundancy Payments Act.

THE JOB RELEASE SCHEME

While there is technically no compulsory retirement age in Britain (except as imposed by individual firms) custom reinforced by pension policy has effectively created one. A state pension may be claimed from the age of sixty by women and from the age of sixty-five by men. For many years deferred retirement was encouraged and even today social security pensioners can defer drawing their pension for up to five years, resulting in a pension that can be up to 37% greater (one seventh for each week of deferment). Within these five years those who choose to draw their pension may still continue working up to an earnings limit before losing from their pension. After five years the earnings limit is dropped (Fogarty 1980: 30; Cooper 1980). This applies to the state pension scheme; the position in occupational pension schemes varies. Occupational pension schemes increased from covering 49% of full-time employees in 1972 to covering 64% in 1979 (*General Household Survey* 1980). Their arrangements in this respect are becoming increasingly important, particularly if their coverage continues to expand. Policy up until 1977 offered positive inducements to older workers to remain in employment if they were part of the state pension scheme. As unemployment increased, arguments began to be put for reducing the age of retirement and consequently reducing the size of the labour force. These have not been restricted to industry. The TUC is committed to reducing the age of retirement for men to sixty, particularly in hazardous industries. The EOC favours an equal pension age between 60 and 65 for all. The major problem with a lower retirement age is that unless pensions are improved, it will increase the incidence of poverty and dependency among the elderly – which is already great on existing pension levels (Walker 1980). Also, it will further diminish the degree of choice which older workers have with respect to retirement age.

In January 1977 the Job Release Scheme (JRS) was introduced to reduce the labour supply and, therefore, the level of registered unemployment. The JRS is politically significant as a low-cost method of reducing unemployment. It enables older workers to withdraw from the labour market before they reach the state pension age if their job is filled by someone from the unemployed register. An indirect replacement can occur if, for example, the vacancy is filled by internal promotion which releases another job, but this makes it difficult to monitor the scheme. Initially the JRS was restricted to certain Assisted Areas. It was later extended to all people in full-time work within one year of the state retirement pension age and men with disabilities aged 60–64. It was extended for a temporary period to cover men aged 62–64. (Makeham and Morgan 1980; Robertson 1982). People on the JRS receive an allowance until they reach the age of 60 or 65 (women and men). There are certain anomalies regarding the allowance. It is higher than for single people on a state pension but lower than for married couples on a state pension. The allowance is higher for men with disabilities but is taxable, whereas it is lower and tax free for the able-bodied. In the March 1983 Budget, a variation to the scheme was announced. The same group of older workers (men aged 62–64, women aged 59, men with disabilities aged 60–64) were offered a weekly allowance if they changed to part-time work. The aim was to create more part-time jobs for unemployed people, at the same time cutting unemployment by 40,000 over two years.

In a survey of 2,800 JRS applicants in late 1978, 30% would have preferred the option of working part-time. The single most important reason given for applying for the JRS was health. It may be, therefore, that a number of older workers do not positively wish to stop working but do require work that is less strenuous and so require a balance between what Fogarty has described as a continuing work commitment and disengagement on which achievement and satisfaction in retirement are likely to depend (Fogarty 1975: 14).

In the first three years of its existence, some 100,000 individuals entered the JRS (Metcalfe 1982: 47). The scheme attracted only a small proportion of those eligible to apply – about 12% for males aged 62–64, who form the majority of applicants. This does not appear to be due to a lack of awareness of the scheme but due to the allowance being set at too low a level. A survey by National Opinion Polls suggested that if the allowance was higher, so would be the take-up. A 23% increase in the allowance was found to induce a 53% increase in the proportion of people who would definitely consider applying (Makeham and Morgan 1980: 28). As might be expected, a high proportion of applicants are semi-skilled and unskilled manual workers who tend to be low paid. Despite this, most applicants experienced a reduction in household income by taking up the scheme. Many semi-skilled and unskilled workers joined the JRS for reasons of ill health, which may explain this finding. The desire for leisure was a more important reason for non-manual workers joining the scheme. Extending the right to choose early retirement has a strong appeal. However, as long as the choice is influenced by financial and health constraints, it will simply continue to reflect inequalities and differentials in access to resources and in access to healthy working conditions. Early retirement may well result in avoiding the need for policies which are aimed at preventing occupational ill health.

There is little information on the effectiveness of the JRS in reducing unemployment – its prime motivating force. In 1980 a survey of 500 employers taking part in the scheme was undertaken. There was a considerable degree of replacement by young workers: 40% of people coming into the jobs were under twenty-six years of age. Almost three-quarters of disabled workers were replaced by people without disabilities, thus increasing the unemployment of the disabled. As far as reducing the unemployed register was concerned, in 40% of cases no reduction occurred due to posts not being filled, being filled internally, being filled by an employed person or by the replacement being made redundant (Robertson 1982). In many cases, therefore, the JRS did not succeed in reducing the supply of labour.

REDUNDANCY AND AGE

Although only a minority of people become unemployed as a result of redundancy, those who do tend to be substantially older than most other people who become unemployed. Age is also the strongest influence on people's experiences after becoming redundant. Older people are more likely to take longer to find jobs and are more likely to find jobs that are inferior in level of skill and earnings to the one they lost. Age, for instance, has a greater influence than the level of local unemployment or people's job or skill level and this is usually a negative effect (Daniel 1981c: 7). In a sample of notified redundancies, the Department of Employment found that the largest number occurred in the 60–64 age band followed by the two preceeding age bands, 55–59 and 50–54. The age pattern of redundancy by industry largely reflected that which is found overall. In twenty-three industries representing 83% of all redundancies, the largest single number occurred in groups over the age of fifty (Jolly *et al*. 1980: 101–2). Age seems to have become an acceptable criterion upon which to base redundancy. It is facilitated by the Redundancy Payments Act 1965. In the first two years following the Act, the proportion of older workers who received benefits under it was much higher than that of younger workers. This pattern has persisted. In a study of redundancy and subsequent levels of unemployment in a major shipbuilding industry, the Department of Employment found that the proportion of older, longer-service workers volunteering for redundancy was very high. Forty per cent in the age band 50–59 volunteered as against 13%–15% in the younger age bands. This pattern is repeated (although not with such disparity) in redundancies occurring in all industries. It would appear that older, longer-service workers will be induced to volunteer under a system in which lump-sum payments increase with age. The problem that arises is that older, longer-service workers may be less prepared for the process of looking for another job and may suffer more from leaving an environment which they have known and liked (MacKay *et al.* 1980).

The impetus behind the Redundancy Payments Act was the need to assist industry to adapt to a changing economic and technological environment in which certain industries were declining while new ones were developing. The Act aimed to promote the movement of labour in situations where it was in surplus. It was thought that payments to individual workers would enable industries to shed labour and remain competitive. It achieved this by making provision for statutory payments as compensation for people losing their jobs. The Act requires an employer to make a lump-sum payment to any employees under age 65 (males) or 60 (females) who are dismissed because of redundancy after at least two years service since the age of 18 and who have been working for more than 20 hours a week. A redundancy payment is calculated with reference to age, length of continuous reckonable service (up to a maximum of 20 years) and weekly pay (up to a limit reviewed annually). Employees nearing retirement age have their redundancy payments reduced progressively. This may lead to extensive reductions. In addition, employers may, if they choose, offset pension and lump-sum payments made under occupational pension schemes against redundancy payments. This too may affect older workers particularly badly. To mitigate the cost to individual employers and to encourage them to use the legislation, a Redundancy Fund was established, financed by an allocation from employers' social security contributions. Employers could then claim a rebate from the fund for any redundancy payments made. Initially the amounts refunded increased over a certain age in order that employers should not stop hiring older workers because of their potentially higher rates of redundancy.

From the start redundancy payments were calculated according to a sliding scale which always gave the older, longer-service worker higher compensation. The Redundancy Fund in effect paid an older

worker's premium, contributing to an age-oriented approach to redundancy. Jolly *et al.* suggest that the 1965 Act contributed to social acceptance of age as an element of redundancy. Prior to 1965
both unions and employers used the criteria of LIFO, i.e. last in,
first out, with the interests of older and more experienced workers
being protected. This is no longer the case. There has been a significant shift towards a climate of opinion which sees older workers
as being natural candidates for redundancy because (*a*) they will
have a greater redundancy payment, (*b*) they will be retiring anyway, and (*c*) they may not be as productive. As a result 'for many
older workers the mobility that the Redundancy Payments Act facilitated was mobility out of the active labour force' (Jolly *et al.*
1980: 98).

In 1969, however, the legislation was amended, effectively transferring the age premium from the Redundancy Fund to the employer. It was felt that this would act as a disincentive to making
predominantly older workers redundant but it in fact had no noticeable effect. It is likely that making an older worker redundant
as a kind of early retirement will be perceived to be more legitimate
in a period of mass unemployment than sending workers at the start
of work or in the prime of their working lives into the certainty of
unemployment.

DISCRIMINATION

The older worker suffers discrimination in two ways. When there
is substantial unemployment, older workers tend to be treated as
a secondary and disposable workforce. This is likely to occur to an
even greater extent when policies exist which *appear* to result in no
financial loss to the worker concerned. Secondly, with high unemployment, the recruitment of older workers will decline in favour
of younger workers. It is more likely to occur if the employment
of older workers is seen to entail immediate costs. Older workers
suffer both from direct discrimination in 'hiring and firing' decisions and from defects in manpower policy in selection procedures,
training facilities, job design and the pension system. Ironically,
there is a higher level of job satisfaction among workers over 65
(*General Household Survey* 1980) and a substantial group of older
workers who would have liked to continue beyond the age at which
they gave up working (Hunt 1978: 63; Fogarty 1982: 174). There
are, therefore, strong reasons for thinking that high rates of withdrawal of older workers from the labour force are often involuntary.

Among those who have left the labour force voluntarily, ill health is usually the principal reason. Many may have wished for the opportunity to move to jobs more suited to their capacities or to part-time work. There are powerful barriers, however, to older worker's mobility, of which discrimination by employers is only one. Occupational pension losses are potentially high for people who change jobs many times, particularly older workers, especially if preserved pension rights are not index-linked. If their pension rights are not transferable or if there is not some equivalence between one employer's pension scheme and another, older workers will be reluctant to move. Fogarty reports that over a certain period 81% of exits from pension schemes led to a loss of pension entitlement. In addition, new employers taking on a worker close to retirement age face pressure to level up that worker's pension to that of others in the organisation (Fogarty 1975: 90). Additional mobility difficulties which exist as one gets older are the costs of moving home and the availability (if at all) of short-term mortgages. Moving to part-time work is only likely to exacerbate these problems.

An *a priori* question concerning worker mobility, however, is the ability of older workers to enter new employment at all. There is growing evidence that older jobseekers have fewer chances of success due to the 'practices, policies and beliefs regarding the use of, and capabilities of, older workers that prevail among employment service agencies and among employers and their representatives' (Sheppard 1976: 301). Walker found similar 'informal' policies in operation with regard to handicapped school-leavers (Walker 1982b). While employers may profess willingness to employ experienced workers, there is some evidence that they will distinguish between employees already in service and those seeking it. This suggests that in firms with an internal labour market older workers will suffer less discrimination. Those older workers likely to be seeking work may find themselves confined to lower-skilled jobs in the secondary labour market (Makeham 1980b: 42).

Some of the most extensive work undertaken on discrimination against older workers has been with regard to the use of age limits in employment. In a survey made of advertisements appearing in the Professional and Executive column of a British national newspaper over a number of years, age discrimination was found to increase. In 1957, 19% of all advertisements specified men under forty and 26% specified men under fifty. By 1970 these had increased to 32% and 41% respectively (Slater 1973). A more comprehensive survey has analysed a sample of age-qualified vacancies notified to the public employment service in Britain (Jolly *et al.* 1978). Of 16,000 vacancies notified and either filled or cancelled, 28% were qualified by an upper age limit. The proportion of all age-limited vacancies was 39%. However, one in four of the people placed in these jobs was outside the limits specified. This was more likely for the lower limits than for the upper limits, indicating that employers were more ready to accept someone younger than they had intended than someone older.

The construction industry had fewer upper age qualifications in its vacancies than other industries, while distribution had considerably more. The occupational group with the highest proportion of upper-age qualified vacancies was 'other non-manual' which is largely confined to the distributive trades, making it consistent with the industrial pattern. General labouring work also had many upper age restrictions. Enforcement of the age limits varies. The manual trades appear to be more flexible while the non-manual are more rigid, particularly the category of 'other non-manual'. Some writers have ascribed this to the more highly developed internal labour market that exists in the non-manual group, supporting the contention earlier in this chapter that older workers seeking employment may find themselves forced into downward mobility. They are also female-dominated occupations and age limits are more closely associated with female employment.

Jolly *et al.* examine the effect of age restrictions in relation to the supply of labour in various age groups and conclude that, contrary to appearances, the discrimination contained in them is indeterminate. While 35% of age-restricted jobs are for those over forty, only 15% of submissions for work come from this group. On the basis of an analysis on these lines they conclude that there is no need for age discrimination legislation in Britain. However, the effect of age restrictions both explicitly in job vacancy advertisements and implicitly in general opinion about who is entitled to work is likely to erode the supply of older workers even before they submit themselves for jobs at the employment service (Jolly *et al.* 1978).

Anti-discrimination measures in the USA and Europe

In Britain most governments have generally taken the view that the interests of older workers are best served by encouraging employers not to discriminate against them rather than by establishing protective legislation. The Watkinson Committee, for instance, recommended that quotas not be adopted because they suggested that there was something inherently uneconomic about employing older workers. By contrast the United States has attempted to remove age discrimination in the labour market by statutory means but without going so far as to impose quotas. The same concern that prompted the establishment of the Watkinson Committee in Britain led to the passing of the Age Discrimination in Employment Act (ADEA) in the USA in 1967. The impetus for this legislation came from the Civil Rights Act a few years earlier which had prohibited discrimination on the grounds of race, sex, religion or nationality. It also directed the Secretary of Labor to investigate and report on age discrimination. At the time nineteen individual states had already taken legislative action on age discrimination. The Secretary of Labor's report to Congress found that half the vacancies advertised for the private sector were for people below the age of fifty-five. Age discrimination was considered to be widespread. This caused concern in its own right but legislative action was precipitated by the pressure which early retirement was placing on social security funds (Jolly and Mingay 1978).

The Act's purpose was: 'To promote employment of older workers based on their ability rather than age; to prohibit arbitrary age discrimination in employment; to help employers and workers find ways of meeting problems arising from the impact of age on employment.' Originally it covered the civilian labour force from the age of 40 up to 65. In 1974 federal employees were brought within its scope. In 1978 it was extended to cover all those from 40 to 70 and lifted all age limits on federal employees. The National Council on the Ageing, however, pressed for the extension of ADEA coverage to all those over 40 without exception (Jolly *et al*. 1980: 113). Employers of less than twenty people and unions with less than twenty-five members are exempt.

The ADEA makes the following provisions: No employer can 'fail or refuse to hire, discharge or otherwise discriminate against any individual with respect to his compensation, terms, conditions or privileges of employment because of age'. No employment agency can 'fail or refuse to refer for employment or in any other way discriminate against anyone due to his age'. No employment advertisements are allowed which quote age limits or use phrases such as 'recent graduates'. A list of prohibited phrases is available for advertisers, but advertisers and employment agencies are liable for illegal wording as well. There are certain exemptions to the legislation such as when age is a bona fide qualification for the job, when a genuine apprenticeship programme is under way or a seniority system is being observed, and when an individual is being discharged or otherwise disciplined for a good cause. In addition, certain employment and training programmes sponsored by federal or state employment services permit positive discrimination in favour of specific age groups (Jolly *et al.* 1980: 13). The latter exemption and the apprenticeship exemption were introduced subsequent to the Act and possibly reflect growing concern with high rates of unemployment among the young as in Britain.

Anti-discrimination legislation now operates in virtually all American states. These laws take precedence over ADEA, which was essentially a safety net in states where protection of older workers was either inadequate or missing. Certain states have superior protection: Alaska has no upper age limit. The Act was amended and improved in 1978. There were four main changes. Firstly, the upper age limit was raised to 70 except for certain exemptions such as the police, the fire service, tenured professors and senior executives entitled to pensions over a certain amount. Secondly, the upper age limit for federal employees was lifted. Thirdly, the right of ADEA litigants to a trial by jury was guaranteed. Fourthly, ADEA enforcement was transferred from the Department of Labor's Employment Standards Administration to the Equal Employment Opportunities Commission. This is the body responsible for enforcing legislation on race and sex discrimination (Jolly and Mingay 1978).

The crux of employment protection legislation is the extent to which it is complied with (as can be seen in stark terms in the following chapter on people with disabilities). The US Department of Labor employed twenty-seven specialists to work on ADEA compliance and 5% of the time of its more than 1,000 general compliance officers. Like the British disablement resettlement officers (Ch. 8) they must provide both information and advice to employers and employees as well as ensuring compliance. The Civil Service Commission is responsible for enforcement with regard to federal employees. There is some disparity between federal and non-federal efforts. The Employment Standards Administration of the Department of Labor was authorised to spend $5 million for this purpose but by 1977 had only spent about half this amount. It was criticised for this and directed to spend up to the limit of its budget by a Congressional Select Committee on Ageing. Despite enhanced resources, however, a large backlog of complaints awaiting investigation has arisen. Excluding federal cases, the number of complaints increased fivefold between 1969 and 1976 (Jolly *et al.*

1980: 14). The Secretary of Labor or any aggrieved person can take action under ADEA. Before any court action can be brought, however, the Secretary of Labor must attempt conciliation. But the Act does not specify at what point conciliation is exhausted, entitling the claimant to go to court.

The ADEA is part of the United States' civil rights legislation. Its strength lies in its recognition that age discrimination occurs both as far as job opportunities are concerned and with regard to premature retirement. Its effect on employment appears to have been small despite the increase in the number of complainants coming forward. These are important considerations with regard to its appropriateness as a policy for Britain. Its limited effect may have stemmed from features particular to the Act itself rather than from a general limitation of this kind of policy. However, it is clear that protective legislation requires the backing of a strong enforcement agency and the resources to carry out that enforcement efficiently and quickly. A question that arises is how successful such a policy would be in a country without the legislative traditions of the United States.

Variations on this particular theme of employment protection exist in Sweden and Germany. In Sweden the County Labour Market Board has powers to monitor employment practices with regard to, among other things, age, sex and nationality. It may call on an employer to increase the proportion of older recruits, for instance, and in the case of a dispute may refer the case for arbitration to the National Labour Market Board. Each firm of over fifty employees has an 'adjustment' team which plays an important advisory role and consists of representatives of the employer, the union and the local employment office. In Germany, the responsibility for avoiding age discrimination rests with employers and the Statutory Works Council. They are specifically required to take account of the needs of older workers. The Works Council can intervene to protect workers' rights, including having the right to take cases to arbitration and appeal for a binding decision (Fogarty 1975: 118–19). Although there are no equivalents to the adjustment team or the Works Council in Britain, these are useful illustrations of the variety of methods by which employment rights can be protected and discrimination avoided. They are in sharp contrast to the lack of employment protection currently provided for Britain's older workers.

The experience of many older workers remains precarious, particularly in periods of high unemployment. Once unemployed they often face tremendous difficulties in their attempts to get back into the labour force. Myths continue to proliferate about their inefficiency and their access to other forms of financial support, most noticeably pensions, which give legitimacy to calls for early retirement. There are pressures in Britain for a reduction in normal retirement age. If the reserve pool of young people overflows while employment continues to drop, it is likely that attention will turn even more readily to this part of the disposable labour force. The debate over the future of older workers, like that over the role of married women or the future of school-leavers, is part of the more general and far reaching debate over the quality of life and work and the shape of Britain in the years to come.

Chapter eight
DISABLING POLICIES

INTRODUCTION

Government intervention in and regulation of the labour market has many different forms and purposes, including the promotion of greater efficiency, control of the labour force and the promotion of social justice. The development of rehabilitation and employment services for people with disabilities gained impetus after both world wars when there was political and moral appeal in making such provision as well as a shortage of labour. Public assent for statutory provision was not difficult to muster after a war, particularly one which had involved conscription. Government training centres were established in 1919, primarily to rehabilitate and resettle those disabled by the First World War. They were later extended to the civilian blind. The major impetus for employment policy for people with disabilities occurred, however, after the Second World War. An Inter-Departmental Committee on the Rehabilitation and Resettlement of Disabled People (the Tomlinson Committee) was established and reported on its findings in 1943 [doc 20]. Their report was to become the bedrock of policy for the next forty years. Its recommendations were embodied in the Disabled Persons (Employment) Act 1944 which is still in operation. In one comprehensive measure the Act made provision for

* a disabled persons employment register
* assessment, rehabilitation and retraining
* a specialised employment placement service
* a quota scheme for registered disabled people
* designated employment
* sheltered employment
* national and local advisory committees.

Additional legislation has amended, added to or repealed provisions made in the 1944 legislation. The Disabled Persons (Employment)

Act 1958, in accordance with the view that sheltered employment was not therapeutic but a means of obtaining a livelihood, transferred responsibility for it from the National Health Service to the Department of Employment. The Chronically Sick and Disabled Persons Act 1970 made provision for a wide range of welfare services and a local authority register of people with disabilities (see Topliss and Gould 1981 for a review of this legislation). The 1973 Employment and Training Act repealed the key section of the 1944 Act relating to industrial rehabilitation courses, replacing it with a general power to provide such training for all people 'suitable for their ages and capacities'. Finally, the Disabled Persons Act 1981 made provision for educational buildings and other public places to be made more accessible to people with disabilities, thus indirectly facilitating their employment opportunities.

The latter piece of legislation illustrates quite clearly how virtually all policy relating to people with disabilities has been oriented towards the physically handicapped. There is a numerical basis for this but the proportion of people handicapped by mental illness or mental subnormality is growing. In addition, there is some evidence that they are suffering from unemployment disproportionate to their size as a sub-group of the disabled. An employment policy, therefore, which is biased towards physical handicap may not be meeting the needs of substantial sections of the disabled population.

There are two registers of people with disabilities, one kept by the Disablement Resettlement Service (DRS), a branch of the employment services, the other by all local authorities. Both are based on a statutory definition of disability. Under the Disabled Persons (Employment) Act 1944 a disabled person is defined as someone who 'on account of injury, disease, or congenital deformity, is substantially handicapped in obtaining or keeping employment or in undertaking work on his own account, of a kind which apart from that injury, disease or deformity would be suited to his age, experience and qualifications . . .' The expression 'disease' is construed as 'including a physical or mental condition arising from imperfect development of any organ'. Although the physiological bias is clear, in practice this has been taken to include individuals who suffer from psychiatric illness and mental subnormality as well as physical disability. The disability must be likely to last at least 12 months and the person must wish to take on remunerative employment and have a reasonable chance of doing so.

The local authority register of people with disabilities is based on a definition contained in the National Assistance Act 1948 which is accepted under the Chronically Sick and Disabled Persons Act 1970. It refers to 'persons who are blind, deaf or dumb, and other persons who are substantially and permanently handicapped by illness, injury, or congenital deformity or such other disabilities as may be prescribed by the Minister'.

Both statutory definitions focus on the limitations which the disablement places on individuals, as indeed does the very word 'disabled' itself. They concentrate on the loss, the abnormality or the functional limitation. Townsend suggests that disability can be defined to mean socially deviant behaviour or a more generally defined social status which, by contrast, would focus attention on the social perception of disability (Townsend 1979: 686–7). The importance of this distinction in policy making is crucial since different types of provision and different kinds and degrees of mandate – in this case, on employers – flow from the concept we hold of disability.

Over 1 million people are registered with local authorities as disabled, about one-third of whom are of working age. Almost half a million people are registered with the employment service although this has declined by about one-third from the 1940s when the Act was still new. Estimating the size of the population with disabilities is fraught with difficulty, to say nothing of estimating those eligible for employment (see Lonsdale and Walker 1982). Since registration is voluntary and biased towards physical impairment, it is very likely that the register underestimates the real size and nature of the disabled population. Because of the inadequacies of the register, the government conducted a survey in 1969 to arrive at a more accurate figure (Harris *et al.* 1971). The survey suggested that there were 3 million adults living in private households who were impaired. Half of the estimated 1.3 million of working age were in the labour force. Subsequently, the Department of Employment and the MSC accepted that there were probably considerably more disabled people in the labour force. The survey severely underestimated the size of the mentally handicapped and mentally ill populations and excluded those living in institutions, although some may have been within sheltered employment schemes. Other surveys including the *General Household Survey* have produced higher estimates. In an independent study, Townsend estimated that the scale of disability was far higher than government estimates suggest. He suggested that 15.5% of the population over the age of ten years, representing some 7 million people, had some appreciable or severe incapacity. About 2 million of these were of working age (Townsend 1979: 695–9).

This was in sharp contrast to government estimates which for some time have ranged around 0.5 million people. Regular information is published by government sources on the numbers of people in this group who are unemployed and the number of people placed in employment by the DRS. Over 200,000 people are recorded as unemployed, including 12,000 judged to require work under sheltered conditions. However, only a small percentage of these are ultimately found work by the DRS staff. The number of registered disabled people has been declining while the number of unregistered disabled people seeking help from the DRS has been increasing. A high and growing number of people with disabilities are becoming or remaining unemployed. If increasing the job opportunities available for people with disabilities was perceived to be necessary in 1944 when there were shortages of labour, then there is an even stronger argument for increasing those opportunities in periods when they experience a disproportionate share of unemployment.

THE PROBLEM: UNEMPLOYMENT AND DEPRIVATION

People with disabilities of all kinds have always experienced high rates of unemployment [doc 21]. In periods of full employment such as during the 1960s there was still some residual unemployment that was more than frictional or temporary as individuals searched for appropriate jobs [doc 7]. There were pockets of unemployment, discouraged workers who had withdrawn from the search for work and workers who found it difficult to obtain and keep jobs because of discrimination and prejudice. The disabled were among these. Not only have they been subject to more unemployment but once in work they are often in low-status, low-paid jobs.

There is increasing evidence of an association between occupational status and ill health generally. The incidence of chronic morbidity, high mortality and disability generally are greater lower down the socio-economic scale, particularly among unskilled manual workers (DHSS 1980). The *General Household Survey* records a rate of chronic illness for all unskilled and female semi-skilled workers more than twice as high as the rate for professional workers. Chronic illness often leads to more severe disability and is also often very disabling in itself. The occupational status of the impaired population tends to be lower than that of the population as a whole, with a greater proportion of disabled people working a manual jobs (Buckle 1971).

It is particularly noticeable that the prevalence of chronic illness is higher among women of most occupational categories. The problem of women's health and the higher prevalence of female disability cannot be taken only to reflect their dominance among the higher age groups. It is increasingly coming to be seen as evidence of occupational stress and poverty and the position of women both at work and at home, issues which have only recently begun to be taken seriously.

In an assessment of the occupational profile of unemployed disabled people, the MSC has found that many more unemployed disabled people were looking for unskilled jobs than unemployed people as a whole. Twenty-nine per cent of able-bodied people were seeking manual work and 32% general labouring work, compared to 21% and 60% of disabled people. There is also evidence that at every age unemployed disabled people are likely to have been unemployed for considerably longer periods of time than others, again partly a reflection of their occupational status. More than three times as many disabled people as able-bodied (excluding the severely disabled) have been unemployed for more than two years (MSC 1982f). Despite the association between disability and age, younger workers are also affected by unemployment. A study of handicapped school-leavers indicated a substantial amount of under-employment and disadvantage (Walker 1982b). Table 8.1 shows the greater incidence of long-term unemployment among disabled people compared to the general population.

What are the factors which contribute to the overrepresentation of people with disabilities lower down the occupational scale and in unemployment? It could be suggested that low levels of skill or

Table 8.1. Proportion of registered disabled people unemployed for more than a year compared to the general unemployed population, (percentages)

	Young people	*Women*	*Men*	*Total*
Disabled	11.0	47.3	51.5	50.1
General	4.4	17.8	25.4	19.2

Note: While the figures refer to 1980, they represent a common pattern over a number of years

Source: House of Commons, *Hansard* WA, 23 July 1981, cols. 230

ill health contribute but the choice of jobs available also narrows after the onset of disability due both to discrimination and to the low priority given to people with disabilities in the job market. In Buckle's survey, seven out of ten workers interviewed felt that their choice of jobs had been restricted while four out of ten felt they had been forced to take a job in which they did not have the opportunity to use their skills or qualifications (Buckle 1971: 22, 28). In a survey of multiple sclerosis sufferers rates of unemployment increased dramatically, with 42% being out of work in contrast to only 3% being out of work prior to the disability (Davoud and Kettle 1981). Placements by the MSC resettlement staff have been falling rapidly: in the case of registered disabled people, placements in work have halved since 1979, whereas for those who are unregistered they have fallen to a third (Hansard 1981b).

People with disabilities suffer considerable disadvantages in the labour market. They often face many additional cost-of-living expenses which their able-bodied counterparts will never experience. The costs of extra heating, special foods, special clothing, medication, additional transport are only some and have been well documented (Durward 1981). Extra spending needs must be seen in relation to income and many disabled people rely on inadequate wages or inadequate benefits. When they do find work they are often more likely to be lower paid. The OPCS survey of disabled people found that half of those households with a single income had incomes of less than 42% of average earnings and a quarter had incomes of less than 32% of average earnings (Buckle 1971). The earnings of those in sheltered workshops are often notoriously low (NACEDP 1980). The low wages which people with disabilities receive may also be due to their being forced into homeworking because of mobility or other problems. Fatigue, for instance, is a little recognised feature of disability requiring certain adaptations to the work routine which homeworking would permit.

Increasing levels of unemployment, however, mean that many more disabled people are being forced to rely on inadequate state benefits. In addition, some disabled people are forced out of work due to a feature of the benefits system itself. There is no provision for a person who is disabled to work part-time without losing their entitlement to state benefit. There is a small exception where someone can earn up to a certain amount of 'therapeutic' earnings without forfeiting their benefit. However, this is limited to certain people as it is clearly seen to be part of the rehabilitative process rather than part of earning a living. Aside from this, people with disabilities must either work and receive a wage or they must apply for invalidity benefit. There is no recognition in policy of the growing number of people who are not completely incapacitated for work but who can only manage to work if their hours are flexible or limited. It has recently been estimated that about 100,000 people have this need. This gap in policy had been recognised by the Multiple Sclerosis Society whose members face this problem, as do those with degenerative diseases and those recovering from a severe illness or major surgery. They have put forward proposals for a new partial incapacity benefit which would enable certain groups of people to both work and claim benefit (Economist Intelligence Unit 1982).

THE RESPONSE: INDUCEMENT OR REGULATION

Policy since the 1944 legislation has concentrated on creating job opportunities for people with disabilities. To increase job opportunities policy makers have recourse to 'carrot' strategies which include a range of financial or other inducements offered to employers to take on individuals they might not otherwise employ. They also have recourse to 'stick' strategies whereby regulations compel employers to take on certain people. A third approach involves promoting voluntary equal opportunity campaigns and educational campaigns aimed at proving the worth of marginal employees to employers. These, however, do not necessarily replace compulsory measures but may accompany them. Financial inducements include limited or temporary recruitment subsidies or longer-term subsidies. They may take the form of tax credits or payroll tax cuts. Compulsory measures include quotas, positive discrimination and designated or reserved employment. A number of Western European countries have compulsory measures, the most common pattern being quotas: Britain 3%, West Germany 6%, Italy 8.5% and France 10%. The USA uses tax credits as an inducement to take on certain groups of people, including those with disabilities. None the less there is a growing number of legal regulations governing the employment of people with disabilities in the US as well as a number of subsidies in Britain.

The concept of financial inducement as a means of reducing unemployment generally has been around in theory and in practice for some time. Not surprisingly it is an idea which is popular in periods of economic crisis and, as such, has been revived in recent years. As already shown, Britain is inundated with a range of these kinds of measures, most of which have been directed towards saving or creating jobs generally. As far as people with disabilities are concerned, there are some subsidies available. The Job Introduction Scheme is intended to give disabled people a chance to prove their worth to an employer. Firms agree to take on someone with a disability (selected by the Disablement Resettlement Officer (DRO) and agreed by the firm) for 6 weeks, paying them the normal rate for the job. At the end of the trial period the firm can claim a subsidy from the MSC. There is no obligation on the employer to either continue to employ the person afterwards or even to employ them for the full 6 weeks. Although 80% of employees were retained in the first year of the subsidy's operation, the scheme has been cut back to a third of its size. It has been criticised for its withdrawal of normal forms of job protection for those disabled people participating in the scheme. The Job Rehearsal Scheme permits the tax-free allowance paid to disabled people on rehabilitation courses to continue for three weeks to allow a trial period of employment. Yet another scheme pays a training allowance to employers who agree to train a disabled person and who guarantee to continue to employ them for a further 6 months.

Other financial inducements to employers include the Capital Grants Scheme which provides funds for employers to redesign and adapt their workplaces to make them more accessible for those with disabilities. There is very poor take-up for all these schemes, in particular the Capital Grants Scheme. Originally £0.5 million was allocated for this purpose, of which only 2% was disbursed among twenty-six projects. Although an increasing proportion of the grant was applied for, within five years the amount allocated was reduced to less than one-third of its original amount. The low take-up of the Capital Grants Scheme lies both in the way it is administered and in ignorance of its existence.

The arguments for employment subsidies as an instrument for keeping and getting people into work range from reducing the costs of labour and, therefore, stimulating employment without lowering wages or increasing prices, to being a cheap alternative for government to the costs of social security payments and lost tax revenue. The arguments for subsidies to reduce unemployment generally and the arguments for subsidies targeted at specific groups may need to be separated – in that it is possible to assess the impact of one more favourably than the other. One of the characteristics of unemployment is the marked extent to which it is concentrated on certain groups in the labour force. This is so with regard to incidence and recurrence of unemployment but is especially so with regard to duration or length of time that someone is unemployed. While people with disabilities take their place alongside school-leavers, women, older workers, immigrants, black workers, and unskilled workers as far as the incidence and recurrence of unemployment is concerned, they have a special place when it comes to being unemployed for long periods of time. If long-term unemployment is taken as an indicator of severest disadvantage – both materially and psychologically – it will harm people with disabilities more than others. This in itself could be a case for selective assistance.

Even with subsidies targeted at people with disabilities, there are a number of inherent problems. The very act of giving employers a financial incentive to take on specific workers could be seen to suggest that the group concerned, in this case people with disabilities, have less to offer employers than others. This contradicts the notion that they have the same right to jobs as anyone else. Some people might argue that there will be a spin-off for disabled workers in any event without selectively aiming subsidies for their advantage, but it seems that this is far less likely in periods of high unemployment. A second problem may occur if people are hired for as long as they qualify for a subsidy and are then replaced by other target workers. A third problem could be that of the employment of target workers leading to the dismissal of non-target workers. Both this and replacement were problems faced under the YOP scheme, for instance. Employers are often reluctant to take on subsidised workers of whatever nature because they perceive, often correctly, that they will incur extra costs in administration (applying, filing reports, claiming subsidy, being investigated, etc.) and with all subsidies there is the possibility of firms taking on workers they may have hired anyway. But for people with disabilities this is probably less so than for young workers.

In the USA a subsidy has taken the form of a tax credit called the Targeted Jobs Tax Credit. In this programme, private employers are paid a subsidy for two years for workers who are disabled as well as other designated workers such as war veterans and young people. In addition to the subsidy having a very low take-up, there is some evidence that the physically and mentally disabled did not do as well as other groups. A high proportion of those hired did not retain their employment for very long – possibly an example of the replacement problem mentioned above (Halberstadt and Haveman 1981).

Generally there is evidence of a low take-up of subsidies. This calls into question the success of inducement strategies since the essence of a 'carrot' policy is that it attracts the donkey in the first place! Notions of equity and social justice do not appear to be strong enough to displace traditional attachments to profitability through low costs and efficiency. They may also not be strong enough to overcome stereotyped ideas about the productivity and capacity of workers with disabilities. Compulsory measures such as quota employment or legal regulations are more compatible with the view that people with disabilities have the same right to employment as anyone else – at least part if not all of the problem is recognised as being one of discrimination. By contrast, implicit in the notion of subsidies is a definition of the problem as being one of deficient demand. But there has always been higher unemployment for people with disabilities even when demand was high. If the problem is defined as discrimination or incorrect assessments of the effect of disability, then the policy required is one of public education and intervention backed by law.

Finally, on subsidies, if employment of target-group workers results in an increase in labour force participation of people who were formerly discouraged workers, official measures of unemployment may not decrease. This may not be an overriding concern for social policy but it may attract the interest of policy makers who are concerned primarily with reducing unemployment.

REHABILITATION FOR EMPLOYMENT

The MSC has identified two different conceptions of what employment rehabilitation is. One is preparing people who have become sick or disabled for employment as part of their overall rehabilitation. The other is facilitating the re-entry into employment of people who have lost their basic work aptitude but not necessarily because of disability (MSC 1981h: 3, 7). The Tomlinson Committee, which laid the foundations of employment rehabilitation, was much clearer about what the service should be and who it should serve. Its view was that most disabilities were physical, that the disability was of recent origin and that the service would deal with people just out of a course of medical treatment. Rehabilitation was viewed fairly simply with recommendations that special centres be established 'with facilities to assist full recovery to physical fitness by the provision of fresh air, good food, physical training and exercises, together with a limited amount of useful indoor occupation' (*Tomlinson Committee* 1943: para 43). Less attention was paid to people with degenerative diseases, to people who had accumulated diverse problems because of lengthy illness or multiple handicaps, or to socially rather than physically disadvantaged people and the complex problems that arise as a consequence.

The first Employment Rehabilitation Centre (ERC) opened in 1943. Within a few years there were fourteen and today there are twenty-seven. In addition to these, but with a different function, the MSC supports four residential training colleges for people with disabilities. Run by voluntary organisations, these colleges developed in response to the neglect of handicap in general educational settings. Changes in attitudes, however, have led to greater integration rather than segregation of the disabled in education. Retraining courses for able-bodied workers are often just as suitable for people with disabilities, particularly those involving new technology. The ERCs on the other hand tend to offer assessment facilities. They have been criticised for focusing on rehabilitation to manual or lower-level skilled work which perpetuates the occupational pattern and movement into lower status positions of disabled people. The ERCs provide just under 3,000 places at any one time. They were traditionally equipped along the lines of a factory and production work was obtained from local firms or government departments, although this contract work has declined. Initially most clients were referred by medical sources. Today this has changed dramatically, with fewer being referred from medical agencies and the majority being recruited from the MSC's unemployed clients. A third of the people undergoing rehabilitation no longer fit Tomlinson's category of newly physically disabled but either have no obvious disability or are mentally disabled (MSC 1981h). In addition, a high proportion of clients have been out of work for a long period of time: 48% for more than one year, 31% for more than two years. This suggests that ERCs are moving away from working with the recently disabled towards assisting people who have poor work records.

The change that has occurred in employment rehabilitation is reflected in its advertising material, in which the ERC is billed as helping people get back to their old job after an illness or injury or as helping people to find a new job after a long period away from work. Rehabilitation is now being interpreted as also facilitating re-entry into employment for people who may have lost confidence or the aptitude for work. This has enabled attention to be paid not only to degenerative diseases but also to mental illness and other social conditions. Consequently, the concept of rehabilitation has become more diverse and more complex.

ADULT TRAINING CENTRES

Adult Training Centres (ATCs) are run by local authorities specifically for mentally handicapped adults. The majority of severely mentally handicapped school-leavers go on to ATCs. Over 40,000 are now attending about 480 centres. In theory the function of the centre is training for employment and, like the ERC, should be a bridge to employment. In practice, however, very little rehabilitation or training occurs and virtually no movement to open employment. One study of ATCs revealed that only about 4% of trainees entered employment during the course of a year, despite staff estimates that 37% were capable of either open or sheltered work (Whelan and Speake 1977).

Initially ATCs provided craft work as a form of training. During the 1960s the centres began to take on sub-contract work which was far more repetitive and monotonous. An issue which has become of great concern is the wages the trainees receive for the work they do. While some centres pay their trainees an established rate for the job, there is increasing evidence that many receive extremely low wages. Faced by shortages of work in the 1970s and in competition with sheltered workshops, centres began to take sub-contract work at unrealistically low costs. There is no statutory requirement on centres to pay their trainees and many encouraged their trainees to take up social security benefits instead. The limit on earnings (after which deductions are made on benefits) acts as a disincentive to increase wages beyond this point. Consequently, in Whelan and Speake's survey only 1% of trainees earned more than the then earnings limit. Fifty per cent earned less than half the then earnings limits and 3% were unpaid. Other evidence indicates that trainees work on average between 30 and 39 hours a week (Walker 1982b: 49).

The problems in ATCs appear to be more fundamental than simply a temporary response to external economic pressures. For a number of years their training and rehabilitative objectives have been allowed to lapse while the provision of employment, often exploitative, grew. The need to return to a more creative approach was recognised by an independent advisory group, the National Development Group for the Mentally Handicapped. They recommended a comprehensive programme of reform including planned learning, developmental exercises and continuous assessment in order that the ATCs return to having an educational and rehabilitative role which would foster the employment potential of trainees (National Development Group for the Mentally Handicapped 1977). Their recommendations were not pursued, the group was disbanded and the monotonous, exploitative work continued.

THE DISABLEMENT RESETTLEMENT SERVICE

The Disablement Resettlement Service (DRS) represents a half-way point between policies which induce and policies which compel employers to take on people with disabilities. Nowhere is this duality more obvious than among the Disablement Resettlement Officers (DROs) who must both administer and police the service. The cornerstone of the DRS, and many believe for disablement employment policy generally, is the quota scheme. Under the Disabled Persons (Employment) Act 1944 all employers with twenty or more workers are required to employ 3% of registered disabled people in their workforce. This means that a central register of all people with disabilities must be kept as well as employers being required to maintain records on the operation of their quota. Contravention of the quota requirement can make an employer liable to a fine or a term of imprisonment. However, the employer is only breaking the law at the point of hiring someone if the firm is below quota and a registered disabled person is not hired. It is also an offence to dismiss a registered disabled person if this would render the employer below quota, but no penalty is fixed here. The maximum fine for breaking the quota, £100, was set in 1944 and has remained unchanged. Only ten firms have ever been prosecuted out of the 8,000 to 10,000 firms illegally below quota. One case was dismissed, two received the maximum fine and the remainder received fines of £5, £25, or £50. About two-thirds of all employers fail to comply with their quota obligations. Just under 22,000 firms have been granted permits entitling them to be below quota legally under the provisions which exist for employers to make such applications.

The proportion of employers fulfilling their legal obligations has dropped steadily since the 1960s. The proportion of employers granted permits to be below quota has increased steadily. From 1972 onwards the number of firms issued with permits began to exceed those complying with the quota and has continued to do so ever since (Lonsdale 1981). Block permits are issued so liberally that the process of permit application has become a matter of routine for many companies. It is not only firms in the private sector who evade the quota scheme. Although the Disabled Persons (Employment) Act does not technically apply to the Crown, one Minister for the Disabled stated that government departments were expected to obey a 'moral duty' in this respect. Despite this, only three government departments meet the 3% quota requirement in Britain. None of the departments in Northern Ireland do so. Many departments in Britain have fallen behind their compliance in previous years. No nationalised industry, Electricity Board, Regional Water Authority or Regional Health Authority fulfils their quota. Few local authorities do (Lonsdale 1982). In addition, a large number of prominent private employers do not employ their full complement of registered disabled people including the TUC, the CBI, several major trade unions, newspaper groups and television companies and those who first made the law, the Houses of Parliament (*Hansard* 1978).

The DRS was created both to place individuals with disabilities in work and to supervise the quota scheme. There are 565 DROs who must, therefore, ensure that quota obligations are being met and decide applications for permits as well as place people in work. In addition to being time-consuming, the supervision of quotas casts the DRO in the position of being policemen and women. There is a fundamental contradiction in their work. On the one hand they must build up a rapport with local employers in order to persuade them to take on disabled workers. On the other hand they must police the actions of those same employers and decide on prosecution if they fail to obey the law. Each DRO is reported as having on average more than 260 workers for whom he or she must find work (*Hansard* 1980) but there is some evidence of DROs with as many as 700 workers. This placement function leaves little time for the police function.

In the face of this worsening situation, the quota scheme has come under increasing criticism. Two main explanations have been put forward for the steady erosion of its original intentions: a falling registration rate and the failure to enforce it. The number of people with disabilities registering under the 1944 Act has declined steadily since the 1950s. This does not appear to be due to a fall in the numbers of 'registrable' individuals in the workforce, particularly since there has not been a similar decline in local authority registration. The consequences of this for quota compliance is whether a national rate of 3% of registered disabled people is still possible. On the basis of a falling registration rate, the Department of Employment and the MSC have attempted twice to abolish the quota scheme in favour of voluntary placements. On both occasions the attempt was unsuccessful due to protests from people with disabilities themselves and organisations representing them. The first attempt in 1973 was abandoned with the scheme retained unmodified. The second attempt over the period 1979–81 was altogether better orchestrated. Although it too failed, history may well show us that it was indeed the beginning of the end [doc 22].

It took place in the context of two government campaigns known as 'Positive Policies' and 'Fit for Work'. Both were based on the belief that voluntary action by employers could do more to get people with disabilities jobs than statutory employment protection. Consequently, in 1977 a campaign known as 'Positive Policies' was launched. It aimed to persuade employers, by means of publicity and visits by DROs, to develop enlightened internal company policy which would improve the employment prospects for those with disabilities. Publicity material was sent to 55,000 firms encouraging them to recruit disabled workers. Six main guidelines were put forward:

1. Full and fair consideration of disabled people for all types of vacancies.
2. Retention of newly disabled employees wherever possible, after rehabilitation or training if necessary.
3. Equal opportunities for disabled workers for training, career development and protection.
4. Modifications to equipment, the use of special aids to employment and job restructuring, if needed to help the employment of disabled workers.
5. Adaptation of premises where necessary.
6. Close co-operation with the local DRO.

The promotional approach of 'Positive Policies' had very little effect and was followed two years later by a 'Fit for Work' campaign in which up to 100 awards were to be made each year to firms that 'made outstanding achievements in the employment of disabled people'. The award lasts three years and includes a presentation plaque, citation, desk ornament and the right to use the award's emblem. The award was based on the same six guidelines. Even more than 'Positive Policies', the 'Fit for Work' scheme extended the change in emphasis from statutory protection and equal rights to beneficence and official approbation. In 1980 a third initiative was added to the enveloping tide of persuasive policies. Under the Companies (Director's Report) (Employment of Disabled People) Regulations 1980, the annual reports of companies employing more than 250 people must contain a statement of the company's policy towards employing people with disabilities – covering recruitment, training and career development.

Having set the stage for persuasive non-statutory policies, the MSC published a discussion document on the quota scheme in which the question was raised: is special employment protection for disabled people by statutory means still necessary and justifiable for the future (MSC 1979a)? Although a number of policy options were put forward including both statutory and non-statutory provisions, the document was clear that those administering the quota scheme were highly critical of it and saw it as lacking credibility. Three surveys – of employers, MSC staff operating the quota and disabled people themselves – showed that all, none the less, favoured retaining statutory protection.

One of the arguments put forward against the quota scheme has been and is that the declining register makes it possible for employers to reach a quota compliance of only just over 2%. However, if the much larger number of unregistered disabled people was taken into account this would no longer be the case. Also, while there are still thousands of firms illegally below quota and thousands of unemployed registered disabled people, it could be said to be inappropriate to argue that the declining register explains lack of quota compliance. The argument fails to take into account the reasons why people with disabilities do not register. There are no incentives to register other than to get employment and while the quota scheme is not enforced, employers do not seem to feel compelled to obey the law. In addition, the MSC acknowledge that the increase in the issue of permits has been a response to the decline in registration. A vicious circle appears to have been established where disabled people fail to register because they feel it is a waste of time and where MSC actions make that feeling a reality. This contrasts sharply with the quota system in West Germany where quota compliance is much higher. Their model of operating a quota offers a most useful example: employers who do not fulfil their statutory obligations pay a levy into a special fund, the Equalisation Fund, which is used to finance a range of projects promoting the employment of disabled people. Unlike the UK, the number of registered people in West Germany has risen continually since the registration requirement was introduced in 1974. This may be due to other incentives, such as rights to additional leave, to refuse overtime work and protection against dismissal, as well as to its assiduous enforcement. There have also been attempts to increase the levy for each unfilled post (Massie 1981; Semlinger 1982). Although the USA has a system of 'affirmative action' rather than a quota scheme for disabled people, the machinery adopted to ensure compliance and its aggressive enforcement of the legislation is in sharp contrast to the British situation.

In its report on the responses it had received to its discussion document the MSC recommended that the quota scheme should be abandoned if favour of a largely voluntary scheme supplemented by a weaker form of statutory protection. This was to take the form of a general statutory duty to promote equality of employment opportunity for disabled people and a statutory disclosure of company policy (which had already taken effect). It was suggested that the general duty be linked to a code of practice. The new proposals were vague and essentially unenforceable (MSC 1981i). They were surprising on two counts. Firstly, they were flying in the face of EEC policy which had earlier in the year passed a resolution which considered 'issuing directives to Member States on a "workable" quota system' (EEC 1981). Secondly, they were contrary to the views of most organisations involved with disablement and to the strong support for the quota scheme among the general public (Weir 1981). As a consequence, a substantial body of opinion expressed their opposition to the report's proposals. Exactly one year later, the Secretary of State for Employment issued a statement in response to this pressure announcing that the quota scheme would be retained for the time being but that the matter would be kept under review. This stay of execution, however, was accompanied by an instruction that the MSC draw up a code of practice, a draft of which it duly published. The draft code again represented little more than an 'educational' approach offering 'guidance and suggestions' rather than establishing strong rights to employment protection. A working group was established to consider how the quota scheme could be made more effective, again intimating that the struggle over its existence was not yet over (MSC 1982g).

INSTITUTIONALLY SECURED EMPLOYMENT

There are two forms of institutionally secured employment for people with disabilities, both provided for under the 1944 legislation. The Act permitted certain jobs to be designated as open only to people with disabilities. People occupying those jobs could not be counted towards that employer's quota. Two jobs have been designated as reserved employment under the Act – car-park attendant and electrical passenger-lift attendant. The policy has attracted much criticism because it has reserved only jobs which are of low status. The more significant form of secured employment has been sheltered employment and sheltered industrial groups.

Sheltered employment was originally conceived as providing a bridging experience to the open market for severely handicapped people. Many of the early workshops were envisaged as providing welfare or therapy rather than employment and, therefore, took their place as part of what rehabilitative arrangements there were. The foundations of sheltered employment were laid in section 15 of the Disabled Persons (Employment) Act 1944. This enabled the establishment of sheltered workshops which would be run as non-profit-making companies subsidized by public funds. A special company, Remploy, was initially set up and today has very much the same form as it did in the 1940s. Remploy is heavily committed to furniture manufacture but has in recent years moved into large-scale contract work in order to reduce its overheads. Remploy also works in textiles and knitwear and in packaging and assembly. In the latter, it has begun to take on short or seasonal production runs. Because of its need to remain labour-intensive. it takes on labour-intensive tasks which other companies might rule out (Reardon 1982: 194). It has ninety-two factories providing work for 8,500 people, including a homeworking scheme. The government's subsidy to Remploy in 1980–81 was over £42 million including interest-free loans, but is a relatively open-ended commitment.

Local authorities also run sheltered workshops as subsidized companies. The Disabled Persons (Employment) Act 1958 altered what had been a power to provide sheltered employment in their geographical locality to a duty on local authorities. Local authorities provide these either directly or indirectly through the agency of a voluntary organisation. This duty is discharged through the Social Services Committee of the local authority, reinforcing the rehabilitative function of sheltered work, although the Social Services Committee must negotiate with the Department of Employment through the MSC. In 1980–81 public monies subsidizing local authorities for this purpose were over £9 million. In addition to this, the government also subsidized voluntary bodies to the extent of some £2 million. Local authorities and voluntary bodies provide employment for 5,300 people in 130 sheltered workshops.

The net cost of sheltered employment is reduced by the flow back to the Exchequer from taxation, national insurance payments and savings in social security. Government subsidies include capital expenditure grants, deficiency grants paid towards trading losses, grants for 'approved' workers and training grants (MSC 1980c). Grants may only be made in respect of workshops approved by the MSC; the conditions necessary for such approval are supposed to relate to the workshop's efficiency and viability. The financial help is only available for disabled people who are registered under a separate Section II Register and who are formally approved by the MSC. Grants to local authorities are paid up to a maximum amount. A loss of more than this amount, therefore, represents a charge upon the ratepayers. This is intended to act as an incentive for local authorities to keep their losses down.

An analysis of the costs and benefits of sheltered employment on a national scale has been carried out by the Research and Planning Division of the Department of Employment. Excluding the value of the output produced, the psychological benefits for the individual and the value of a rehabilitative service, a financial analysis examined the cost to public funds of providing sheltered employment compared with the cost of providing the social benefits necessary for severely disabled workers if unemployed. Making certain assumptions (regarding the inability of disabled employees to find work and the demand for currently produced output from sheltered employment not requiring extra employment), the net cost to public funds was estimated. Remploy involved a net financial cost of £133 per disabled worker, blind workshops a cost of £716 per disabled worker, while workshops of sighted workers involved a net saving of £105 per disabled worker (Morgan and Makeham 1978: 19). While these figures vary over time, they do suggest that the net cost of sheltered employment to public funds is considerably less than the gross cost.

There has always been an uneasy compromise between the economic and the humanitarian goals of sheltered employment. The service and non-profit-making orientation of the legislation, the extensive government subsidies and the administrative responsibility of the Social Services Committee all suggest humanitarian goals and objectives, but in their actual operation many workshops face straight industrial and commercial problems. This issue has never really been resolved and, consequently, sheltered workshops find themselves caught up in a vicious cycle. The legislation and their administrative position under the Social Services Committee all reinforce the notion that sheltered employment has predominantly a charitable function rather than primarily an industrial and commercial purpose. In the long run the effects of this makes the workshop even more unprofitable or unsuccessful which then reinforces the argument that it is a shelter, a charity, a humanitarian enterprise. In 1973 a major and comprehensive review of sheltered employment took the position that its *raison d'être* was social rather than economic (Department of Employment 1973). There is no evidence that this view has changed.

The separation of social and industrial or economic objectives suggests that they are somehow opposed to one another. Today the perspective increasingly being adopted in policy terms is to look at the relationship between the two in an attempt to improve the economic performance of workshops by socially acceptable means. One of the avenues explored for doing this was the possibility of the public sector underwriting the production of sheltered workshops. In 1979 a body called Sheltered Employment Procurement and Consultancy Services (SEPACS) was established to help small sheltered workshops find outlets for their products. So far the progress of SEPACS has been disappointing. Only a year after having been set up, their management consultants were publicly advising workshops to look to the private sector for outlets for their goods (Drummond 1980). There have been, therefore, increasing calls for a significant strengthening of what has become known as a priority suppliers scheme (Grant 1982). The National Advisory Council for the Employment of Disabled People (NACEDP) which includes representatives of employers. unions, the medical profession and disabled people themselves, has argued the case for government purchasers to give preference to sheltered workshops when placing contracts (NACEDP 1977). Their report to the MSC on the extent to which sheltered workshops received business from the public sector indicated that this was generally very low. The majority of work done in workshops is obtained from the private sector.

Government purchases from sheltered workshops are extremely small. The latest figures available suggest this is in the region of 1%–2% of the products that are made there. The amount government spends on purchasing the products of sheltered employment is about 2%–3% of the millions of pounds it spends on subsidizing their losses. The majority of government business is with Remploy.

The difficulty managers of sheltered workshops have in finding work must be exacerbated by the effects of inflation on their costs and the effects of the recession on their markets. But there are other factors which contribute as well. One of these is the inability to tap the public sector. A working party set up by the Joint Advisory Committee on Local Authority Purchasing and the Blind Advisory Service recognised that a possible solution to the problem of poor performance in sheltered workshops lay in 'harnessing the enormous purchasing power of local government in a rational system whereby local authorities' purchasing policies could guarantee a reliable market' (Association of County Councils 1979). Despite SEPACS having been established to persuade the public sector to give sheltered workshops priority, there is no legislative backing to ensure that this happens.

The NACEDP report also recommended that central government request local authority associations to urge their members to adopt resolutions to give their own local workshops reasonable priority in the allocation of official orders and to follow procedures under which no order could be withheld without consultation with the Social Services Department. However, it is still not mandatory on local authorities to give any priority to sheltered workshops. The present contracting arrangements exist as an exhortation to government departments, not a statutory duty.

Sheltered Industrial Groups (SIGs) are part of the sheltered employment programme. They first began in 1960 but the numbers of disabled people involved in them have always been small. The groups are also intended to give severely disabled people the opportunity to work. In this case, they do so in small groups of approximately six to eight people who work in an 'enclave' within the setting of an ordinary industrial or commercial environment. Most of them have consisted of either epileptic or mentally handicapped people working on fairly modest labouring jobs for local authorities. However, this is how they have developed and is not necessarily how they will or should proceed (Wansborough 1980). SIGs are intended as a bridge to open employment, just as sheltered workshops are. In both cases, this original aim has been so rarely translated into practice that the rehabilitative objective of both seems to have been forgotten. In many instances the more competent workers in both situations are vital to the successful functioning of the group or the workshop. Consequently, they are specifically retained in order to protect its viability. The MSC's advertisement for SIGs goes even further and states that if 'after a fair trial period, it is clear that a SIG employee is unlikely to make the grade, he or she would be replaced' (MSC 1980a).

Given the unsatisfactory nature of sheltered employment at present, a question increasingly being asked is whether sheltered work-shops should continue to be provided predominantly for disabled people. It has been suggested that a mixed workforce consisting of both severely disabled and fit workers would have two major ad-vantages. On one level the enforced segregation of disabled people could be said to be discriminatory and damaging. On another level, a mixed workforce would be more productive and would reduce the current high deficits. This approach does entail recognising shel-tered employment predominantly as a productive rather than a so-cial service. This would not mean withdrawing subsidies but rather moving to a position of providing subsidies which are directed to-wards creating a viable industry rather than towards disabled in-dividuals. Instead of the deficiency grants for 'approved workers', more emphasis would be placed on capital subsidies and marketing subsidies such as the priority supply arrangements referred to above.

Already some sheltered workshops are moving towards a mixed workforce with apparent success but these are few in number (Grover and Gladstone 1981: 32–3). The problems to be faced are the inevitable reduction in places for the disabled initially and the potentially harmful effect of reducing places for those more hand-icapped than others. However, the overriding principle of integra-tion as a philosophy to underpin employment policy for people with disabilities is strong outside the employment service itself. It is after all the basis of equal opportunity policy and positive discrimination such as the quota [doc 23].

Chapter nine

RACIAL DISCRIMINATION AND EMPLOYMENT

INTRODUCTION

Recent estimates of the black population in Britain suggest that it is a sizeable minority of 1.85 million or 3.4% of the total population (Runnymede Trust and Radical Statistics Race Group 1980: 4). Most black adults were born outside Britain and are generally of Indian, Pakistani, Bangladeshi or Caribbean origin, with a smaller number from Africa and the Far East. Demographically the black community has a younger age profile than the white community. There are fewer elderly people at present (although this will obviously change) which is of importance because of the significant role which grandparents often play in the country of origin. There is also a higher proportion of males, particularly among the Pakistani group. This is initially likely to have been due to the circumstances of their employment in the textile industry. Single men were hired in certain parts of the wool industry in Yorkshire because the installation of new machinery required intensive shiftworking for it to be profitable. Pakistani men were prepared to work the long unsocial hours because they had no family commitments in England and wished to accumulate savings (Cohen and Jenner 1969) [doc 24]. Apart from the usual tendency for immigrants to be single adult males, restrictions on bringing dependants into Britain have exacerbated this. All of these things combine to produce a lifestyle which is often different, more difficult and more lonely than the one adopted in their countries of origin.

Like the Jewish and Polish groups before them, these minority groups have tended to settle in big cities in pursuit of jobs, housing and friends. The black population of Britain has tended to settle in London and the South-East or in the West Midlands and Yorkshire. For example, 32% of white people live in Greater London or the metropolitan counties as compared to 81% of West Indian or Guyanese people and 68% of Indians, Pakistanis, or Bangladeshis (*Social Trends* 1983). Within the cities, however, the black community is often concentrated in ghetto areas or in decaying inner-city districts. Much of this is a consequence of discrimination in the housing market or of poverty and deprivation itself (Duncan 1976). For over twenty years a number of studies have provided growing evidence that the black population tends to live in lower standard housing and to experience more unemployment (Daniel 1968; Smith 1974, 1976, 1981; Runnymede Trust and Radical Statistics Race Group 1980). In addition, the cultural assumptions underlying many other services such as health and education may discourage those not of Anglo-Saxon origin from making effective use of them.

Patterns of black employment and especially unemployment differ in many important respects from the general population. Some of these differences are due to the different age profile of the two groups, e.g. a higher proportion of black men and women are economically active. But the differences may also reflect differences between the cultural sub-groups, e.g. the economic activity rates of Pakistani women are far lower than those of white women whose rates in turn are lower than those of West Indian women (Runnymede Trust and Radical Statistics Race Group 1980: 59). Other differences are the result of racial discrimination. It is important to establish what the profile of black employment is in order to assess whether disadvantage and discrimination are decreasing in the light of certain policy measures to reduce this. However, as with the other disadvantaged groups already mentioned, black workers may be recruited into lower-paid and inferior jobs that were *already* in existence. The presence of immigrant groups or racial discrimination does not in itself create such jobs, but immigrants and black people are often forced into providing replacement labour for jobs which indigenous workers are no longer able or willing to fill. Discrimination aids in effectively perpetuating a less desirable sector of work by closing other job opportunities to certain groups, in this case black workers.

HISTORICAL CONTEXT OF IMMIGRATION

Employment policy and its effect on the black population of Britain must be understood in terms of the circumstances under which recent immigration has occurred and the legislative controls which have been placed on immigrant labour. Virtually all immigration from the newer Commonwealth countries occurred during the

1950s and 1960s. Until this time the number of black residents in Britain was small. Although entry into Britain had been restricted under the various Aliens Restriction Acts of 1905, 1914 and 1919 (aimed largely at Jewish immigrants), under the British Nationality Act of 1948 all citizens of the British Commonwealth were permitted to enter the UK freely, to settle, to work and to bring in their families. The motives were both economic self-interest and a liberal concern with justice and tolerance. With encouragement from the government and many employers who were facing labour shortages after the war, substantial numbers of Commonwealth citizens flowed into Britain. From the Indian sub-continent, from the Caribbean territories, from Guyana, the African colonies, Malaysia and Hong Kong, Britain's imperial past returned to settle in the country which had once claimed theirs for its own. Many British firms like London Transport and the British Hotels and Restaurants Association recruited directly from the West Indies to meet their staff shortages.

The declining need for labour and the increase in immigration during the 1950s led to concern about their effect and agitation for control. The 1960s saw Britain not only retreating from the liberal principles of the 1948 legislation but introducing a form of preferential treatment for white immigrants. Initially this took the form of employment vouchers which were oriented away from semi-skilled or unskilled workers who had made up most of the immigrants from the West Indies. It then took the form of a concept known as patriality. Patriality meant that individuals with a close connection to the UK, usually by way of a spouse, a parent or a grandparent born in the UK (and, therefore, usually white) had a freedom of movement which others did not. Others came under a work permit scheme which, once certain conditions had been fulfilled, was largely discretionary and depended on the desire of employers to hire the particular individual. The largest single group of work permit holders have tended to be from the USA, followed by other highly developed economies (Rees 1979: 85). The strongest determinant of immigration rapidly became economic need combined with the preference of individual employers.

Government policy on race relations has been equivocal and double-edged since 1962. On the one hand there are the various Acts on immigration which are essentially negative forms of legislation controlling and discouraging black people from coming into the country. Individual immigration officials are afforded considerable power, which has led to discriminatory treatment at the point of entry into the country. In addition, individuals who are restrained from entering the country are not accorded the same civil liberties as a British citizen. On the other hand there is a body of legislation on race relations which attempts to encourage better race relations and restrict discrimination against black people. The effectiveness or otherwise of the latter will be dealt with below, but it can be argued that with two sets of such contradictory legislation one is bound to fail.

The political pressure for controls on black immigration began in the late 1950s. Evidence of racial harassment and fears of white racism seem to have played a part as did the declining shortage of labour. The Commonwealth Immigrants Act 1962 established a voucher system which was related to labour demand and which was restricted in number. However in 1967, 66,000 Asians living in Kenya but with British citizenship began to take up residency in the UK when the Kenyan government decided to grant them only temporary status. This led directly to the Commonwealth Immigrants Act 1968 which withdrew the right of entry from British passport holders unless they had a close tie to Britain – defined as having a parent or grandparent or being themselves born in Britain. Since many more whites than blacks were likely to have the required close connection to Britain, the Act clearly intended to discriminate on the basis of race. This was recognised by the European Commission on Human Rights who referred to the singling-out of people for differential treatment on the basis of race as an 'affront to human dignity' (Runnymede Trust and Radical Statistics Race Group 1980: 34). Nevertheless the pattern continued. In 1969 dependent wives and children had to obtain entry certificates to join their immigrant husbands, which could be an extremely lengthy and difficult procedure. In 1971 a new Immigration Act, replacing the 1962 and 1968 legislation, introduced the concept of patriality and was far more restrictive in its control of Commonwealth immigration. A sign of the changing economic priorities of the country was the complete freedom of movement accorded EEC nationals while workers from the new Commonwealth countries became subject to the same regulations as aliens.

Despite the considerable restrictions on black immigrants, racism and discrimination persist, fuelled by individual politicians, groups such as the National Front and prejudiced media reporting. Persistently drawing a colour bar in immigration legislation has undoubtedly also made a contribution to negating the effects of race relations legislation. In 1983 a new Nationality Act came into force replacing all other nationality laws. It created three types of citizenship which reflect the closeness of the individual's connection with the UK and, again, their 'whiteness' in some circumstances. One lesser category of citizenship, that of British Dependent Territories (such as Hong Kong) excludes the Falkland Islands and Gibraltar, whose populations are largely white. After 1988 certain Commonwealth citizens stand to lose their current right to remain in Britain unless they have paid £200.00 and registered. Registration is discretionary, giving black immigrants no protection against discrimination. In addition, the fee may be prohibitive for poorer members of the population and those in more vulnerable and lower paid jobs. Aspects of the new law such as these have led to claims that it discriminates on the basis of race as did its predecessors (Dummett and Martin 1982).

Powerful organisations like the TUC, the recognised representative of labour, have not always acted to help their minority group members. Miles and Phizacklea have documented the poor record of the TUC over the period when most of the above legislation was being enacted. Until 1973 the General Council of the TUC held a negative and defensive attitude towards immigration due to a combination of xenophobia and a fear that immigrant labour would undercut wages. This took the form of failing to 'acknowledge that there existed considerable hostility towards black workers among white trade unionists' and adopting the position that 'problems arose from the immigrants' refusal to 'integrate' (Miles and Phizacklea 1977: 3). Both the TUC and the CBI were strongly criticised by the Select Committee on Race Relations and Immigration in 1974 for failing to take adequate steps to counter racial discrimination. In 1975, however, the policy and practice of the General Council began to change. It moved from focusing on attempts to 'integrate' immigrants into British customs and way of life towards focusing on the existence of racism and discrimination at work (Miles and Phizacklea 1978). The documentation of discrimination at work, however, has not noticeably come from the trade union movement but from other independent sources. None the less, the current policy of the TUC is no longer to promote integration at work but to eliminate racism at work, evidence of an important shift in emphasis.

EMPLOYMENT AND UNEMPLOYMENT

The collection of statistics on the basis of colour or ethnic origin is surrounded by controversy, as was evidenced in the debate over whether a question on racial origins should be introduced in the 1981 census (it was finally decided against). Statistics have been collected on immigration for some time but certain sectors of the public and media interest in black immigrants have tended to reinforce a terminological confusion between being an immigrant and being a member of a racial minority. This can and has been used to legitimise discrimination. However, the absence of recent census data on race may create serious obstacles to investigating the extent of discrimination both in employment and in other fields in the years to come. One survey which does provide such information is the *Labour Force Survey* which is organised by the Statistical Office of the EEC and is carried out by all member states every two years in the spring. Information in Britain is collected by personal interviews from a representative sample of households. In the 1981 *Survey* there is evidence of disparity in socio-economic status between whites and those of West Indian, Guyanese, Indian, Pakistani or Bangladeshi origin. A smaller proportion of white men and women are to be found in manual work, especially unskilled work (*OPCS Monitor* 1981).

These findings confirmed an earlier study by Barber based on the *National Dwelling and Housing Survey* (Barber 1981). Not only is there a higher proportion of black people in manual and unskilled jobs, but there is evidence that they take longer to find jobs, are often in jobs which are unpleasant, low-paid or unsocial in working hours, tend to work more on shiftwork, are more vulnerable to redundancy, and are particularly vulnerable to high unemployment (Dex 1979; Runnymede Trust and Radical Statistics Race Group 1980; Smith 1974; Smith 1981) [doc 25]. According to the *Labour Force Survey* for 1981, 10% of economically active males between the ages of 16 and 64 were unemployed in the white group compared to 21% in the West Indian or Guyanese group and 17% in the Indian, Pakistani, or Bangladeshi group. Unemployment was particularly high for black youngsters. The differences in female unemployment, as with female socio-economic status, were not as marked as they were for males except with regard to young workers.

The findings on socio-economic status and unemployment show the same discrepancies. As was shown in Chapter three, the risk of unemployment increases lower down the socio-economic scale, with those in manual work more at risk than those in non-manual work. In addition, according to Smith, those who have difficulty finding a job because of discrimination may compensate by accepting a less attractive job (Smith 1981: 2). None the less, the group of unemployed black people in his sample were more highly qualified than the white unemployed group (Smith 1981: 17).

For some time there has been an assumption that immigrant labour is largely to be found in old labour-intensive or under-capitalised industries which have not invested in new machinery in order to save costs. To some extent this is correct. Many small companies have started to form a new low-wage sector in response to the decline of established industries in the inner city. These firms depend on operating at low cost margins which means paying their labour force rates which are usually below the minimum rates agreed for that particular industry. One of the ways of doing this is to have a non-unionised workforce. The company may, therefore, try to recruit weak non-unionised labour who will not complain about low wages. Immigrants, whether black or white, tend to provide such labour. Workers who are recent immigrants may be more concerned in the first instance with getting adequate housing and settling in than with improving the quality of their employment (Craig *et al.* 1979: 100–1). Secondly, if recent immigrants speak little English they are less likely to have much knowledge of their rights as workers such as wage agreements nor of their rights to organise protection for themselves by way of joining a union. There is some evidence that low-paying firms such as these consciously recruit their employees from certain vulnerable groups in society such as non-English speakers, disabled workers or married women (CDPPEC 1979, 1980).

Immigrant labour was recruited to meet the labour shortages of the 1950s and in a variety of ways was incorporated into the low-wage sector. Many years on, the ethnic minority groups descending from that immigrant labour have been some of the first to suffer from rising unemployment. Smith documents this vulnerability on the basis of trends in both the first and the second half of the 1970s. His findings show that as total male unemployment rises, the unemployment of males in minority groups rises even more quickly. The main differences emerge for non-manual and skilled manual workers, with rates of unemployment showing greater similarity for unskilled and semi-skilled workers (Smith 1981: 5; Barber 1981: 38). One of the most striking features is the extent of youth unemployment among minority groups. Since the majority of these young people are likely to have been born or at least schooled in Britain, the explanations for their vulnerability cannot easily be seen in terms of language or cultural difference. Neither can their higher unemployment be put down to having fewer qualifications than white youths. One study of all 16–20 year-olds in selected neighbourhoods of London, Liverpool, Manchester and Wolverhampton found that their black respondents had left school with higher qualifications than the whites, were more ambitious and more likely to enrol in further education. Despite this, their unemployment rate was 36% greater than that of the whites (Roberts *et al*. 1981: 16).

One of the key factors operating to cause such deprivation in employment is racial discrimination. The most direct evidence of the extent of discrimination was obtained in 'situation' tests carried out in 1966 by PEP (Political and Economic Planning). People of equal qualifications, background and appearance but of different colours or countries of origin were sent to apply for jobs and their experiences were monitored. The applicants were white English, white immigrant (Hungarian), West Indian or Asian. The tests were carefully controlled, taking steps to ensure freedom from bias. In most cases apparently incontrovertible evidence was provided of discrimination on the basis of race. In addition, a sample survey of 1,000 immigrants found a high incidence of reported discrimination, particularly by West Indians (Daniel 1968). Later surveys confirmed this experience of discrimination (Smith 1974; 1976; 1981). In most cases the victim has no means of ascertaining absolutely that he or she was discriminated against in, for instance, recruitment for jobs, promotion or redundancy. Most discrimination is covert, especially since the introduction of legislation to outlaw it. The provision of a procedure to adjudicate claims of discrimination has, however, brought to light many instances of discrimination at work The Commission for Racial Equality regularly publishes details of such instances [doc 26].

There have been a number of measures designed to improve the position of black people in employment. Recent government policy has been twofold, based on the perception that there are two key problems. The first problem is seen to be that of discrimination – which has been challenged by anti-discriminatory legislation. The second problem is seen to be that of deprivation – this has been challenged by inner area policies and specific statutory instruments.

ANTI-DISCRIMINATORY POLICY

Britain has no written constitution which guarantees and protects the rights of individuals. Instead it has pursued a policy of outlawing discrimination against specific groups in society. The Sex Discrimination Act is an example of this, as is the race relations legislation. Three Race Relations Acts have been passed over a period of twelve years – in 1965, 1968 and 1976 – each one progressively offering more protection than the last. Prior to 1965 attempts had been made to legislate against racial discrimination but the 1965 Act was the first to make discrimination on the basis of race, colour, ethnic or national origin illegal and established a Race Relations Board to investigate complaints about alleged discrimination. The second Act of 1968 specifically detailed discrimination in employment and housing and in the provision of public services. The Race Relations Board had to resolve disputes by conciliation and was the sole body with power to start litigation. The Act also established the Community Relations Commission to promote good race relations.

From 1968 onwards, as has been shown, increasing evidence began to emerge of discrimination against ethnic minorities. The PEP group undertook a number of studies which indicated that discrimination, particularly in employment, was widespread despite the Act having been in existence for six years. Much of this had to do with the nature of the legislation and the procedure. For instance, small firms of less than twenty-five workers were excluded from the Act which meant excluding 20% of the working population (in 1970 this changed to 10%). A special procedure applied to employment complaints, which first went to the Secretary of State for Employment. Only if suitable non-statutory machinery was not available to deal with the complaint was it referred to the Race Relations Board (Bentley 1976). The Race Relations Board then had the total responsibility for investigating complaints, making a judgement, effecting a conciliation, awarding damages and sometimes defending their judgement in court.

These weaknesses led to the final and existing Race Relations Act of 1976 which replaced both the previous pieces of legislation. This Act replaced the Race Relations Board and the Community Relations Commission with the Commission for Racial Equality (CRE). With regard to employment it has made two important new departures. A complainant has the right of direct access to an industrial tribunal and may be supported by the CRE in taking a complaint to the direct legal machinery. Secondly, the definition of discrimination is extended to include 'indirect' racial discrimination, for which the CRE alone may institute proceedings. This includes treatment which is discriminatory in effect, in that even if it is applied to all people, it effects proportionately more of one racial group or cannot be justified aside from race (Little 1977: 98). An example might be a test for employment which effectively excludes black applicants and cannot be shown to be related to the needs of the job. The Act also prohibits discrimination in recruitment to employment, discrimination in training, promotion, transfer and other benefits of existing employees. It embodies a concept of positive action in making provision for programmes to remedy the effects of past disadvantage but positive discrimination remains unlawful. Although a local authority can choose to regard membership of a particular ethnic group as a qualification for a post, the Act generally makes provision for equality of opportunity (Young and Connelly 1981: 47). One of the ways this has been taken up has been in the form of a code of practice for employers. In 1983 a draft code was submitted by the CRE to the Secretary of State for Employment after some controversy over whether small firms should be exempt from such a code. It was felt that their exclusion could reduce the effectiveness of the code given the large proportion of black workers in small firms.

The CRE now has a strategic function which includes instituting legal proceedings in respect of persistent discrimination and conducting formal investigations where discrimination is suspected, as well as promoting better race relations. In the first year of its operation it received 862 applications for assistance. In the same period only four industrial tribunal cases were won by complainants. The compensation awarded was never more than £250 (Runnymede Trust and Radical Statistics Race Group 1980: 45). While the 1976 Act is more comprehensive in its efforts to combat racial discrimination in employment and elsewhere, its effectiveness is questionable. Some writers question the likelihood of equal opportunity legislation being a sufficient condition to eliminate inequality in employment between majority and minority groups because of the strength of segmented labour markets. Racial or sexual discrimination is seen as subsidiary to (or convenient to) the forces in operation which have created a secondary labour force (Jain and Sloane 1980). It is clear, however, that some equal opportunity legislation is more effective than others. In a study of seventy-four companies in the private sector undertaken in the Department of Employment, Hitner *et al.* found that despite all having a commitment to the promotion of equal opportunity for racial and ethnic minorities, 'no relationship between policy and practice could be discerned'. They conclude that 'the most damaging indictment of this elaborate equal opportunity policy is that since 1975, there is virtually no evidence to suggest that the policy has had any effect on the employment and promotion prospects of ethnic minorities' (Hitner *et al.* 1982: 23–5). The most startling aspect of this finding is the criteria upon which the companies were selected. They were companies with a good employment record including a better than average occupational distribution of black staff, a written equal opportunity policy and special facilities for ethnic minorities such as language training, extended leave arrangements and time off for religious holidays. None the less, in a detailed investigation of twelve of the companies, discrimination, some of it inadvertent, in selection and promotion was found. The authors suggest that this was due to the policies being conceived independently of the workforce, i.e. without consultation and separately from employment issues in general.

The shaping of the Race Relations Act 1976 was influenced by equal employment policy for minorities in the United States both in its reference to indirect discrimination and in permitting individuals to bring complaints to the law (Jain and Sloane 1980). Both these provisions have been accepted in the United States for some time. In a number of important respects there appear to be procedural and substantive obstacles in the British legislation which are reducing its effectiveness. These relate to compensation, the inability to bring 'class action' suits, the lack of record keeping, the lack of priority funding and the small budget allocated to enforcement (Boggs 1982).

Firstly in Britain, damages awarded for discrimination can only date from the time of alleging discrimination. There is no provision for backdating compensation to a period of time when financial loss was suffered. To date, the awards made by tribunals are often very small and usually only given for injury to feelings, which must act as a disincentive both to complain and to comply with the law. Tribunals have also been reluctant to speculate on the loss of future earnings.

Secondly, unlike the United States, Britain has no provision for 'class actions'. This entails a legal action by which the rights of a group of people rather than an individual can be adjudicated for at the same time. A 'class action' can be taken for an individual on behalf of a larger number of people who are similarly situated and have suffered as a result of the same practices. It can lead to settlements on a corporate wide basis (Jain and Sloane 1980; Boggs

1982). Thirdly, British companies are not required to keep records of their black (or female) employees, which makes it more difficult for the CRE to identify targets for investigation or to place individual complaints in the overall record of the company. Fourth, there are no sanctions which can be brought to bear on companies who do not employ people from minority groups such as the federal funding requirements outlined in Chapter eight. Firms not complying with the law in the United States face considerable financial penalties.

Finally, the budget for the CRE is extremely small. It is not geared in financial or staff terms to vigorously and systematically enforcing the law. For instance, in the financial year 1982–3 its budget was just over £8 million, of which £3 million was disbursed to Community Relations Councils and local groups. Its staff was 226. Two full-time lawyers are assigned to support formal investigations and complaint work. By contrast, in the United States the federal agencies dealing with civil rights enforcement have a budget in excess of $359 million and a staff of 6,000. A total of 540 lawyers are employed by the Equal Employment Opportunity Commission and the Civil Rights division of the Department of Justice. Even taking into account population differences, the disparities are significant (CRE 1982; Boggs 1982).

INNER AREA POLICIES

In 1975 the Labour government published a White Paper, *Racial Discrimination* (HMSO 1975) which led to the 1976 legislation. The White Paper identified racial discrimination as the major problem faced by members of the black community in Britain. It also identified a cycle of cumulative disadvantage by which low-paid and menial jobs accompany a depressed environment and poor overcrowded living conditions. Consequently, it called for a more comprehensive strategy for dealing with multiple disadvantage as well as one for dealing with discrimination. The notion of multiple deprivation in the inner city was not new. Since 1968 a number of programmes had been aimed at improving the inner city which can be referred to under the umbrella term of the 'Urban Programme' (Higgins *et al*. 1983).

The Urban Programme was first announced in a speech on race relations and immigration by the Prime Minister in May 1968. While the policy was new, there was a precedent for it in the Local Government Act 1966. Section 11 of the Act empowered the Home

Secretary to make grants for the employment of staff by local authorities whose areas contained substantial numbers of Commonwealth immigrants whose language and customs differed from the general community. By 1969 the grant was 75% of approved expenditure. Ten years later, eighty-eight local authorities and the Inner London Education Authority were claiming £40 million under this legislation. The majority was for education, and for teachers in language and remedial skills. By then, however, local authorities were receiving a general Rate Support Grant from central government of about 65% of all expenditure and the significance of a 75% grant had lessened. An attempt to introduce more flexible grant aid power was lost during the change of government in 1979 (Young and Connelly 1981: 174).

In 1968 the Urban Programme was transferred to the Home Office. This suggests that a stimulus for concern was as much the maintenance of law and order in the inner city as poverty and deprivation. The Urban Programme of 1968, the Community Development Projects of 1969, the Urban Deprivation Unit of 1973 and the Comprehensive Community Programmes of 1974 were all the responsibility of the Home Office. It was only in 1977 that the Urban Programme was again transferred, this time to the Department of the Environment. It appears that the same duality of control and concern that oscillates between the immigration and race relations legislation is also present in the Urban Programme. It is also present in more recent reports such as the Scarman Report, which while acknowledging discrimination and the disproportionate effect of unemployment and deprivation on black people, had as its terms of reference, policing (Scarman 1981).

Most of the early Urban Programme focused on education, housing, health and welfare. Unemployment and income received virtually no attention. In 1976, however, the programme was criticized for not coming to grips with underlying social and economic forces. The Secretary of State for the Environment called for a greater emphasis on the loss of jobs from the inner city and the need to regenerate the economic infrastructure of those areas (Higgins *et al.* 1983: 63). From that time more projects developed which were concerned with employment, job creation, training and economic regeneration. However, in 1973 the MSC had been established with prime responsibility for the first three of these, which possibly drew away some of the impetus to focus on employment. The implicit intention of much of the Urban Programme seems to have been that as a result of its projects, inner-city children would eventually do better at school, become qualified, get better jobs, earn higher wages and have more security. Evaluating whether the projects actually have this effect is a difficult and long-term task, one which many American writers were doubting was possible from their own experience of the 1960s (Marris and Rein 1967; Moynihan 1970). It can also be argued that many projects implicitly assumed that the problem of unemployment was one of lack of skills or 'human capital' as outlined in Chapter one. It was accepted that possession of such skills was hampered by the social environment of the inner city but not by the nature and structure of the labour market itself. However, a continuous rise in unemployment has accompanied the Urban Programme from its very beginning, as has a period of public expenditure restraint. The panacea of improving selected neighbourhoods has not worked with regard to either unemployment or racial disadvantage, suggesting the existence of a 'national structure of unequal resource allocation' through the process of job allocation and racial discrimination (Townsend 1976).

The projects of the Urban Programme have often been introduced in the context of race relations but they are aimed at all populations living in certain geographical areas. A White Paper published in 1977 faced the problem of the inner cities in terms of how government could secure their economic revival (Department of Environment 1977). It suggested that this would have to be done by a partnership between central and local government. As far as a strategy to overcome racialism was concerned, this was seen to be a side issue, one that was best dealt with in legislation and through the CRE. In so far as the Urban Programme benefited the inner cities and in so far as these continued to have a concentration of black residents, such a policy was perceived to be improving racial disadvantage. The inner-city programme remained largely unchanged over the next few years apart from experiencing reductions in their budgets as part of general public expenditure restraint.

In 1981, as a result of major disturbances in Brixton, the heart of one of London's inner-city partnership areas, the issue of the inner city, race and employment again came to the forefront of government attention. Over a weekend in April a few hundred young people, most but not all of whom were black, rioted on the streets. In the subsequent inquiry into the events, two views were predominantly expressed about their cause. One put the disturbances down to oppressive policing and harassment of young blacks. The other put them down to the experience of frustration and deprivation of young people in a racially divided society (Scarman 1981: 14). One of the conclusions of the inquiry was that unemployment is 'a major factor in the complex pattern of conditions which lies at the root of the disorders in Brixton and elsewhere'. The solution was seen to be part of wider economic policy, including the programmes of the MSC. The *Report* of the inquiry also recommended projects to clean up and regenerate the inner city for young people in place of current unemployment and social security programmes (Scarman 1981: 169). The implication of such self-help programmes is that they are usually a form of cheap labour and not 'real' jobs. They may be a short-term expedient but do not solve the unemployment which comes from discrimination and deprivation. Relying on the training programmes of the MSC, too, does little for the trained black youngster who, when he or she goes for a job, faces discriminatory hiring practices. The employment disadvantages of blacks in Britain are more likely to be aided when legislation is no longer contradictory, when laws against discrimination are firmly enforced and adequately financed, and when the structural constraints of the labour market itself are broken down.

Part four
THE PERSISTENCE OF INEQUALITY

Chapter ten
ASSESSMENT

INEQUALITY AT WORK

A great deal of poverty and inequality persists in Britain. About one in nine people live on or below the government's poverty line. Much of this deprivation is due to unprecedently high levels of unemployment which have forced several million people to rely on the inadequate support provided by state benefits. However, poverty is something experienced both in work and out of work. There is also a great deal of inequality at work, experienced mainly in low wages. One million adult male workers earn low wages (defined as two-thirds median male earnings) although they are employed full-time and work overtime as well. Two and a quarter million adult female workers working full-time are similarly low paid (Byrne *et al.* 1983: 5). Part of the reason for this has been the effect of high rates of unemployment which have depressed wages and decreased the amount of overtime work available. Another reason has been the government's policy since 1979 of jettisoning or weakening many existing employment protection policies and altering the balance of power in industrial relations through, for example, the Employment Acts of 1980 and 1982.

However, inequality at work is not new or particular either to certain periods of recession or to certain governments. A low wage sector has been in existence for some time. Increasing research has suggested that the labour market is segregated into different sectors. The most common formation proposed is that between a primary sector of secure, well-paid employment and a secondary sector of insecure, low-paid employment. There are variations on this theme and differences in the explanations put forward for the origins and operations of a structured labour market. But there is common agreement about the existence of a sector which is disadvantaged and relatively powerless, consisting of jobs that are menial and susceptible to forces beyond the control of those who occupy them. This low-wage sector appears to play an important supportive role to the large monopoly corporations which have grown up during this century. The low-wage sector is concentrated in a narrow range of industries, usually consisting of small firms offering semi-skilled or unskilled work. They provide areas to which large firms can sub-contract simpler aspects of their production as well as transferring certain business risks. They also constitute a competitive sector which is maintained alongside a monopoly sector. This keeps down wages and hinders the effective organisation of workers by providing a pool of cheap and competitive labour. Some workers are, therefore, less protected against economic and industrial changes than others.

The actions of both employers and well-unionised primary sector workers have served to keep workers who are perceived to be marginal or less desirable out of more favourable jobs. This has usually been seen to occur through the operation of an internal labour market whereby recruitment is limited to the lower grades of work and promotion is internal to the organisation. But it may also occur through selective recruitment which discriminates against specific kinds of workers such as black or female applicants. When certain roles are socially ascribed to individuals on the basis of their sex, race or physical and mental condition, such discrimination is facilitated and given legitimacy – especially when the roles give rise to sexist, racist and ageist attitudes which become internalised even by those who fill them. The pervasiveness of such attitudes, particularly when combined with industrial requirements, are not overcome by legislation and policy. The difficulty facing women and black workers trying to enforce their rights to equal opportunity is a case in point. Even a policy of positive discrimination, such as that contained in the quota scheme for people with disabilities is insufficient to overcome such convention backed by ideology. Even so, it is in the pursuit of workable policies that a considerable part of the struggle for greater equality takes place.

A theme thus far has been that there is a hierarchy of employment in which certain groups of people are susceptible to low-paid low-status jobs, poor working conditions and a greater risk of unemployment. Women, younger and older workers, workers with disabilities and immigrant or black workers are particularly vulnerable because of the positions they are ascribed in the ideological framework dominant in our society. This is one which accepts that certain groups are inferior or dependent by virtue of their physical attributes: their sex, their age, their disability, their race. These attributes are often related to assumed levels of productivity.

Concentrating on specific groups of people should not be taken to suggest a belief that focusing on the supply of labour will give us a complete explanation for the disadvantaged position of these groups in the labour market. They have been used to provide a framework for the discussion of policy because policy measures are usually directed at certain groups. In addition, these groups experience discrimination and disadvantage in society which in turn both legitimises their employment at the bottom of the hierarchy of jobs and ensures a supply of workers ready to meet the demands of a stratified labour market. While it is important not to abstract the problems of such groups from wider issues of inequality, focusing on them in this way enables us to understand the role policy plays in ensuring a reserve of labour for the secondary, low-wage sector. It is not sufficient, however, for a complete understanding of how the labour market works.

Certain groups are perceived to have an employment status that is marginal, i.e. their attachment to the labour market is seen to be a loose one in that they have primary social roles other than that of worker. For women this is the 'housewife', for young people it is the 'student' or the 'dependant', for older people it is the 'pensioner', for people with disabilities it is the dependent 'sick' role and for immigrants it is that of 'citizen of another country'. They are, therefore, seen to have access to other resources such as pensions, husband's or father's wages and so on. Consequently, unemployment or low wages are seen as less of a problem than they would be for a prime age, white, able-bodied male worker. The concentration of these groups among the unemployed or in a low-wage sector of work is then easily legitimised. None the less, in periods of labour shortages women and immigrants in particular have been recruited and the struggle for greater equality has gained a new impetus. Equal opportunity policies have been fought for and often enacted and enforced. The demands of work in times of a labour shortage have had to be adjusted to meet the needs of, for example, older or disabled workers or women with children. In periods of labour surplus these same workers are the ones who are discarded or discouraged. Policies which make it easier for industry to ease out the surplus are enacted, such as the redundancy scheme or the Job Release Scheme and younger workers are dispensed into training schemes. Although equal opportunity policies remain on the statute books, their use declines because they fail to be enforced

– as evidenced by the decline in tribunal applications under the Equal Pay and Sex Discrimination Acts. The surplus or shortage of labour itself is to a large extent determined by the decisions of companies or governments (not always local) regarding the organisation and rationalisation of production including the opening or closure of plants. These are usually decisions which are taken on the basis of criteria which are unrelated to the needs of the workforce or the community in which the company operates. They are commercial decisions about what can be most profitably produced rather than social judgements about what individuals and communities need to have produced and how they want to produce them.

SOCIAL POLICY AND EMPLOYMENT

The subject of social policy has often been late in taking on board issues *directly* related to employment and unemployment. It has largely confined itself to dealing with the principal resource system for those out of work, i.e. social security or income maintainance. The nature of government intervention in the labour market has been 'confined to helping the interaction of labour supply and demand, rather than attempting to mitigate the social and economic inequalities generated by the market system' (Showler 1982: 177). This reflects a policy concern with efficiency rather than equity. The lack of response by social policy reflects its tendency to react to events rather than to initiate them. It is also a measure of the extent to which unemployment as a social issue has been ignored. None the less, two seminal thinkers in the field did place employment issues firmly on the agenda for social policy after the Second World War. In the *Report on Social Insurance and Allied Services* (1942), William Beveridge stated that without the maintenance of full employment his plan for social security could not succeed. In *The Social Division of Welfare* some fourteen years later, Richard Titmuss asserted that systems of fiscal and occupational welfare existed alongside social welfare and often undermined what redistribution the latter might achieve. Occupational welfare referred to the provision of a system of benefits for those in work over and above both their remuneration and what they may have received from social welfare. He saw it as being more available for some than for others, reinforcing a hierarchy at work. Beveridge's concern for the maintenance of full employment, and Titmuss' concern that occupational benefits offset the benefits of the welfare state, remain dominant in social policy.

Work and inequality

BEVERIDGE, SOCIAL SECURITY AND EMPLOYMENT

Until the end of the nineteenth century unemployment hardly existed as a concept because of the assumption that work was available if people wanted it. Garraty suggests that the concept of unemployment has a social dimension and the lack of such a concept last century, therefore, indicated that the condition of being without work was regarded as a personal rather than a social issue (Garraty 1978: 4). The role of the Poor Law, for instance, was one of maintaining the supply of labour. There was general acceptance of the view that in a competitive economy there was an automatic tendency towards a full-employment equilibrium. So long as prices, wages and interest rates were flexible, the market was held to be self-regulating. Government intervention, although minimal, did go so far as to create labour exchanges to facilitate the tendency to equilibrium. Beveridge, for instance, in analysing unemployment as a problem of industrial change (rather than an individual problem) recommended the labour exchange as a means of managing the reserve of irregularly employed labour (Garraty 1978: 137–40). It was only after the Second World War that governments accepted a more positive responsibility for employment and economic activity generally, leading to unprecedented levels of intervention in the labour market. Full employment became a feasible policy option, something which was in the power of governments to choose and determine.

Beveridge, while best known for his contribution to social policy through the *Beveridge Report*, had long concerned himself with unemployment. His initial approach to the problem was an attempt to devise a system of financial relief such that the efficiency of workers could be maintained while they were unemployed. He later adopted the view that the key problem of unemployment was not individual relief but the re-organisation of a faulty labour market. This was based on the view that unemployment was not so much due to the decline of certain industries, for instance, but the failure of the labour market to re-direct employees to alternative employment (Harris 1972: 21–4). As a consequence he proposed that labour exchanges collect and publish information about employment. In addition, the exchanges and the merging social security system were linked. Those out of work had to prove to the exchanges that they were genuinely seeking work before they could claim benefit. The identification of the labour exchange with the administration of benefits for the unemployed grew during and because of the depression of the 1920s and 1930s and continued into the 1960s. It was undoubtedly aimed at those individuals who were thought to be wilfully and irresponsibly avoiding work. Beveridge, however, finally came to the conclusion that the link between employment and social security was not simply one of deterring scroungers from applying for benefit by providing jobs. In his attempt to establish a system of social security, he concluded that full employment was not just necessary for its own sake but possible and, most importantly, necessary to enable his plan for social security to work.

The *Beveridge Report on Social Insurance and Allied Services* was published in 1942. It was drawn up by a committee which had been established about 18 months previously as part of a general surge of interest in social issues after the war. The *Report* was a major comprehensive survey of the existing system of social insurance. It set out a plan for social security such that 'every individual, on condition of working while he can and contributing from his earnings, shall have an income sufficient for the healthy subsistence of himself and his family, an income to keep him above Want, when for any reason he cannot work and earn' (Beveridge 1944: 17). The main feature of the 'Plan for Social Security' was to be a scheme of social insurance against interruption and destruction of earning power. Three assumptions lay behind the plan without which Beveridge considered it would not work. One of these was full employment. Full employment was necessary so that the insurance fund would not be depleted. The kind of unemployment which had followed the First World War would undoubtedly have made a plan based on insurance contributions and flat rate benefits, such as this one, impossible. This assumption was the key to the success of his plan for social insurance and is the reason for its manifest difficulties since the mid-1960s when unemployment began to rise above its average rate of 1.7% after the war.

There was a very deep concern at the end of the war that the dole queues of the 1930s should not return. The coalition government of 1944 published a White Paper on employment policy in which the maintenance of a high and stable level of employment was accepted as a primary aim and responsibility of government. At the same time, Beveridge published a sequel to the *Report on Social Insurance and Allied Services*, on full employment (Beveridge 1944). His report was more radical and far-reaching than the White Paper. Beveridge proposed a radically new budget which would use fiscal policies, government borrowing and deficit financing to determine levels of public spending as well as investment decisions

(Harris 1977: 438). One of the issues debated at the time was whether full employment could be sustained without elements of control and coercion and in a 'free society' (Deacon 1981a). Beveridge too was concerned with the possibility of achieving full employment while retaining essential liberties of citizenship. He had come to believe that deficiency of demand and misdirection of demand caused unemployment and that state policy could influence private spending through fiscal policy and its annual budget. He laid out a long-term programme of planned output, controlled industrial location and organised mobility of labour to achieve full employment under the title *A Full Employment Policy for Peace* (Beveridge 1944: 29, 123–93). His views on the demand for labour did not extend to institutional factors which influenced it nor to those factors which segregated the workforce into privileged and unprivileged groups [doc 27].

The post-war government, however, was initially faced with an acute shortage of labour. It appealed to married women to go back to work and selective immigration of foreign workers was encouraged – in interesting contrast to the period of mass unemployment of the 1980s which led to demands for the return of women and immigrants to their homes or homelands respectively. There were some fears that the shortage of labour would lead to an increase in demands for higher wages and less discipline on the shop floor. The White Paper, consequently, spoke of the need for moderate wage claims to accompany full employment. The commitment to full employment was common to both parties and remained the main objective of all governments for well over the next quarter of a century.

Beveridge and the Webbs made the political and social case for a labour market policy which reduced 'the pain' or the price of industrial competition (Beveridge 1944). Keynes made the economic case for government policies to create the expansion in consumption he considered necessary for full employment. Certain economic arguments for a labour market policy which contributed to flexibility in the system and the preservation of an efficient labour force, were also seen to be compatible with the view that there is a natural tendency for supply and demand to be in equilibrium. Labour market policies can be evaluated in terms of their contribution to either of these economic goals – full employment or efficiency. They can also be evaluated in more social terms of their relief of suffering or the extent to which they open up opportunities for disadvantaged groups ensuring that unemployment (and employment disadvantages generally) are not experienced disproportionately.

OCCUPATIONAL WELFARE

In 1955, only a few years after the introduction of some of the major pieces of social legislation which were to have made up the 'golden age' of the welfare state (including those proposed by Beveridge), Richard Titmuss questioned how these collective interventions were serving society and how the distribution of resources and power was being affected by them. He concluded that three systems of welfare existed: one though the social services, another through the fiscal system and another through the occupational system. These he called the 'social division of welfare' because they had arisen out of a complicated division of labour which threw up different needs requiring different forms of organisation to deal with them. Occupational welfare benefits were seen to include occupational pension schemes, personal expenses, fringe benefits such as motor cars, medical expenses, holidays and so on. He described these as 'an incalculable variety of benefits in kind ranging from obvious forms of realisable goods to the most intangible forms of amenity' (Titmuss 1958: 51). Most importantly, the ultimate cost of these benefits falls, if not on the consumer, then on the Exchequer, making them a system of welfare. The significance of the social division of welfare is that the same or similar needs are defined differently and attract a different response because they are dealt with in a separate system of welfare. This can be illustrated by the different kinds of help available, through the three systems, for individuals losing their jobs: the social welfare system provides a taxed unemployment benefit or means-tested benefits; the occupational welfare system provides redundancy payments; through the fiscal welfare system redundancy payments are tax free up to a certain amount for the recipient and can be set against the employer's liability to corporation tax on profits (Sinfield 1978).

Most of the cost of these benefits ultimately falls on the taxpayer (or on the consumer in the case of occupational welfare). The most obvious implication to draw from the existence of an occupational welfare system is that its benefits are only available for those in employment. There is additional evidence that manual workers and low-paid workers are less likely to have access to occupational benefits than non-manual workers, thus also creating inequalities among those who are in employment. Manual workers, particularly women, have less coverage by occupational sick pay schemes (Lonsdale 1980: 6–8). Few manual workers belong to occupational pension schemes (Field 1981: 139). Redundancy schemes are often considerably more generous for top employees (Field *et al.* 1977). Women are often doubly disadvantaged in occupational welfare: because many are not in formal employment they are simply excluded from the start; even when in employment, their uneven work patterns place them at a disadvantage with regard to benefits such as pension schemes or redundancy payments.

When viewed in relation to fiscal and occupational measures which both perpetuate and legitimise social and economic inequality, the post-war system of social welfare proposed by Beveridge to abolish poverty seems merely symbolic. With increasing levels of unemployment, two major streams of inequality have developed. One relates to those at work as before. The other relates to the mass of people who do not have a job. The social division of welfare, however, has not only perpetuated inequality. It has disguised the fact that a great many resources in society are flowing to the already rich and powerful while a semblance of redistribution to the poor is allowed to continue. It is no longer possible to accept the concept of the welfare state as a mechanism for either overcoming poverty or redistributing wealth. At certain periods and in certain ways it has represented both a humane response to need and the outcome of hard-fought battles for access to resources. Overall, however, it has served to obscure many actual lines of power and wealth in society while acting as a servant to economic growth. One of these lines of power and wealth is to be found in the social division of labour.

LABOUR MARKET POLICY

If social policy is 'the institutional control of services, agencies and organisations to maintain or change social structure and values' (Townsend 1981: 23) then an analysis of the institutional forces which influence the labour market must also include the growing role played by the public employment service, most notably in the form of the MSC. Labour market policy can be evaluated in terms of any of the following objectives: (*a*) its contribution towards maintaining a 'natural' balance between supply and demand for labour; (*b*) its contribution towards maintaining full employment; or (*c*) its contribution to the relief of suffering experienced by the casualties of the economic system (Hill 1981: 91).

Since the establishment of the labour exchanges at the beginning of this century, British labour market policy has adopted the first objective, that of keeping government intervention in the labour market to a minimum and leaving the objective of full employment to the arena of fiscal, monetary and incomes policy. The MSC continued this policy, although in 1978 it adopted the third objective by establishing a Special Programmes Division to assist groups in the labour market who were thought to be vulnerable. The growth of 'manpower' policy in the early 1970s was in sharp contrast to the reductions in public spending that were occurring almost everywhere else. It signified a definite response to the growth of unemployment and a decision to move beyond the approach of minimal intervention without taking on board the creation of full employment. The initial involvement of the MSC in job creation soon gave way to a concern for training. Fulfilling the objective of assisting the market system to operate smoothly became increasingly more difficult as unemployment rose. As Showler says, 'to be fully effective, manpower policy in its traditional form needs to operate in a labour market with adequate total demand for the available supply of labour'. Instead of being able to complement a policy for employment, labour market policies were adopted as a substitute for it (Showler 1982: 177). As a result training programmes implicitly promised work, as did special programmes which in reality were no more than temporary *ad hoc* schemes to alleviate the effects of unemployment.

Implicit in much labour market policy is the view that unemployment derives from lack of skills and an insufficiently or untrained workforce. The neoclassical model of the labour market is that the individual qualities of job applicants are assessed in terms of their potential productivity which is judged on the basis of education, training and experience. Although there is growing evidence that most workers, particularly manual workers, are selected on a far more subjective basis, there is a strong bias towards training and work experience in most MSC programmes. Almost all the youth training schemes on offer over the past few years have accepted the neoclassical model and have as their aim better qualified or experienced individuals. Official publications usually deny that the Youth Training Scheme has anything to do with growing unemployment among the young: it is still placed in the context of prosperity and growth which 'cannot be achieved with an under-qualified, under-trained' workforce (MSC 1982e) and is available not only for school-leavers but for unemployed 17 year-olds. If a young person is still unable to find work after a stint on the Youth Training Scheme, the implication will clearly be that they have only themselves to blame. Given the low demand for labour to fill both good jobs and low-paid insecure ones, policies which rest on a rationale of personal inadequacy will do little to alleviate unemployment or inequality. Until the mid-1970s the programmes created and administered by the MSC were often short-lived and usually *ad hoc*, uneven and rudimentary. With the development of the Youth Opportunities Programme and the subsequent Youth Training Scheme, intervention in the labour market became more calculated and ambitious in scope, at least as far as training was concerned. But, importantly, the Youth Training Scheme also represented a move towards 'voluntarism' or privatisation since it replaced the previous statutory training system. This reflected the belief that government's role should be one of enabling or facilitating private industry to meet its own needs.

CONCLUSION

Labour market policy has largely aimed at maintaining a 'natural balance between the supply and demand for labour in order to ensure the efficient functioning of our market economy. To this end policy has concentrated on incentives to employers to encourage them to expand their demand for labour, training schemes to improve the supply of labour and arrangements to dispose of surpluses of labour when they arise. The one radical departure from this approach was arguably the establishment of a quota scheme for the employment of people with disabilities which placed a statutory obligation on employers to positively discriminate in recruitment. The quota scheme represented a very real attempt to direct employment and was in contrast to the belief that market forces should be left to reach their own equilibrium. It is probably not surprising that in the context of an overall policy approach of minimal intervention, this attempt at more rigorous regulation has not only failed to be enforced but has regularly been threatened with abolition (Lonsdale 1981).

Other attempts to influence and direct employment have taken the form of anti-discriminatory legislation which gives people the right to seek redress or damages if treated unfairly with regard to employment. In Britain this has concentrated on sexual and racial discrimination while in the United States it extends to discrimination which occurs on the basis of age and disability as well and is part of a civil rights programme. Anti-discriminatory policies and policies of positive discrimination have variable rates of success. They depend crucially on the political will to enforce them and the budgets and staffing which make enforcement possible. In addition, they are orientated towards those factors which influence the supply of labour and have a limited influence on the conditions of production which determine how much and what kind of labour is required at different times. Their importance may lie in undermining and deflecting the inequalities generated by the market system such that, for instance, workers are not always divided against each other on the basis of their race, age or sex. Such policies may be necessary in the struggle against inequality but are insufficient in themselves to overcome it. Similarly, the minimum wage policy operating through wages councils, which set minimum rates of pay, has done little to overcome inequalities in earnings. Like positive discrimination, it requires enforcement to be successful. And like the quota scheme for disabled workers it has been poorly policed and is now threatened with abolition. None the less, these policies are essential to protect some of the most vulnerable people in our society against discrimination, poor working conditions, low wages and unemployment while the struggle for better conditions of production continues.

THE SOCIAL FOUNDATIONS OF WAGE POLICY

More significant socially are the issues raised in cost of living claims by the fact that attempts to measure absolute standards of living are inevitably conditioned by the whole gamut of conventions implied in our social hierarchy: their absolutism is indeed quite specious. Occasionally these conventions are explicitly acknowledged, and the cost of living is frankly defined as the cost of maintaining an appropriate social position. As the spokesman of one set of claimants put it, 'No matter what way of life one has to live one gets used to that way of life.' In another case a wage advance was asked for – in order to enable the recipients 'to dress in a manner befitting their vocation'. The terms of reference of the Spens Committee, which was appointed to make recommendations as to the remuneration of the various branches of the medical and dental profession, included an instruction to have 'due regard to . . . the desirability of maintaining the proper *social and economic status*'[1] of the professions concerned; and in the public discussion of the Government's proposal early in 1953 to increase the salaries of Her Majesty's judges, the same argument was freely used. After pointing out that the puisne judges had enjoyed no increase of salary at all since 1832, a leading article in *The Times* went on to remark that 'there are practically no rich men nowadays – as the subjects of King William IV understood riches – and it is far beyond the capacity of public funds to endow the present judges with the opulence that their predecessors enjoyed a century ago. *But it is of first-rate public importance that they should continue to be men of substance and security. The vast moral authority of the law in this country is bound up in the public mind with the visible dignity of the men who dispense the Queen's justice.*[2] Ten days later *The Times* returned to the topic in a second leading article. By this time a good deal of public outcry against the Government's original proposal to make any advance free of tax had made its impression, and *The Times* was disposed to prefer a method, if such could be found, which did not involve gross increases ranging from £5,000 to £30,000 a year, according to the rank of the judge in question; but the argument that 'the dignity of the Bench must be upheld by a certain way of living which must extend as much to the judges' home lives as, for example, to the manner in which they travel to and from the courts'[3] remained. Justice, it seems, must be rich as well as blind: travel by bus would threaten her – but not by Rolls-Royce. Commenting on the same proposal a few days later, Sir Hartley Shawcross (who occupies a seat in Parliament on the Labour front benches) observed that 'we do not live in an egalitarian society'.[4] Evidently not; but in the present ostensibly democratic age it is unusual to say so quite so candidly.

The admissibility of such arguments turns, of course, entirely on the degree of sanctity attached to the present social hierarchy. It is perhaps a fair summary of present attitudes to say that frank challenge of conventional standards is today about as unusual as are the unabashed acknowledgments just quoted. For the most part, established standards are accepted, so to speak, by default; and the common phenomenon of inability to live on salaries of widely differing size is explained by the fact that the verb 'to live' is tacitly redefined at every level.

1. Inter-Departmental Committee on the Remuneration of Consultants and Specialists, *Report*, Cmd.7420, HMSO (1948) [*Italics mine* – B.W.]
2. *The Times*, 14 March 1953 [*Italics mine* – B.W.]
3. *The Times*, 24 March 1953.
4. In a letter to *The Times*, 30 March 1953.

From: B. Wootton, *The Social Foundations of Wage Policy*, George Allen & Unwin (1962)

Document two
LABOUR MARKETS AND THE LABOUR PROCESS

The labour market is an abstraction from numerous processes of allocating people to jobs: an abstraction from a multiplicity of organizational decisions concerning hiring, firing, promotions and job transfers. But the labour market is more than an abstraction, it has a palpable existence. For most people there is a vast difference between being *in* an organization, and being *in* the labour market, and for the school-leaver, the job-changer and the redundant the labour market does exist as a set of social institutions – the employment exchange, the newspaper job column, the personnel office and the grapevine. For many the return to the labour market comes as a sharp shock. As Allen puts it, 'People of all income levels and status are compelled to cart their skills around in varying forms when confronted by unemployment.'[1] One does not need to see the shuffling queues of casual catering workers in the twilight London streets nor the undernourished building workers in Mexico City, each with a card proclaiming 'carpenter', 'bricklayer', 'labourer', to realize that the labour market is one part of economic theory which bears heavily on the individual.

It is in the labour market, then, that the buyer and seller of labour power meet, but the cards around the necks of the Mexican building workers tell us that buyer and seller meet in terms of skill. On the face of it labour power is obtained for its skill content (whether dexterity, job-knowledge or innovative abilities) and we have already noted that there are large variations among sellers in these respects. However, the concept of a labour market does not enable us to reject non-objective notions of skill *because there are different conceptions of labour market processes*. I will briefly set out three perspectives in tabular form and consider their relevance to deskilling.

The neoclassical model stems, of course, from Adam Smith and assumes that human beings interact more as isolated individuals than as group members. In general, labour has always proved to be a difficult factor to bring under the control of market theory. The inadequacies of the neoclassical view have often led to an alternative perspective – that of a carve up of the labour market by occupational groups. We can see here a correspondence to sociological theories of skill: the neoclassical model links with objective conceptions of skill, whilst the social construction theory of skill entails some notion of occupational regulation of the labour market. The theory which finds no counterpart from our survey of the literature on skill is that of dual labour markets. It is worth examining dual labour market theory in more detail.

Dual labour market theories have been developed by Doeringer and Piore (1971), Piore (1972) and Gordon (1972) to explain an assumed fundamental split in the labour market. According to these writers there are primary and secondary labour markets. The primary sector is composed of jobs in large, oligopolistic firms (IBM and ICI for example) in which the internal labour market plays a dominant role in job allocation. In this market there are 'jobs with relatively high wages, good working conditions, chances of advancement, equity and due process in the administration of work rules, and above all, employment stability'. In contrast, in the secondary sector:

jobs tend to be low-paying with poorer working conditions, little chance of advancement, a highly personalized relationship between workers and supervisors which leaves wide latitude for favouritism and is conducive to harsh and capricious work discipline, and with considerable instability in jobs and a high turnover among the labour force.[2] In the secondary sector the external labour market is the major job-allocator.

---

1. Allen 1977: 66.
2. Piore 1972: 3.

From: C. Littler, *The Development of the Labour Process in Capitalist Societies*, Heinemann Educational Books (1982)

Document three
SECONDARY JOBS AND SECONDARY WORKERS

This chapter is concerned with two issues: the characteristics of secondary-type jobs and the processes that generate a supply of labour for secondary sector employment. These two issues are crucial to an analysis of the policy implications of the existence of low pay and labour market segmentation. If workers are low paid because of their low level of skill and efficiency the emergence of new forms of secondary-type employment could be interpreted as a response to 'distortions' in the wage structure as trade unions act to raise the minimum rates for unskilled jobs above the efficiency wage which is determined both by the skill content of the job and the efficiency of the worker. Alternatively, if secondary employment forms are a means of 'exploiting' the disadvantaged position of particular groups in the labour market, so that low-paid workers are efficient relative to their costs, the analysis of the structure of the labour supply takes on a new importance in the labour market segmentation debate.

Segmentation analysis disputes the neoclassical view that the structure of pay reflects primarily the structure of relative labour efficiency, and argues that the number of good jobs in the economy is mainly determined by the development of the industrial and technological structure largely independent of labour supply. The structuring of the supply of labour serves to determine which groups are confined to the low-productivity secondary sectors of employment, but it does not follow that the least efficient workers are necessarily relegated to these low productivity sectors. The existence of non-competing groups has important implications for the structure of employment. Barriers to mobility mean that there is no equalisation between groups of the relationship of pay to labour productivity. In these circumstances firms can claim labour from segments where pay is low relative to labour productivity in order to compete more effectively and can possibly retain otherwise obsolete techniques. The existence of segments of the labour force with different labour market status may also create the situation where jobs are classified not by their content but according to the labour market position of the workers normally undertaking the work. Thus jobs are secondary because they are performed by workers generally considered secondary: jobs are regarded as unskilled because they are feminised and not feminised because they are unskilled. Moreover, the existence of non-competing groups may be of considerable social and political importance for the maintenance of labour market segmentation. The role of class divisions and racial and sexual discrimination as a means of legitimising and enforcing inequalities in the labour market is central to the radical approach to labour market segmentation but there has been relatively little consideration of how far these sources of low-paid, disadvantaged and 'passive' labour can be maintained in the future.

From: C. Craig *et al.*, *Labour Market Structure, Industrial Organisation and Low Pay*, Cambridge University Press (1982)

Document four
THE END OF FULL EMPLOYMENT

In August 1980 unemployment in the United Kingdom reached 2 million in the official figures. Since then the total has risen even faster: no one is predicting any significant reduction in 1981, and most forecasters expect the numbers out of work to grow and remain very high throughout the decade. Even those who foresee an improvement in the economy and a reduction in inflation offer no hope of a decline in unemployment with present policies. Others draw attention to changes they see occurring very largely outside governments' control that will maintain high unemployment and increase it further still. The collapse of work is now seen by an increasing number of people as a sombre and by no means far-fetched or hysterical forecast for the next decade.

From the deepening gloom has emerged a consensus that the days of 'full employment' are not only over; they are now as much a part of social history, which we may regard with nostalgia or contempt according to taste, as hoolahoops and spats. Whatever the disputes and conflicts among those expecting the permanent change to higher unemployment, this belief has become much stronger during the last few years. It is part of the reality that must be accepted as we attempt to tackle the major economic, social, political and industrial problems facing Britain in the last two decades of the twentieth century.

There are many arguments put forward to support this view. All tend to point to the inevitability and/or desirability of the abandonment of full employment as an objective of economic policy and a goal for society. Varying weight is given to different reasons but among the main ones are the following six:
1.   The long-term impact of the world recession and the dramatic growth in economic and political power of the oil-producing countries of the Middle East. There are some 7 million out of work in the European Community and unemployment had been rising in many other industrial societies. The calculation of unemployment is more difficult in Third World countries, with large rural populations trying to maintain an existence from the land, but well over 300 million people are without any form of regular work.

2. The specific changes within Britain resulting from major and pro-longed economic and industrial problems. They include the long-term decline in our share of world markets with our decreasing competitiveness, inadequate increases in productivity and excessive levels of inflation -- and the failure of successive governments in their economic policies and industrial strategies to make any impact on these problems. Whether the achievements of undeviating Tory monetarism will bring us to a 'brave new world' or simply convert a cyclical recession into a chronic slump, we are already being encouraged not only to expect, but to accept, current and even higher levels of unemployment.

3. The coming crisis of the micro-electronic revolution. This will hit Britain most severely just as the advantages of North Sea oil are flowing away and will dramatically reduce the need for workers, let alone absorb any of the unemployed.

4. The labour force will continue to be swollen by more young and inexperienced school leavers and by the return to work of more married women. These are both groups with a traditionally higher level of unemployment, and one must expect this vulnerability to increase with our diminishing capacity to create new jobs.

5. A new vigour to the critique of employment and the work ethic. This is coming from many directions and takes many forms. Supporters of the new technology draw attention to its potential for increasing the opportunity for leisure. Others point to the drudgery and toil of many jobs, the inadequacy of the reward and the triviality of the products. There is renewed criticism and rejection of a society that measures worth by the work that you do and not by the sort of person you are. Some at least see an opportunity to counter this as the amount of work to be done diminishes and believe the years of full employment helped to reinforce the class-ridden dominance of the work ethic.

6. A women's movement that emphasises how much vital work is neglected and given no recognition. In particular, the unpaid labour in the home, which is carried out predominantly by women, is both taken for granted and undervalued. We also continue to assess the status of a whole family by what the husband does and deny any real equality to women. Some believe that full employment was for men only and reinforced the gulf between home and work; others that it created or reinforced the dual careers of paid employment and unpaid housework that lay an unequal burden on women.

From: A. Sinfield, *What Unemployment Means*, Martin Robertson (1981)

Document five
THE MEANING OF FULL EMPLOYMENT

3. What is meant by 'full employment', and what is not meant by it? Full employment does not mean literally no unemployment; that is to say, it does not mean that every man and woman in the country who is fit and free for work is employed productively on every day of his or her working life. In every country with a variable climate there will be seasons when particular forms of work are impossible or difficult. In every progressive society there will be changes in the demand for labour, qualitatively if not quantitatively; that is to say, there will be periods during which particular individuals can no longer be advantageously employed in their former occupations and may be unemployed till they find and fit themselves for fresh occupations. Some frictional unemployment there will be in a progressive society however high the demand for labour. Full employment means that unemployment is reduced to short intervals of standing by, with the certainty that very soon one will be wanted in one's old job again or will be wanted in a new job that is within one's powers.

4. Full employment is sometimes defined as 'a state of affairs in which the number of unfilled vacancies is not appreciably below the number of unemployed persons, so that unemployment at any time is due to the normal lag between a person losing one job and finding another'.[1] Full employment in this Report means more than that in two ways. It means having always more vacant jobs than unemployed men, not slightly fewer jobs. It means that the jobs are at fair wages, of such a kind, and so located that the unemployed men can reasonably be expected to take them; it means, by consequence, that the normal lag between losing one job and finding another will be very short.

5. The proposition that there should always be more vacant jobs than unemployed men means that the labour market should always be a seller's market rather than a buyer's market. For this, on the view of society underlying this Report – that society exists for the individual – there is a decisive reason of principle. The reason is that difficulty in selling labour has consequences of a different order of harmfulness from those associated with difficulty in buying labour. A person who has difficulty in buying the labour that he wants suffers inconvenience or reduction of profits. A person

who cannot sell his labour is in effect told that he is of no use. The first difficulty causes annoyance or loss. The other is a personal catastrophe. This difference remains even if an adequate income is provided, by insurance or otherwise, during unemployment; idleness even on an income corrupts; the feeling of not being wanted demoralizes. The difference remains even if most people are unemployed only for relatively short periods. As long as there is any long-term unemployment not obviously due to personal deficiency, anybody who loses his job fears that he may be one of the unlucky ones who will not get another job quickly. The short-term unemployed do not know that they are short-term unemployed till their unemployment is over.

6. The human difference between failing to buy and failing to sell labour is the decisive reason for aiming to make the labour market a seller's rather than a buyer's market. There are other reasons, only slightly less important. One reason is that only if there is work for all is it fair to expect workpeople, individually and collectively in trade unions, to co-operate in making the most of all productive resources, including labour, and to forgo restrictionist practices. Another reason, related to this, is that the character and duration of individual unemployment caused by structural and technical change in industry will depend on the strength of the demand for labour in the new forms required after the change. The greater the pace of the economic machine, the more rapidly will structural unemployment disappear, the less resistance of every kind will there be to progress. Yet another reason is the stimulus to technical advance that is given by shortage of labour. Where men are few, machines are used to save men for what men alone can do. Where labour is cheap it is often wasted in brainless, unassisted toil. The new lands empty of men are the homes of invention and business adventure in peace. Stimulus to labour saving of all kinds is one of the by-products of full employment in war.

---

1. This definition is taken from the Nuffield College Statement on *Employment Policy and Organization of Industry after the War*. The Statement adds that full employment in this sense 'cannot be completely attained so long as there exist structural maladjustments needing to be put right'.

From: W. Beveridge, *Full Employment in a Free Society*, George, Allen & Unwin (1944)

PURPOSES

The statistics on the unemployed serve a variety of purposes – economic, social and administrative. There is often too great an emphasis on the figures for the total of the unemployed and perhaps also on unemployment figures alone. It is the published totals that make the greatest public impact since they are most often at the centre of political debate as to whether the Government should pursue different economic and social policies or measures.

There are some whose concern with unemployment leads them to emphasise the importance of looking at figures on the widest possible definition, partly in order to stimulate the Government into actions which they wish to see pursued: but there are others who see merit in narrower definitions and see the danger of precipitate action based on an over-estimation of the extent of labour reserves or of the 'genuine' unemployed.

Different uses of the figures call for emphasis on different aspects and elements of the figures as the paragraphs which follow show. There is ample scope for debate about certain groups or categories of people who should be included as unemployed or not, and on the form in which the figures are presented. So far as the definitions are concerned, it is essential to have great regard to what can be measured with reasonable accuracy, particularly on a monthly basis, in order to reduce the area of debate and have general acceptance of the figures. It is also convenient to have reasonable continuity and avoid frequent changes in definitions, even though these need to be reviewed from time to time as circumstances change.

Economic indicators. The unemployment figures represent one of several related *economic indicators*, including employment, vacancies, output and earnings, which are important for evaluating economic performance. Indeed, until recent years, there was a tendency to use unemployment as a principal indicator in this group of figures. This stemmed partly from its intrinsic economic significance but also its speedy availability and considerable detail. More recently, however, the relationships between the various economic indicators have become less close, and less weight can be placed on unemployment figures in isolation as an indicator of the state of the economy. The sustained appearance side by side of high unemployment and inflation, not only in this country but in many industrialised countries, adds weight to this caution. Nevertheless the unemployment figures remain a major indicator of great importance . . .

A measure of labour reserve. The unemployment figures have often been used as an indicator of the supply of unused labour in the economy, or of the degree of slack to be taken up by reflationary measures. The number of unemployed is clearly an important source of labour reserve but there are other sources including changes in working hours, the drawing of people from outside the labour force, people having more than one job and better utilisation of those already employed. The labour supply is not homogeneous and its economic value will depend, for example, on the skills that could be offered and could be utilised, the willingness to accept the jobs that may become available and the geographical distribution . . .

A measure of social distress. The numbers unemployed are a matter of major social concern as a determinant of hardship and distress. But unemployment is only one of the sources of these and other social problems. In some periods, more especially before the war, unemployment has been regarded as a proxy measure of the degree of and change in social distress. Now, benefits and social security, more secure housing, the presence of more than one earner in the family and redundancy payments may form some cushion against hardship; also for a more complete picture of social problems it is necessary to take into account other factors, such as health, disablement or low incomes at work or in retirement.

However, unemployment is often a disturbing experience and represents a severe handicap when it is for more than a temporary period between jobs, particularly for the young, the one-parent families and the longer-term unemployed. Thus when looking at the unemployment figures, it is necessary to look deeper than the overall totals to take into account the duration of unemployment, the age of the unemployed, their family circumstances, and the like.

Administrative or operational use. Apart from its use as an indicator, or at least as a guide, to changes in labour reserves and social distress, the actual figures of registered unemployed are of course used for *operational purposes* in guiding the management of the employment and benefit services. They are also used for *administrative purposes*, including helping to delimit those areas of the country which are treated as assisted areas, and the figures have sometimes also entered into formulae used in calculating rate support grants. They are also of importance to local authorities, in planning control and land use contexts.

From: *Employment Gazette*, 'A review of unemployment and vacancy statistics', May 1980.

UNEMPLOYMENT: FRICTIONAL, SEASONAL,
STRUCTURAL

'Frictional Unemployment' is unemployment caused by the individuals who make up the labour supply not being completely interchangeable and mobile units, so that, though there is an unsatisfied demand for labour, the unemployed workers are not of the right sort or in the right place to meet that demand.

'Seasonal Unemployment' means the unemployment arising in particular industries through seasonal variation in their activity, brought about by climatic conditions or by fashion.

'Structural unemployment' means the unemployment arising in particular industries or localities through a change of demand so great that it may be regarded as affecting the main economic structure of a country. The decline of international trade after the first World War, involving drastic contraction of the demand for labour in British export industries, is a leading instance of structural change of this character. The northward movement of industry in Britain before the first World War is a less striking instance, though perhaps sufficiently great to be called a structural change. Structural unemployment may or may not be a form of frictional unemployment.

On the definition given above there cannot be actual frictional unemployment, unless there is an unsatisfied demand for labour somewhere. If the total demand for labour is less than the total supply, those who are unemployed are so because of deficiency of demand not because of friction.

This does not mean that the problem of industrial friction, that is to say friction in adjusting the supply of labour to the demand, is unimportant. Assuming an unsatisfied demand for labour there may still be frictional unemployment, arising in several ways:

(*a*) Through technical change, that is the development of new industries, machines and methods, superseding old industries, machines and methods. Innumerable small technical changes take place constantly. Assuming that they do not diminish the total demand, but only change its character or location, the extent to which they result in unemployment depends on the ability of the labour supply to adjust itself to the changes in the character of the demand, that is to say on the adaptability and mobility of labour.

The amount of unemployment will vary with the strength of industrial friction.

(b) Through local variations of demand. So long as production is conducted by a number of independent businesses, the demands of different employing units may vary, one rising and the other falling, even though demand remains adequate and steady in total. How much frictional unemployment will result from this depends on the degree of mobility of labour and the way in which the engagement of men is organized. The chronic over-stocking with labour of the casual labour industries . . . represents an acute form of frictional unemployment.

(c) Through seasonal variations of demand. Nearly all industries are seasonal to some extent, though to very different extents, but the slack and busy seasons respectively of different industries do not coincide. The amount of unemployment involved in the seasonal variations of separate industries depends therefore on the extent to which they are separate for the purpose of labour supply, i.e. the ease or difficulty with which men can change from one industry when seasonally slack to another which is seasonally busy. Assuming adequate total demand, seasonal unemployment is a form of frictional unemployment.

Whether structural unemployment should be regarded as a form of frictional unemployment or not depends on the effect of the structural change on total demand for labour. Where, as between the wars, the structural change destroys demand for labour of one kind without adequate compensating increase of demand for labour of another kind, it brings about unemployment due to deficiency of demand, rather than to friction. If the structural change involves both a great decrease of demand for one kind of labour and a compensating increase of demand for another, the unemployment which results through men not being qualified or willing to meet the new demand is frictional unemployment.

The degree of industrial friction, relatively unimportant when total demand is deficient or weak, becomes of decisive importance when demand is strong, as in war, and would be of great importance under a full employment policy in peace.

From: W. Beveridge, *Full Employment in a Free Society*, George, Allen & Unwin (1944): Appendix D

Document eight
SPECIAL EMPLOYMENT MEASURES

Around 3.25 million people in the United Kingdom are unemployed. In some towns, and among certain sections of the labour force, unemployment rates are above 25 per cent. The 3.25 million figure represents a trebling in unemployment since 1975 and a doubling since 1979.

The potential labour force is also growing. Entries to the labour force are high as the large birth cohorts of the early 1960s reach the age of 16–18 and exits are low, reflecting the low birth rate during World War I. The labour force participation rates of married women have also grown secularly over the last two decades. The actual growth of the labour force has been tempered by the recession, which has particularly reduced both the numbers of married women and of men aged 60–64 in the working population. These 'discouraged' workers resulted in the Department of Employment (DE) reducing its labour force projection for 1985 by as many as one million people between 1978 and 1981. Nevertheless the DE calculates that in the four years 1982–85 the labour force will grow by around 0.7 million. Thus if unemployment is to be cut to 2 million by 1985, around 1.7 million extra jobs need to be created between now and then. This is equivalent to some 1,200 jobs a day, twice the fastest previous rate of growth of employment experienced between 1960 and 1965.

Necessary as it is, traditional reflation is unlikely to generate jobs on the scale required. The National Institute of Economic and Social Research recently (1981) produced figures which indicate that a cut of £5 billion in income tax or in employers' national insurance contributions would raise employment by only 190,000 – a gross cost per job of over £26,000 a year. Increases in public spending create more jobs than equivalent tax cuts but the magnitude of the extra spending required would surely be inflationary, the more so because both the Labour and Conservative Parties continue to rule out a well developed incomes policy.

Intervention at the micro level is therefore bound to continue. The Department of Industry (DoI) helps preserve and create jobs by selective industrial assistance but this is not analysed here. The DE and Manpower Services Commission (MSC) operate special employment measures and these are our concern. It may be helpful to think about these measures in the following way: the government is worried about inflation and so it sets a financial target for the government deficit (public sector borrowing requirement (PSBR)). The special employment measures are then a way of getting most employment consistent with the inflation and PSBR targets.

Both the MSC[1] and the Institute of Fiscal Studies[2] calculate that in 1981–82 each unemployed person cost the Treasury around £4,500 (1981–82 prices) and aggregate unemployment cost the Chancellor nearly £13 billion, made up as follows:

	£ billion
loss of income tax	3.1
loss of national insurance contributions	2.6
loss of indirect tax revenue	2.6
unemployment and supplementary benefits, etc.	4.6
TOTAL	12.9

These figures suggest that there is plenty of scope for special measures. Providing such measures are concentrated among groups or in areas where the labour market is weak – like youths, the long-term unemployed, high unemployment regions – such spending should not compound the wage inflation process.

Some special measures raise the demand for labour through wage subsidies or job creation, and in the case of youths are specifically targeted to their particular problems. Other measures reduce the labour supply either by reducing numbers in the labour force – early retirement, for example – or by reducing the annual hours of those in the workforce. Spending on these measures is now over £1 billion a year. So they clearly have macroeconomic implications. In what follows, therefore, we shall periodically compare the impact of the measures on unemployment, output, inflation, employment, the balance of payments and income distribution with the impact of alternative uses of the money such as a cut in income tax.

As we proceed, the cost per job created is sometimes presented, but the whole question of the optimal scale of the special measures is difficult.[3] It is likely that the marginal, and hence average, cost rises with the number of jobs to be created. Therefore while the cost per 100,000 jobs (say) may be calculated in a straightforward way it would be wrong to assume that the cost per job would be the same if one million jobs were to be generated by the same measures.

The peak coverage of the special measures occurred in February 1982 when 1.2 million people were covered (of whom 960,000 were on the Temporary Short Time Working Compensations Scheme) and this directly reduced unemployment by 370,000. In May 1982 the coverage of the measures was as follows:

Temporary Short Time Working Compensation Scheme	106,000
Job Release Scheme	67,000
Youth Opportunities Programme	180,000
Community Industry	7,100

Young Workers Scheme	61,000
Community Enterprise Programme	29,500
Training for Skills	35,000

The total number covered was 486,000 and it is estimated that the schemes directly reduced registered unemployment by 270,000.

1. Manpower Services Commission, *Draft Corporate Plan 1982–86* (February 1982)
2. N. Morris and A. Dilmot, 'The cost of unemployment', *Fiscal Studies*, November 1981
3. For a recent attempt to address this problem see House of Lords, *Report of the Select Committee on Unemployment*, Vol. 1, 142, HMSO (1982) Chs. 9, 10 and p. 162

From: D. Metcalfe, *Alternatives to Unemployment*, Policy Studies Institute (1982)

STRUCTURE OF MANPOWER SERVICES COMMISSION

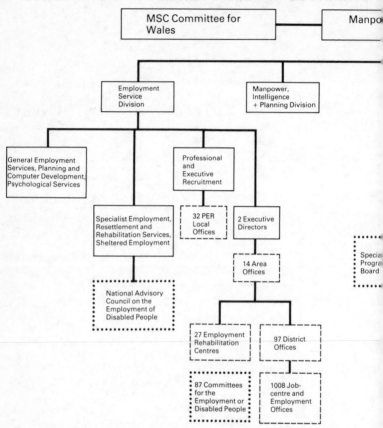

MANPOWER SERVICES COMMISSION
Headquarters and local organisations (June 1

```
┌─────────────────────────┐        ┌──────────
│ MSC Committee for       │────────│ Manpo
│ Wales                   │
└─────────────────────────┘

        ┌──────────────────────┐         ┌──────────────────────┐
        │ Employment           │         │ Manpower,            │
        │ Service              │         │ Intelligence         │
        │ Division             │         │ + Planning Division  │
        └──────────────────────┘         └──────────────────────┘

┌──────────────────────┐   ┌──────────────────────┐
│ General Employment   │   │ Professional         │
│ Services, Planning   │   │ and                  │
│ and Computer         │   │ Executive            │
│ Development,         │   │ Recruitment          │
│ Psychological        │   └──────────────────────┘
│ Services             │
└──────────────────────┘     ┌───────────┐   ┌──────────────┐
                             │ 32 PER    │   │ 2 Executive  │
   ┌──────────────────────┐  │ Local     │   │ Directors    │
   │ Specialist Employment│  │ Offices   │   └──────────────┘
   │ Resettlement and     │  └───────────┘
   │ Rehabilitation       │        ┌──────────────┐       Specia
   │ Services, Sheltered  │        │ 14 Area      │       Progra
   │ Employment           │        │ Offices      │       Board
   └──────────────────────┘        └──────────────┘

   ┌──────────────────────┐  ┌──────────────┐  ┌──────────────┐
   │ National Advisory    │  │ 27 Employment│  │ 97 District  │
   │ Council on the       │  │ Rehabilitation│ │ Offices      │
   │ Employment of        │  │ Centres      │  └──────────────┘
   │ Disabled People      │  └──────────────┘
   └──────────────────────┘  ┌──────────────┐  ┌──────────────┐
                             │ 87 Committees│  │ 1008 Job-    │
                             │ for the      │  │ centre and   │
                             │ Employment or│  │ Employment   │
                             │ Disabled     │  │ Offices      │
                             │ People       │  └──────────────┘
                             └──────────────┘
```

From: *Manpower Services Commission Annual Report, 1981–82*, p. i

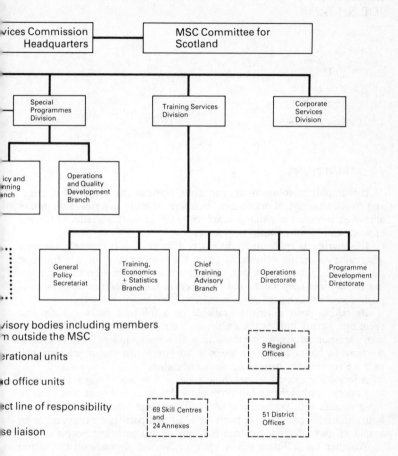

~vices Commission Headquarters	MSC Committee for Scotland

Special Programmes Division

Training Services Division

Corporate Services Division

~icy and ~nning ~nch

Operations and Quality Development Branch

General Policy Secretariat

Training, Economics + Statistics Branch

Chief Training Advisory Branch

Operations Directorate

Programme Development Directorate

9 Regional Offices

69 Skill Centres and 24 Annexes

51 District Offices

~visory bodies including members ~m outside the MSC

~erational units

~d office units

~ct line of responsibility

~se liaison

Document ten
JOB SHARING

3.1 DEFINITIONS

It is important to avoid any confusion between the terms 'job-sharing' and 'work-sharing'. Work-sharing is a term used to describe attempts to alleviate the impact of rising unemployment by spreading a reduced volume of work among an existing workforce.

Job-sharing is quite different. It is a form of part-time employment whereby two people voluntarily share the responsibility of one full-time position. The salary and fringe benefits are divided between them according to the time they work, and each person holds a permanent part-time post.

By taking posts normally available on a full-time basis and dividing them up, usually into two, each person's terms and conditions of employment are normally pro-rata those of a full-timer, and as long as each is working 16 hours or more a week in any week that they work they will each be covered for certain employment rights.

A job-sharing situation can come about in a variety of ways: two people may apply jointly for one full-time job; individual employees may come to an agreement with management which allows them to reduce their working hours and management to appoint an additional part-time employee; or an employer may advertise for 'one full-time or two part-time people'.

Whether the full-time job is 'split' or 'shared' depends on the nature of the post and the degree of interaction necessary between the job-sharers. In some cases the job may be split in two and become two virtually separate part-time jobs needing very little interaction; in others where a high level of co-operation and communication may be needed between the sharers, the job is truly shared. There are various ways in which the working week may be divided: for example, split days, split weeks, alternate weeks or alternate days.

3.2 JOB-SHARING AND EQUAL OPPORTUNITIES

As has been seen, part-time work is at present characterised by low pay and poor working conditions and is concentrated in the lowest occupational grades. This means that when women wish or need to take part-time work because of family commitments they often take a job which is below their level of skill or qualification; their pay and job status may drop because part-time work is not available in those fields in which they may be qualified and/or experienced. Job-sharing is a way of increasing access to professional, skilled, and rewarding work for people who choose or are only able to work part-time. In addition, job-sharing may provide women who have been out of the labour force for a number of years while caring for children, with the opportunity of a way back into employment. Job-sharing therefore has the potential to improve women's job opportunities and help break down occupational barriers.

At present it is of particular relevance to women, but it may also be a way of creating more flexibility in the work patterns of those men who wish to spend more time looking after their children but are currently unable to do so because there are few part-time opportunities in their areas of work. Thus in the widest sense job-sharing can contribute towards equality of opportunity between men and women.

By opening up the possibility of almost any job being suitable for either one full-time or two part-time employees, job-sharing presents an imaginative variant on the norm of the full-time '40 hour' working week. It may therefore be of use to older people who would like to ease into retirement, to those who wish to study or follow up other interests, and to anyone else who, for whatever reasons, chooses not to work full-time. In addition it can give some people the chance of working who might otherwise be unable to work at all, for instance single parents, disabled people and those caring for sick and disabled dependants.

From: Equal Opportunities Commission, *Job Sharing*, EOC (1981)

Document eleven
WORK AND WOMEN

Explanations for the nature of sexual divisions and the place of women in the economic system which point to the operation of the capitalist system or which utilize the concept of patriarchy come from two basic theoretical perspectives – those of socialist feminists and of radical feminists. To characterize these positions crudely, socialist feminists favour class as the basic category in their theorizing, and radical feminists favour gender. Socialist feminists vary considerably amongst themselves in the precise positions they take, which range from a primary concern with a Marxist analysis and the application of this analysis to women's position, without basically questioning the Marxist categories, to the position that there are fundamental problems with Marx's theoretical formulations in so far as they can be applied to women and that some articulation of the interaction between class and gender through the economic, political and ideological moments of the social formation is necessary. In the latter case they frequently turn to the concept of patriarchy as a starting point for articulation, arguing that the patriarchal principle pre-dated capitalism, and that capitalism grafted its own divisions onto the sexual divisions which already existed.

The attempt to take a basic Marxist economic analysis and apply it directly to the problem of women and their work in the family was the starting point for a long and ultimately somewhat fruitless debate on domestic labour.[1] Much of the discussion centred around the question of whether or not theoretical concepts developed by Marx to explain the workings of the capitalist economic system and the free exchange of labour in the market could in fact be applied to domestic labour, and it was argued that this was not a meaningless quibble but had relevance for political action and alliances. If housewives produced surplus value they were part of an exploited group in relation to capital. This debate has been characterized as consisting of those taking an orthodox and those taking an unorthodox viewpoint, the orthodox rejecting the application of such Marxist categories as surplus value and productive labour to domestic labour. From the unorthodox position Dalla Costa and James (1972) argued that in addition to being socially necessary labour, producing use values, domestic labour is productive in the sense that it contributes to the exchange value of the commodity labour power and so to the creation of surplus value; Seccombe (1974) argued that domestic labour produces value but is unproductive labour; Middleton (1974) argued that domestic labour is not marginal to capitalist production, but integral, and that it is productive, producing essential labour power. Proponents of the orthodox view were, for example, Harrison (1973), arguing typically that domestic labour constitutes a mode of production quite distinct from the capitalist mode, a client mode 'created or co-opted by the dominant mode to fulfil certain functions within the economic and social system'.

This debate opened up the areas of contradiction in the position of women, pointing to the contradictory demands and requirements on women as domestic labourers and as workers selling their labour power in the market place. The result of an entirely rational capitalism seeking the most efficient method of utilizing female labour, could be the complete socialization of those parts of the sexual division of labour currently allocated to women through the operation of the patriarchal principle and the incorporation into the labour force of women as free agents selling their labour power in the same way as men. Even if one argues that the basic categories in Marx's labour theory of value are neutral with respect to the sex of the individual agents who take up the places in the division of labour, to understand their operation in any concrete historical instance the fact that particular categories of individuals, e.g. women, immigrants and so on, fall into specific areas requires explanation, and may indeed be the site of contradictions within the capitalist social formation. Foreman (1977) for example, makes the point that the notion of a living wage which would support a non-working wife and family, constituted a victory for working class struggle.

Although much of the work on domestic labour can be described as economistic, the whole debate has drawn attention of the fundamental contradictions in women's position, and to the importance of an analysis of that position which takes account not only of its material basis in exploitation at work and in the home, but also the ideological processes which help to create and maintain that position.

---

1. Molyneux 1979.

From: J. Holland, 'Work and Women', *Bedford Way Papers*, 6 (1980)

COMMUNITY CARE AND THE FAMILY

The cultural definition of women as 'carers' is still strong, and since it is part of a set of assumptions about the sexual division of labour in the domestic sphere, it continues to be reinforced and reproduced by a whole range of social and financial policies which unquestionably embody the notion of women's dependency. Hilary Land's work has been important in establishing that this is the case across a wide range of social policies.[1] In the particular area of family policy, she argues that the overt aim may be to protect the family, but that 'On examination, what is being protected are particular patterns of responsibility and dependencies within the family, and a long-established view of division of labour between the sexes and between generations.'[2] The converse of the definition of women as carers is that men are *not* expected to provide domestic and caring services, either for others or even for themselves: Land argues that 'It is clear that men are not expected to look after themselves as much as women, and they are accordingly given much more help from publicly provided support services. Neither is it assumed that they will be able to look after their elderly and infirm relatives'[3].

There is an important sense in which cultural pressures to provide care apply to *all* women, but those who are married or cohabiting are particularly vulnerable to such pressures; with the assumption of their financial dependency, their employment is traditionally considered more 'expendable' than a man's. Married women in practice are treated as dependants throughout the whole of social security and tax legislation[4] and, if they do give up work to care for a highly dependant relative, they will not even be eligible for the invalid care allowance: a married woman living with her husband or receiving maintenance from him is not entitled to the invalid care allowance, even if she is caring full time for a dependant relative.[5] The assumption clearly is that a married woman's natural habitat is the home where she is financially dependant upon her husband.

The cultural designation of women as carers in the family setting is reflected in the available evidence about what happens in practice: in terms of primary responsibility, wives care for husbands, mothers for handicapped children and daughters for their elderly parents or disabled siblings.

Care is also provided by female neighbours and volunteers. This is not to deny that devoted male carers can certainly be found in each of these categories.

1. H. Land, 'Who Cares for the Family?', *Journal of Social Policy*, 7, 3 (1978), 277,
2. H. Land and R. Parker, 'The United Kingdom' in S. B. Kamerman and A. J. Katz, (1978) *Family Policies*, Columbia University Press, p. 332
3. Land, 'Who Cares for the Family?', p. 268.
4. This point has been demonstrated very clearly by Hilary Land. See H. Land, 'Social Security and the Division of Unpaid Work in the Home and Paid Employment in the Labour Market', *Social Security Research*, papers presented at a DHSS seminar, 1976, HMSO, London (1977).
5. See Land, 'Who Cares for the Family?', p. 265.

From: J. Finch and D. Groves, 'Community Care and the Family: A Case for Equal Opportunities', *Journal of Social Policy*, 9, 4 (1980)

EQUAL PAY AND SEX DISCRIMINATION

SOME CASES THAT NEVER REACHED THE TRIBUNAL

A woman saw a notice in the window of a butcher's shop, stating that two cleaners were required. When she inquired within, she was informed that they really wanted men but knew that they were not allowed to say so on the advertisement. The following day she visited the job centre, reported the occurrence and completed a tribunal application form, complaining of sex discrimination. A few weeks later, she received a visit from a conciliation officer. He pointed out that as she had never worked for the butcher she would derive no benefit from taking the case. She replied that she did not do it for personal advantage but because she wanted the butcher to understand the meaning of sex discrimination. Nevertheless, she agreed to sign the appropriate form to say that she would not attend the tribunal.

A twenty-eight year old woman was sacked from a cleaning job and replaced by a man. With the help of a solicitor, she made an application to the industrial tribunal for unfair dismissal and sex discrimination. The firm offered her £20 to withdraw her case. Meanwhile her husband who worked for the same firm as a driver, gave in his notice for a better job. He subsequently changed his mind but the employer would not allow him to withdraw his notice unless his wife dropped the case. The solicitor warned her that she could face bills of up to £300 if she proceeded with the case and said he would make no charge for his services if she withdrew and accepted the £20 settlement. She withdrew her application.

A woman in her late thirties worked for a wool manufacturer as a credit controller. She asked for a salary increase and was refused. As the breadwinner of a one-parent family, she sought alternative employment at a higher salary. On obtaining another job she gave in her notice. A man was appointed to replace her and she was instructed, while working her notice, to teach him the job. On discovering that he was 15 years younger than her but receiving a salary of £1,200 a year more, she brought a claim for equal pay and sex discrimination against the company. They offered her £10 compensation. The conciliation officer advised her to accept. He telephoned and called at her house several times, telling her that she would not have a leg to stand on in court and would have to foot the bill. She withdrew the case.

A young man worked at a dairy in 'quality assurance', which mainly involved weighing yoghurt pots. He wanted to work in 'quality control', which involved testing the products themselves. All the employees in quality control were female and he was repeatedly informed that there were no vacancies. He made an application of sex discrimination against the dairy, who promised to consider him for the next vacancy. He refused to withdraw his application until he actually started work as a quality controller. A success story? Yes, except that his wages dropped by £9 a week to bring them into line with those of the other quality controllers; and he knew that his career prospects with the dairy had been irreparably damaged by his actions. Having obtained the job experience he desired, he sought other employment and left the dairy.

ATTACKING DISCRIMINATION THROUGH LEGISLATION

The 1975 Sex Discrimination Act (incorporating the 1970 Equal Pay Act) and the 1976 Race Relations Act gave the victims of discrimination the right to seek legal redress in a county court or, in matters relating to employment, at an industrial tribunal. From 1965, complaints of racial discrimination were handled by an official body, the Race Relations Board. After only 10 years, the legislators rejected this system as too paternalistic and sought to encourage women and racial minorities to take the initiative in their fight for equality. The new provisions were welcomed by those who believed that: 'it is right that the individual should have direct access to the ordinary courts and tribunals'.[1] Other commentators were more pessimistic:

'The mind boggles at the almost lunatic kind of courage an ordinary black citizen would need to go into court on his (sic) own against lawyers employed by a large institution on which his future may depend.'[2]

It would seem that a considerable number of people were prepared to indulge in this lunacy. Although the county courts have handled very few discrimination cases, the industrial tribunal figures present a very different picture. Evidently people are less intimidated by the tribunal system, or more determined to take action where the discrimination concerns employment. However, with regard to equal pay and sex discrimination applications, this determination seems to be weakening. (Race relations applications remain steady at about 500 per annum.) The number of equal pay claims has declined sharply from two and a half thousand in the first year of operation to 81 in 1980. This is in line with official expectations: employers were aware of the equal pay provisions for five and a half years before the legislation was made operational. The Act was therefore directed at a limited number of 'deviant' employers who had failed to make the necessary adjustments during that time.

However, women have not achieved equal pay – far from it! They still take home less than two-thirds of men's weekly pay, and still receive less than three-quarters of men's hourly earnings.[3] The impotence of the Equal Pay Act derives chiefly from the requirement that the woman must compare herself with a man employed on the same or broadly similar work (unless the job has been rated as equivalent under a job evaluation scheme). Too many employers used the five and a half year 'adjustment' period to reinforce sex-based job segregation, thereby excluding the vast majority of low-paid women workers from the terms of the legislation. So abysmal is the failure of the Equal Pay Act that the European Economic Community Commissioners are taking infringement action against the British Government for its failure to implement Article 119 of the Treaty of Rome.

---

1. Bindman 'The Law and Discrimination: Third Thoughts, *British Journal of Law and Society*, **3**, 1, Summer 1976.
2. Legum, 'Race Relations: another expensive blueprint for failure?' *The Times*, 17 Aug 1977.
3. Equal Opportunities Commission, *Fifth Annual Report* (1980) Manchester EOC. 1981.

From: J. Gregory, 'Equal Pay and Sex Discrimination: Why Women are Giving up the Fight', *Feminist Review* 10, Spring 1982

Document fourteen
EQUAL PAY FOR WORK OF EQUAL VALUE

The amendment to the Equal Pay Act (EqPA) forced on the Government by a ruling of the European Court of Justice was put before the House of Commons on 20th July. The Government's initial proposals for amending the EqPA fell short of the European ruling in at least five significant respects.[1] The final version that was laid before Parliament fares little better. As Jo Richardson MP observed in the debate on the amendment 'the regulations . . . are riddled with holes, and there is no way in which they can help any woman to achieve the objective which is apparent in the judgment of the European Court'.

However, the Government claimed to have made changes to the amendment that take account of the criticism which greeted the original proposals. The changes cover three areas – date of implementation, the burden of proof, and work already covered by a job evaluation study. Although the Government have now brought forward the implementation date for the proposals by about six months so that they take effect on January 1, 1984, it is a small concession compared with what could have been done since. This country had effectively been in breach of its obligations under European law since 1976. If the Government had introduced the regulations by way of amending legislation not only would a fuller debate on them have been possible but they would also have been backdated in the same way that the 1982 Employment Act's provisions on closed shop dismissals were. In the debate Labour MP Barry Jones referred to this contrast, saying that it represented 'a sneaky and diabolical liberty' and that 'under the regulations women will get a shabby deal'.

The burden of proving that a difference in pay between a man and a woman is due to a difference other than that of sex has been shifted back to the employer but it remains quite a different standard of proof than is required under the existing provisions of the EqPA. Indeed, the language of the regulations in this respect is so weak that it is questionable just what is left of the standard. Unlike under the other provisions of the EqPA an employer facing an equal value claim will not be obliged to show that the genuine material difference that he claims explains the difference in pay is a difference that relates directly to the woman's case and the man's.

Instead the amendment states that, in the case of equal value applicants, the employer only has to show that the difference 'may' relate to the woman's and the man's case and, as Jo Richardson pointed out in the debate, 'when "may" is used, there is no need to bother'. So, although the employer still has to prove that a material defence is genuine, under the equal value heading the defence is much wider. The existence of a material *factor* as opposed to a material *difference* will be sufficient in equal value cases to provide a legitimate justification for a difference in pay.

The Under Secretary of State for Employment attempted to defend the different burden of proof by saying that it was necessary so as to allow account to be taken of 'skill shortages or other market forces'. This highlights the overall inadequacy of the amendment for, as Harriet Harman MP put it, 'the market awards higher pay to a man than it does to a woman because of the undervaluation of women's work in the market. The Minister will be providing a complete let out if he allows market value as a way of excluding equal pay'.

Finally, the actual amendment that was laid before the House differs from the original proposal in one other respect. Whereas the earlier draft had the effect of preventing equal value applicants from pressing a claim if their job had already been covered by a job evaluation study, the actual amendment will allow this if it can be shown that there are 'reasonable grounds for determining' that the system used in the study discriminated on the grounds of sex. Whilst this improvement is welcome, in the context of the amendment as a whole it means very little. As we have seen the burden of proof on the employer is a light one and the introduction of the regulations at so late a date will mean that claimants will have to wait until 1986 before they can claim the full amount of back pay that the EqPA allows. Moreover, the serious procedural difficulties that were a feature of the original draft remain unchanged in the actual amendment and, as a result, there remain grounds for believing that the amendment falls short of the requirements of European law.

---

1. See Dominic Byrne, 'An Act of Inequality', *Low Pay Review* No.13, May 1983.

From:'Equal Pay for Work of Equal Value', *Low Pay Review* No.15, September 1983.

What about the suggestion that young people are now too expensive relative to other groups of workers? While some have argued that young people's earnings have risen relative to those of adults, few would seriously argue that young people are now paid more that older workers for doing the same jobs. Indeed males aged under 18 earned in 1981 only 39 per cent of the male adult rate, while women aged under 18 earned only 53 per cent of the female adult rate. It follows that, for any given level of economic activity, it will always be worth employers taking on young people as long as their productivity is at least half that of adult workers. The Department of Employment study cited above warned against the simple assumption that youth unemployment would rise if young people's relative wages increased. A number of factors need to be taken into account; in addition to the question of whether cheaper alternatives (older workers or machines) are available. These include the response of consumers to a change in price of the goods or services being produced by young people, and the importance of their wages within the employers' total costs' . . . It is of course the absolute level of wages, not their relative level, which is important to young people themselves, and many young workers' earnings are already extremely low. On average young males aged under 18 earned only £54.50 a week in April 1981 while 10 per cent earned less that £34.70 for a full week's work. Girls aged under 18 earned on average £50.60 a week and 10 per cent earned less than £32.00 for a week. Workers in the wages council sector, who have benefited less from the improvements won through collective bargaining, fare particularly badly. We noted above that only 5 wages councils were prepared to award young workers a minimum rate in excess of £40 a week and most pay rates of between £30 to £40 a week. 16 year olds covered by the Aerated Waters Wages Council are entitled to as little as £29.45 while apprentice hairdressers are subject to rates as low as £25 for each week's work.[1] Young people working in shops, one of the largest employers of young people, are entitled to around £35 for a full week's work.

Moreover a large proportion of employers appear to be prepared to extend the exploitation of young workers as far as paying below the legal minima. The Commission on Industrial Relations found that in retailing, for instance, the level of underpayment was far higher for young workers than for adult staff. Almost 13 per cent of employers admitted paying their junior full-time male sales assistants below the statutory minimum rate while 17 per cent paid illegally low wages to their female sales assistants. 51.1 per cent of employers reported paying their part-time junior male assistants below the legal minima, while 39.2 per cent underpaid their young female part-time staff.

The evidence does not support the Government's assertion that young people have 'priced themselves' out of jobs. Indeed, official concern might be better directed at ensuring that young people receive at least the minimum rates to which they are entitled by law. In too many industries, young workers are seen as a pool of cheap and easily exploited labour, a view which is encouraged not only by high youth unemployment but by the Government's own approach.

In a speech last Autumn Mr Peter Harrison, an Employment Minister, admitted that 'the main cause of high youth unemployment is the recession'. But he went on to express the Government's concern about the 'high level of young wages'. He argued that young people should be prepared to accept a lower return for their work as a form of investment in training and therefore in their own futures.

'Greater provision for training should go hand in hand with more realistic wage levels for young people.'[2] As we have shown, most young people already accept low wages, yet youth unemployment continues to rise. We have little doubt that young workers would be prepared to accept these low wages in return for adequate training of the type provided in some other European countries. But they are not being offered that choice . . . Before we ask for still more sacrifices from Britain's young people we must begin to treat them more as an investment in all our futures, and less as a source of cheap labour.

---

1. Labour Research Department, 'Young Workers' Pay'. *Bargaining Report* No.17, Dec 1981.
2. DE, *Employment Gazette*, October 1981.

From: C. Pond, 'Youth Unemployment – Are Wages to Blame?', *Low Pay Review* No.8, Feb. 1982

ADVERT FOR YOUNG WORKERS SCHEME

The Young Workers Scheme offers employers an incentive to employ young people under 18 if their rate of pay is less than £40 a week.

The scheme came into effect on January 4th 1982. Here's how it works.

To be eligible under the scheme, the young people must be in their first year of employment and under 18 on or after January 4th 1982.

If you pay them less than £40 a week for a full time job, we'll give you £15 a week. You can be paid this for each week they work for you, up to one year.

If you have eligible young people earning £40 or over but less than £45 a week, we'll give you £7.50 a week.

This new scheme doesn't only apply to people you employ on or after January 4th, but also to any of your present staff who were eligible on that date and who started working for you on or after July 27th 1981.

Employers will be able to claim for all eligible employees whether or not they have taken part in the Youth Opportunities Programme. The scheme is open to firms of any size in Great Britain except public services and domestic households.

It gives employers the opportunity to look at their staffing needs and to take on any extra workers they may want at a price they can afford.

Find out more about the Young Workers Scheme by sending off for our free leaflet which will give you the full story, or you can get one from your local Jobcentre, Employment Office or Careers Office.

Document Seventeen
PROGRAMME FOR THE YOUTH TRAINING SCHEME

Delivering the programme

Basic description	Funding
Mode A	
Employer, local authority, etc. acts as managing agency. Two variants:	
(1) agency provides complete programme for individual	(1) block MSC grant of £1,850 per head, to include allowance costs
(2) agency sub-contracts out all or some of the elements	(2) block MSC grant of £1,850 per head: sub-contractors get agreed payments for education/training, no payment is made for work experience provision but the agent pays the allowance
Mode B	
MSC acts as managing agency Two variants:	
(1) MSC arranges with sponsor to provide complete programme for individual through training workshop or community project	(1) MSC finances the workshop or project on the same basis as under YOP.
(2) MSC sub-contracts out all or some of the elements	(2) sub-contractors get nationally agreed payments for education/training; no payment is made for work experience provision but the MSC pays the allowance.

From: Manpower Services Commission, *Youth Task Group Report* 1982.

Example	Funding
A major company assumes responsibility for (say) 200 trainees and arranges on its own premises a complete programme of education, training and work experience	company receives block grant of 200 × £1,850, i.e. £370,000
a local education authority assumes responsibility for (say) 500 trainees. It provides them with education and training and arranges for them to be placed, within the authority or with other employers, for periods of work experience	authority receives block grant of 500 × £1,850, i.e. £925,000. The authority pays the allowance even when trainees are on other employers' premises
MSC arranges with a voluntary organisation or a consortium to assume responsibility for (say) 50 trainees and provide education, training and work experience for them in a training workshop.	Total 50 × £3,500, i.e. £175,000
MSC arranges courses of FE or training with local contractors and also arranges linked work experience with employers	all payments are from the MSC, including the payments to young people of the allowance.

Document eighteen
OLDER WORKERS AND RETIREMENT

About a third of older workers were in a job that was not the same as that which they had been doing for most of their working lives. Those who had changed were likely to have become non-manual, personal services or unskilled manual workers rather than skilled or semi-skilled manual workers. Six per cent wanted to change the work they did for their present employer, mostly to more skilled or non-manual work.

Full-time workers more often found their work a strain than part-time workers. Those over pension age less often felt strain than those under, probably because some of the latter who do find their job a strain take the opportunity of retiring at state pension age. More than a quarter of those who thought they would eventually have to give up their present job said they would try to get another job, and there was a strong preference for part-time hours. Only a third rated their chances of getting a suitable job as good.

About half the workers either planned to go on as long as their health allowed or had no intention of stopping work at all. Most of the other half thought they would have to give up at state pension age because of the policy of their employer. Full-time workers under pension age more often thought they would have to give up than did part-time workers. Just over a quarter of workers thought they would have problems – particularly money – if and and when they retired. Nearly half of men workers under pension age, and a third of women, said they would like information about retirement. But older workers were less interested.

Nearly two in five workers under pension age were looking forward to retirement, but more had mixed feelings. Workers over pension age were less often looking forward to retirement. Nearly all workers thought they would miss the money, but a high proportion – especially women – thought they would also miss the people at work. About a third thought they would find it difficult to settle down once they had retired.

Eight per cent of those interviewed as retired had looked for paid work after their last job ended. Most of the men who had retired under pension age who had looked for other jobs had sought full-time work, but other men and most of the women had mainly sought part-time work. Local jobs were preferred, and old age was the most frequent reason for being turned down.

Eleven per cent of the 'retired' thought they might seek work in the future – few of those over pension age but a third of the women under pension age. Over a third of those who might seek work again said more money might make them do so. There was most interest in part-time jobs.

The unemployed differed in some ways from the workers, but not in age and sex distribution. They had a more varied occupational history, were more likely to be receiving an occupational pension, and were keener to have information about retirement. They were less healthy than workers and generally less active.

From: S. Parker, *Older Workers and Retirement*, OPCS (1980)

Document nineteen
THE ACTUAL EMPLOYMENT PREFERENCES OF OLDER WORKERS

The other main ground for reconsidering the trend towards earlier retirement is that there are reasons for thinking that present patterns of withdrawal from employment do not fully represent the preferences of older workers themselves. Even without the special impetus given to involuntary retirement by the high unemployment of the last few years, the rate of withdrawal from work reflects such things as mandatory retirement, absence of suitable types of work, reluctance of employers to recruit or train older workers, and discouragement of older workers themselves by employment and unemployment experiences reaching back into middle life.

In 1977 OPCS found that $1\frac{1}{2}$ million full-time workers aged 55–64 (men) and 50–59 (women) – just over half of all workers in these age groups – expected to have to give up their job at a fixed age. Of these, 425,000 would have preferred to work on, (and another four or five per cent were undecided) primarily for money, but also because of enjoying the work and to avoid boredom. Age Concern, three years earlier, found that 37 per cent of already retired respondents agreed that 'I would have stayed on longer if my employer had let me'; 23 per cent agreed strongly. The self-employed, who can choose their own pace of retirement, do in fact often work on. In 1977 the number of male employees still in the workforce at ages above 65 was 12 per cent of that at ages 50–59, but the corresponding proportion for self-employed men was 28 per cent. Though self-employed married women were less likely than self-employed men to continue in work, they were twice as likely to do so as married women employees. Self-employed 'other' women were the most likely of all to continue in work.

For many older workers it would not be enough simply to offer the opportunity to continue in an existing job. Because of changes in health, personal capacity and family situations, many need to change their occupation, to have their jobs adapted to fit their capacities, and perhaps to change their employer. Many also either need or wish to reduce the time they commit to work. Elderly unemployed men differ little from middle-aged men in their willingness to try new types of work, and are more willing to change to a job with lower pay and in a lower skill grade. They tend on the other hand to be much less willing to move house, travel a long distance to work, or accept bad physical working conditions or 'unsocial hours'. They tend to prefer part time; most men and women who continue in work beyond pension age do in fact work not more than 26 hours a week. In these respects the work preferences of elderly men tend to resemble those of women rather than of men in middle life. The question is whether their chances of finding jobs to match their preferences are as good as those of younger workers, and the evidence is that they are not.

The preference of people over pension age for part-time work has obviously been met to some degree, though only within a limited range of jobs. For men, opportunities tend to be in the service and catering trades (barmen, garage attendants, caretakers, and so on), as storekeepers and warehousemen, in general labouring, gardening and farming and in clerical work and retail distribution. But part time for men below pension age has neither developed of itself on any large scale nor been systematically promoted as under the Swedish law of 1976. In 1971 less than four per cent of employed men aged 60–64 were working part-time, and only 2.4 per cent of those aged 55–59. There is a lack of up-to-date figures on this, which is itself a revealing finding, but it does not seem that the position has changed much. In 1977 the proportion of men of all ages who were in 'main' occupations and worked part time was 2.1 per cent. Below standard pension age, part time is still mainly for women or in second jobs.

Convenient location of jobs is a consideration of which planning authorities do take account, though usually with reference to the interests of married women rather than of older workers as such. Daniel, however, has shown that it may be precisely the elderly unemployed who, because they are a disfavoured group, are most likely to have to accept long journeys to work if they are to get back into work at all.

On the re-design of jobs for older workers, again, it is not clear that the position has changed much since OECD issued its series of reports on *The Employment of Older Workers* in the 1960s. These reports were encouraging as to the cost effectiveness of measures to re-design jobs to fit their changing capacities, but decidedly negative as to action of this kind being undertaken in the UK . . .

The idea that older workers cannot be retrained, or at least not economically, has long been obsolete. There is now considerable experience of successful methods of doing so, thanks notably to the work of the Industrial Training Research Unit at Cambridge. The payback for training at the level, for example, of government skillcentres is from the point of view of the economy often as low as one or two years – and shorter still from that of the trainee – even without allowing for factors relevant to the individual employer such as the relatively high stability of older workers in their jobs.

As regards actually obtaining training, however, today's older workers tend to take a justifiably gloomy view of their prospects. Among unemployed men over 55 in 1981, 13 per cent had seriously considered applying for training, and only 3 per cent had actually applied, compared to 34 per cent and 17 per cent on the average of men in younger age groups. When those who had not considered training were asked their reasons, 85 per cent of men over 55 said simply 'age'.

From: M. Fogarty, 'The Work Option' in M. Fogarty (ed.) *Retirement Policy: The Next Fifty Years*, Heinemann Educational Books (1982)

Document twenty
THE REHABILITATION OF DISABLED PERSONS

5.   The successful rehabilitation of a person disabled by injury or sickness is not solely a medical problem. Rehabilitation in its strictly medical sense means that process of preventing or restoring the loss of muscle tone, restoring the full funtions of the limbs, and maintaining the patient's general health and strength. (This is apart from special rehabilitation treatment required for particular diseases such as Tuberculosis.) The process should begin as soon as possible after injury or operation or, in the case of acute or prolonged illness, as soon as the patient's condition permits, and it should continue not only throughout the period of hospital treatment but also during the subsequent stage of convalescence whether that takes place in hospital or is provided in a separate Centre. Continuity of treatment is essential to achieve the aim of restoring the patient's mental and physical capacity at the earliest possible date and to the fullest possible extent.

6.   When restoration in the medical sense has been achieved the services of the social and industrial expert are required: *first* to determine in consultation with the medical experts whether the patient so restored can return to his previous occupation and, if not, what other type of occupation would be most suitable; and *second* to ensure so far as possible that the restored capacity is used to the best advantage in the field of productive effort, whether in the previous or in some other occupation. During the process of rehabilitation in this wider sense there is a transfer of responsibility from the medical to the industrial services and the industrial service should begin to operate before the medical service ends. This means that there should be the fullest co-operation between the two services throughout the rehabilitation process. A notable step towards this end was taken by the Ministry of Labour and National Service and the Health Departments in the Interim Scheme which for the first time linked hospitals with the Employment Exchange service and provided for the interview of patients in hospital and for consultation with the hospital authorities as to the patient's fitness for employment. This experiment has been subject to the special difficulties of war-time conditions but the experience has been sufficient to prove its value and to warrant its development as an essential feature of any permanent rehabilitation scheme. The measure of co-oper-

ation between hospitals and the Employment Exchange service will be materially assisted if, as the Committee understand is the present intention, the organisation of the hospital services on a regional basis and the principle of concentration into specialised centres or hospitals of particular types of disabilities are to be continued into the post-war period. The present system of hospital interview and consultation should be developed with the aim of conveying to hospital authorities such information as they may require in regard to a patient's employment, and of giving every patient, whose stay in hospital is likely to last beyond a given period or whose injury or disability is likely to affect his employment prospects, an opportunity of interview with an Employment Exchange officer so that in consultation with the medical experts steps may be taken in advance to arrange placing, training or such other action as the case may require.

7. Placing in employment will not complete the process of rehabilitation unless the employment – particularly where there is a serious disablement – is suited to individual capacity and makes the best use of individual skill. The aim was described in the leaflet on the Interim Scheme in the following words: 'It is in the interest of the country as well as of the disabled citizen that he should get back to suitable employment as soon as possible – not to *any* employment but to the most skilled work of which he is capable.' The experience of the Interim Scheme is that a large proportion of persons interviewed in hospital are able in the present exceptional circumstances to earn fairly high rates of wages in employment which is of little value from the long-term point of view; only a small number desire to take up a course of training for a skilled occupation, and of those who do enter training the majority are learning engineering processes connected with munitions work. This is inevitable in war conditions but one of its consequences will be that at the end of the war a considerable proportion of such persons will require training or re-training for other forms of employment. It is important that a permanent scheme operating in peace time conditions should include special measures to secure satisfactory employment for persons handicapped by disablement and should encourage more fully than is at present possible the idea of training for a new occupation. This will require a follow-up service to investigate the results of the first placing. A certain measure of follow-up work is being undertaken under the Interim Scheme but this is necessarily on a limited scale; the development of this service should be an important feature of the post-war scheme.

8. Disablement is popularly associated with visible physical injury of some kind, e.g., limb amputation or injury such as to prevent the full use of a limb, and there is a tendency to regard this type of disablement as more serious and a greater handicap to employment than disablement due to other causes. This is far from correct; the problem of complete rehabilitation and resettlement is more difficult among the medical group of disablements than among the surgical group – for the following reasons:

(*a*) Surgical treatment is, as a rule, carried to a stage which leaves the patient fit and able to undertake work requiring physical effort and technical skill; the injury may prevent employment in certain occupations but there is still a wide range within his general capacity and for these not only is he physically suitable but there is little or no danger of his condition becoming worse through employment. Where however the disablement is due to medical causes, the physical fitness of the patient for employment is, as a rule, impaired and this may be increased through unsuitable employment; there may also be mental as well as physical deterioration. Continued medical supervision is rarely required for the surgical, but it may be necessary for a substantial period for the medical, group of disablements;

(b) A physical injury which is visible commands a greater degree of sympathy and willingness to help than a disablement due to medical causes where the handicap is not obvious and its seriousness may not be recognised and may easily be doubted;

(c) The sympathy extended to the surgical group of disablements often carries with it an under-estimate of working capacity and therefore a tendency to regard the individual as suitable only for the lower grades of employment, whereas with the medical group of disablements there is an all too common tendency to assume that the individuals are in fact fully capable of returning to the pre-disablement occupation;

(d) A disablement which is not obvious may not be a handicap to acceptance for employment but may make it difficult to retain employment and therefore to achieve satisfactory resettlement.

There are of course many individual exceptions but the above distinction between the two main categories of disablement is broadly true and its importance has to be borne in mind in the consideration of measures designed to secure successful rehabilitation and resettlement.

9.   On the general question of resettlement, the Committee wish to emphasise at this stage of their report that the only satisfactory form of resettlement for a disabled person is employment which he can take and keep on his merits as a worker in normal competition with his fellows. The chief and continuous aim of a resettlement scheme must be to secure such employment for the greatest possible number of the total group of persons classified as disabled, and the Committee believe that the realisation of this aim is practicable for the majority of the total. In a highly industrialised country such as Britain the number of separate occupations is so large and their demand on physical activity is so varied that it is possible to find an occupation within the physical capacity of all save a minority of the disabled. This does not mean that the problem is easy of solution; it means only that disablement, however it may limit the choice of occupation, need not of itself constitute a bar to economic employment. The right approach is all-important. A general idea prevails that, apart from a few exceptional cases, full efficiency in ordinary employment is beyond the capacity of anyone who fails to pass a general and theoretical medical test, and from this derives the view that the resettlement of the disabled must be a matter of

philanthropy and good will. This idea is wholly out of date. Granted careful assessment of individual capacity and selection of employment, a large proportion of disabled persons are capable or can be rendered capable of taking their places in industry on normal terms. The realisation that this can be achieved, provided that the resources of modern medical knowledge are fully utilised and supported by machinery which can relate the handicap of disablement to the varying demands of different occupations, demands concerted action. The extent and nature of such action must be determined to a considerable extent by the economic conditions; a period of widespread and continuous unemployment will intensify the ordinary handicap of disablement but a period of great demand for labour will call for no less care because of the inducement to many disabled people – as wartime experience has shown – to prefer immediately profitable employment of a temporary character to a period of training for a skilled occupation with permanent prospects for the future. But whatever the conditions, the campaign for successful resettlement must be based upon a full recognition of the fact that disabled persons, given the opportunity, are capable of normal employment; the use of institutional or sheltered employment must be limited to that small group who cannot hold their own on level terms and under competitive conditions.

10. For these and other reasons it is clear that the scheme which the Committee propose will be dependent upon various factors in the health, social, industrial and economic spheres and may need modification in the light of developments of wider policy which are being considered elsewhere. It seems nevertheless desirable to set out as fully as possible the kind of rehabilitation and resettement scheme the Committee would like to see adopted – subject to such adaptations as may be required by developments in other parts of the post-war Reconstruction plan.

From: Tomlinson Committee, *Report of Inter-departmental Committee on the Rehabilitation and Resettlement of Disabled Persons*, Cmnd. 6415, HMSO, London (1943)

SEVERITY OF UNEMPLOYMENT AMONGST DISABLED PEOPLE

2.18 Given the great difficulties of establishing the 'true' numbers of disabled people unemployed and – more particularly – at work it is virtually impossible to produce an unemployment rate for the disabled which would be comparable with the ordinary published rates for unemployment generally. While 'rates' for those registered under the Act are produced (standing at 16% in April 1981 when the GB overall unemployed rate was 10.3%) the figures on which these are based are highly unreliable.

2.19 Even so all sources point unequivocally to a great liability to unemployment for disabled people Townsend found that whereas 90% of fit men had been employed during the preceding 12 months, the same was true of only 68% of men with minor, and 42% of men with more appreciable incapacities. However this study did not differentiate between those non-employed people who had no realistic prospect of work as a result of their disablement, and those who could be regarded as being within the labour market (in any case a difficult distinction to draw). Another perspective comes from the 1976 General Household Survey which shows 23% of unemployed males and 13% of unemployed females reporting limiting long-standing illnesses, compared with 13% and 11% of employed males and females respectively.

2.20 While there must be doubts about the incidence of unemployment among disabled people, there is no difficulty in establishing that, once unemployed, disabled people are likely to experience much greater problems in regaining work than unemployed people generally . . .

From: Manpower Services Commission, *Review of Assistance for Disabled People*, October 1982

Document twenty-two
IN DEFENCE OF THE QUOTA SCHEME

The present quota scheme is not wholly ineffective nor is it true to say that its abolition would make no difference. There is evidence that its existence does influence the behaviour of some employers, and that to abolish it would further worsen the already poor employment prospects of disabled people.

First, the unemployment figures over the past two years suggest that the existence of the quota has helped to protect the jobs of disabled workers at a time of rising unemployment. Only registered disabled workers are covered by the quota scheme. In the year to July 1981 unemployment among registered disabled workers rose by 19.2%, among unregistered disabled workers by 25.0%. The difference is even greater over a longer period. Between May 1979 and July 1981 unemployment among registered disabled workers rose by 18.3% among unregistered disabled workers by 49.5%. The quota scheme must be given some of the credit for this difference.

Secondly, placement figures show that registered disabled people have had consistently greater success in finding jobs than unregistered disabled people. In each of the last twenty-four months for which figures are available, the number of placements of registered disabled people has exceeded the number of placements of unregistered disabled people – despite the fact that the number of unregistered disabled people out of work is about half as high again as the number of registered disabled people out of work. Over the year to October 1981, 19,422 registered disabled people were placed in work, compared with 15,288 unregistered disabled people. The monthly average for the proportion of unemployed registered disabled people placed in employment was 2.3%: for unregistered disabled people it was only 1.2%.[1]

Thirdly, it is reasonable to suppose that many employers respect the law because it is the law, irrespective of the penalties for disobedience, and that they will make an attempt to fulfil their quota obligation even though the chances of prosecution for non-fulfilment are almost non-existent. If the legal obligation were removed, some employers, while well-disposed in principle, might give less attention than they do at present to recruiting disabled people.

The MSC Report refers to research into employers' attitudes commissioned in 1978, and claims that it 'showed that the Scheme had little impact on the outlook or actions of below-quota firms' (4.6). This claim is somewhat overstated. The MSC's research showed that about one third of those employers below quota were genuinely concerned at not meeting their legal obligations, and took practical steps to improve their performance. Such a proportion is not negligible.

Indeed the MSC does itself concede that the existence of the quota may influence employers' attitudes. Arguing against a reduced quota percentage, the Report says that 'there is a danger that in practice employers would lower their sights and make less effort to employ disabled people. For example, a firm which is currently below 3% but above 1.5% may, under the present Scheme, make some attempt to satisfy the higher level by considering registered disabled applicants, which would be unnecessary at the lower level' (8.8). If a reduced quota carries this risk, the absence of a statutory quota carries it even more certainly.

Fourthly, disabled people themselves give strong support to the quota scheme. The MSC's own research has provided evidence that the great majority of disabled people wish the scheme to be retained . . . The present quota scheme cannot therefore be abolished without risk to the employment prospects of disabled workers. It influences the behaviour of employers despite the failure of the MSC to invoke the penalties for non-compliance. Since the scheme was introduced in 1944 only ten prosecutions have been undertaken, the latest in 1975. The total amount paid in fines by employers since 1944 amounts to no more than £434. We shall argue that with a more effective system of enforcement and a more positive policy of encouraging registration, the quota scheme would enjoy a new lease of life as part of a broader package of measures and promote equal employment opportunities for disabled people.

---

1. Based on House of Commons *Hansard*, 8 December 1981, Written Answers cols. 341–3

From: Disability Alliance, *Comments on the MSC's Review of the Quota Scheme for the Employment of Disabled People*, 1981

EMPLOYMENT AND DISABILITY

The problem of unemployment among people with disabilities is larger and more complex – in relation to the integration of such groups as disabled women, or epileptic, mentally handicapped and mentally ill people, as well as, say, amputees into communities and work forces – than is acknowledged in government statements of policy. In the 1980s the problem of creating sufficient opportunities for employment is huge and affects hundreds of thousands of people with disabilities. The danger is that if the government were to accept the MSC recommendation to scrap the quota scheme, one weak but positive contribution to their employment would be removed. The scheme deserves to be retained but not without also introducing a battery of supporting legislative and administrative measures so that more people would be employed. The measures should include:

(*i*)   The introduction of sanctions against non-observance of the quota. A levy on all employers below quota should be imposed, and a fund built up from these levies, which would allow employers meeting the quota to obtain grants and allowances for training, and adaptations of premises and machinery. There presently exist government schemes, like 'job introduction' (to subsidise the trial employment of disabled people for six weeks), 'job rehearsal' (a tax-free allowance for disabled people attending employment rehabilitation centres), fares to work and capital grants to adapt premises. These remain of marginal value, however. The quota might also be defined on a weighted basis (as proposed by the Snowden Working Party), so that people who were more severely disabled would count more against quota and employers would be eligible to receive higher employment subsidies on their account. Supplementary allowances would be payable to those employing certain categories of handicapped people, including mentally handicapped people.

(*ii*)   The number of places in sheltered and enclave employment should be expanded – at the rate, say, of 5,000 a year for 10 years – especially for mentally ill and mentally handicapped people. Some of these new places should be reserved for those presently living in residential institutions. There is far too little sheltered employment at present, with no evidence of any increase over the last five year (13,755 places in 1976 and 13,666 in 1980).

(*iii*) A new system of capital grants for employers to adapt premises and machinery in order to employ groups of disabled people should be administered by the Manpower Services Commission. The present scheme is derisory: for example £500,000 was allowed for capital grants in 1977–78, and only £11,000 spent. By 1981–82, the allowance had been reduced to £150,000 but, even so, only £16,000 will have been spent. There should also be a parallel system of grants for training within firms. There should be new financial incentives for the nationalised industries, public administration and the public social services to submit proposals for employing groups of disabled people.

(*iv*) Anti-discrimination legislation to establish rights to higher minimum earnings in Remploy, sheltered workshops and in forms of employment in residential institutions and adult training centres. The legislation would secure protection against being treated unfairly in other respects of employment situations on account of disability.

(*v*) People with disablement should, with their agreement, normally be registered. The definition of eligibility for registration would include degree of severity and would correspond with the definition used by social service departments under the Chronically Sick and Disabled Persons Act. All those proposed for registration should receive a letter outlining the benefits and rights resulting from registration.

(*vi*) Provision would be made for an Advisory Council consisting wholly of people elected from the register to review employment policy and advise the Manpower Services Commission. Approval of training schemes, and grants for such schemes, might rest with them.

These represent only some of the main elements of a comprehensive policy. Something on these lines is needed both to stop the current disengagement of people with disabilities from the workforce, and to heal the deep conflict of view between the MSC and the disabled population.

From: P. Townsend, 'Employment and Disability', in A. Walker and P. Townsend (eds) *Disability in Britain*, Martin Robertson (1981)

Document twenty-four
THE EMPLOYMENT OF IMMIGRANTS: A CASE STUDY WITHIN THE WOOL INDUSTRY

In summarizing this study and drawing any conclusions it must be emphasized that we have only looked at a small sample of companies mainly concentrated in one section of the wool industry. The results of this study therefore should be treated with caution and are not necessarily applicable to the whole wool industry or even that part of it concentrated in the West Riding of Yorkshire. It would also be unwise to draw too many conclusions as to the degree to which results can be extended to other industries, although certain aspects may well be applicable.

Possibly the most interesting finding of the study is that relating to capital investment. The degree to which new capital investment and the employment of immigrants go together is surprising and it would be fair to conclude that the employment of immigrants has facilitated new capital investment in the sample of firms under study. This is because new machinery is too expensive to be worked only 40 or 48 hours a week and it must be employed as intensively as possible thus necessitating shift work. This is a trend not confined to the wool industry and may well, in the future, make headway into more white-collar occupations. It is well recognized that there is a general disinclination to work nights or changing shifts and higher rates of pay are the general rule. The immigrant (Pakistani) worker is usually more willing to take this work than local labour for a variety of reasons. Firstly, the undoubted dicrimination in employment against the immigrant restricts his choice of jobs severely. Secondly, his lack of suitable qualifications and language problems further restrict opportunities. Thirdly, one can hypothesize that the immigrant newly established in this country is much nearer the economist's ideal of economic man. The majority of immigrants are single adult males less constrained than the English worker by non-economic factors such as socially awkward hours of work, and are willing to work as long hours as possible to earn as much as possible.[1]

The alternatives to the employment of immigrants are more varied and more difficult to define than any other aspect of this study. One alternative that is not really an alternative would be the employment of another type of immigrant, from other parts of the UK, Ireland, Europe, or elsewhere.

The major alternative to immigrant labour would have been a rise in wage rates to attract more labour into the industry. It is probable that in the absence of Pakistani immigrants there would have been a rise in the wage level of the industry but the degree of this rise is problematical and its scope would have been limited probably by the ability of employers to pass on higher costs to consumers. Within the context of the wool industry the room for manoeuvre of any individual employer to raise prices is very small and the current contraction of the industry would probably have been much swifter but for the presence of immigrant labour.[2] Thus some of the less efficient firms in the industry have been allowed time to become more efficient and modernize and extremely painful and over-rapid contraction of the industry has been avoided. This slowing down of the possible decline of certain firms may have relevance to those companies which used immigrants mainly as labourers and had embarked on a process of modernization but did not have sufficient resources to do the job in one go. It can also be argued that a rise in wage rates, especially for shift work, would have had an inhibiting effect on the rate of new capital investment and it would have remained cheaper to use older machinery. Other alternatives to the immigrant include the setting up of satellite companies and a wider recruitment area for labour but these would seem to be only limited solutions for the problems affecting most companies in the sample.

Generally the immigrant was considered by his employer to be as good as any other labour that could be employed. With the exception of two companies, the immigrant (Pakistani) worker was said to be as productive as his local equivalent and in some cases was considered preferable to the indigenous labour that could be recruited. In general no extra costs were associated with the employment of immigrants and no company found it necessary to provide extra facilities for them such as separate toilets. The training of immigrants was the same as for other labour. The reasons why two companies found immigrant labour worse than local labour could be for a variety of reasons or a combination of them. The immigrant labour could have been worse, or it lacked good supervision, or the companies failed to select and train their staff properly, or the companies were incapable of attracting better immigrant workers, etc. All the companies, with the exception of the two that found immigrants were inferior workers, stated that they were more mobile than local labour.

This study can only be treated as a starting point for the building up of a body of knowledge of what actually happens when a flow of immigrants starts working in an industry and there is an obvious need for further studies of this kind in this and other industries. However, despite the limitations of such a study certain general ideas suggest themselves. Both the industry and the immigrant were in a transitional stage. The industry has to change to survive; the immigrant poised between two cultures is probably more willing to adapt to change. The resistance against change in work routine which local labour has built up through a long history of institutional factors is less relevant for the immigrant. But the flexibility of the immigrant is probably only a short run process and over time institutional constraints will become more important.

---

1   See chapter by Peter Jenner 'Some Speculations on the Economics of Immigration' in *Immigration, Medical and Social Aspects: A Ciba Foundation Report* (London, Churchill, 1966), which discusses some of the points raised here.

2.   It can be argued that the arrival of immigrants has allowed inefficient firms to continue to operate when it would be better for the economy if these companies closed down. This argument does not allow for possible social pressures that may have forced Government to intervene and prop up the industry if the rate of contraction of the industry has been too rapid. Thus it could be postulated that immigration has allowed a contracting industry to modernize without Government intervention.

From: B. G. Cohen and P. J. Jenner, 'The Employment of Immigrants: A Case Study within the Wool Industry', *Race*, **10**, 1968–9

Document twenty-five
DISCRIMINATION IN EMPLOYMENT

There is evidence from a number of reports and surveys of widespread discrimination against black people in British industry. One report suggests that discrimination is not a question of employers simply displaying prejudice against people with black skins, but that employers appear to have mistaken assumptions about the actual abilities of black people.

A survey of nearly 300 plants, comprising case studies and interviews conducted by PEP, showed that more than half the plants practised some form of discrimination and a black person had to make twice as many applications as a white person before finding a job. A second PEP report in the same year stated that substantial discrimination was found, even at the level of recruitment for unskilled jobs; further, more than 30% of Indian and West Indian applicants were discriminated against at the earliest stage of recruitment – the written application stage – in a broad range of white collar jobs. This research included Greek subjects to test the extent to which discrimination related to 'foreignness' rather than skin colour. Its authors stated that the findings in all the tests strengthened the conclusion that it was skin colour which underlay most of the discrimination shown in these cases.

According to a report published by the Tavistock Institute of Human Relations, black people are considerably less successful than whites in applying for jobs and promotion in the Civil Service. The departments studied were the Department of Health and Social Security, the Ministry of Defence and HM Dockyard, Portsmouth. In the London North DHSS Region, out of 317 applications for clerical officer grade jobs between June and November 1976, one-third came from black candidates and two-thirds from whites. Only ten black candidates were offered jobs in comparison with 78 whites: this translates to a success rate of 18% in comparison with 54% for whites. Furthermore, more black than white candidates rejected for interview possessed the minimum educational qualifications. The researchers also found that of 100 clerical officers studied, 30 were 'over-qualified' and of these 23 were black, showing that many black employees accept jobs below their level of qualification.

From: The Runnymede Trust and the Radical Statistics Race Group, *Britain's Black Population*, Heinemann Educational Books (1980)

TRIBUNAL CASES OF RACIAL DISCRIMINATION

1. DAVID CLULOW LTD, VICTIMISATION AWARD

In an important tribunal decision involving the first successful case proving victimisation under the Race Relations Act, an award has been made against David Clulow Ltd, the contact lens manufacturers.

In August 1979 Deirdre Wild, personnel and training manager, recruited Frances Joseph, a West Indian school-leaver, as a receptionist. There is a company rule that employees who wear spectacles should not work in the reception area until they had been fitted with contact lenses. However, Miss Wild requested Miss Joseph to work in reception immediately, even though she wore spectacles, as there was only a week's handover period before the girl from whom she was to take over was due to leave.

The following afternoon Mr Stephens, administration manager of the company, ordered Miss Joseph to work in an office upstairs. He later told Miss Wild that David Clulow, the proprietor, did not like black people working in positions in which they came into contact with the public. Two days later he told Miss Wild that Miss Joseph could not work in reception because she was black. Miss Wild refused to be associated with this decision and insisted that Mr Stephens told Miss Joseph himself, which he did.

A few days later Mr Stephens instructed Miss Wild to re-advertise the receptionist's post and to appoint a white person. When Miss Wild said she would report the matter, Mr Stephens told her that if she made a fuss she would be made redundant, and that if Miss Joseph made a fuss her probation would be terminated by dismissal.

Miss Joseph wrote a protest letter to Mr Clulow; she was subsequently told by Mr Stephens that this had been torn up. She wrote again and copied the letter to Mr Cordrey, Mr Clulow's co-director, who subsequently asserted that Miss Joseph had been removed from reception due to her age (she was 16). Miss Wild was unconvinced by this argument as the 15-year-old daughter of another employee had been given a Saturday job as a receptionist. Miss Wild was instructed not to make future appointments without approval of Mr Stephens or a departmental head.

Miss Joseph approached the CRE for help, who contacted David Clulow. When Miss Wild returned from a holiday in November she was informed she was to be made redundant; subsequently the company offered her a post as receptionist on substantially less favourable terms. She refused and her employment terminated at the end of December.

A London (South) Industrial Tribunal found that Miss Joseph had suffered discrimination on racial grounds. They rejected the Respondent's submission that Miss Wild was redundant and found that, by her dismissal, Miss Wild had been victimised under Section 2(1) of the Race Relations Act:

> 2(1) A person ('the discriminator') discriminates against another person ('the person victimised') in any circumstances relevant for the purposes of any of the provision of this Act if he treats the person victimised less favourably than in those circumstances he treats or would treat other persons, and does so by reason that the person victimised has –
>
> (a) . . .
>
> (b) given evidence or information in connection with proceedings brought by any person against the discriminator or any other person under this Act; or
>
> (c) otherwise done anything under or by reference to this Act in relation to the discrimination or any other person; or
>
> (d) alleged that the discriminator or any other person has committed an act which (whether or not the allegation so states) would amount to a contravention of this Act, or by reason that the discriminator knows that the person victimised intends to do any of those things, or suspects that the person victimised has done or intends to do, any of them.

She had given information to the CRE in connection with the proceedings; had encouraged Miss Joseph to make a complaint; and had alleged to the Commission that the respondents were infringing the Race Relations Act; and subsequently had been penalised. Her dismissal was also judged to be unfair under the Employment Protection (Consolidation) Act 1978.

Miss Joseph was awarded £150 for hurt feelings against each of the two respondents, Mr Stephens and David Clulow Ltd, and a similar award was made to Miss Wild, who was also awarded £262.30 compensation under the Employment Protection Act. No award was made for the re-employment of the applicants in their original positions as Miss Joseph was content to continue working in the upstairs office, and Miss Wild was intending to train as a nurse.

2. EL GRECO LTD, BRADFORD, SETTLEMENT OUT OF COURT

A significant out-of-court settlement has been achieved in a Bradford discrimination dismissal case which was assisted by the Commission for Racial Equality.

In September 1979 Pamela Henry, a UK-born West Indian sixth-former obtained a Saturday job as a waitress in an El Greco Coffee Bar. On October 13 her friend Paulette Thompson, also of Jamaican origin, began similar employment, as did two white girls. A senior manager of the company visited the coffee bar each Saturday; he appeared to avoid speaking to Miss Henry and Miss Thompson.

On collecting their wages on October 13, the two girls were informed their services would no longer be required, although Miss Thompson had only begun work the same day. The reason given was that previous staff were returning to work; yet the two white girls who had begun work that day with Miss Thompson were asked to return the following Saturday. The two black girls had been given no grounds for suspecting their work was unsatisfactory, and therefore could only conclude that the reason for their dismissal was on the grounds of their colour, at the instigation of the senior manager.

None of the coffee bar's previous staff returned to employment, and Miss Henry and Miss Thompson were subsequently replaced by white girls.

After the involvement of ACAS in an attempt to conciliate the two parties as part of the Industrial Tribunal procedure, the two girls agreed to accept £75 each from El Greco Ltd 'in full and final settlement for the proceedings'. Pamela Henry commented she was 'a bit disappointed' that the case was not to be heard in a tribunal but had been advised she was unlikely to receive any greater settlement from a tribunal decision. This is surely some indictment of the low levels of compensation which even successful complainants can expect in racial discrimination cases.

3. BRITISH LEYLAND, DISCRIMINATION IN DISMISSAL PROCEEDINGS

Mr Khaliq worked at West Yorkshire Foundries as a moulder from March 1977 until his dismissal in December 1979. On 19 December his foreman, Mr Kenneth Oxley, instructed him to do a labourer's job. Mr Khaliq queried the instruction as labouring was not part of his normal work, and Mr Oxley told him to go home and, in doing so, swore at him. Mr Khaliq was subsequently dismissed and he appealed against his dismissal through his firm's procedures.

Mr Khaliq told the tribunal that, at his appeal on 15 January, he told the management that he had a witness, Mr Allah Dad, who had heard Mr Oxley swear at him. However, Mr Paul Brunner, the Production Manager who conducted the appeal, refused to let an independent interpreter be present when Mr Dad appeared at the appeal hearing. Mr Brunner also said in dismissing Mr Khaliq's appeal, that Mr Dad would have been little help to the hearing as he had no command of English.

Mr K. Oxley, Mr Khaliq's foreman, told a Leeds Industrial Tribunal that Mr Khaliq, who was represented by the Legal Adviser of Leeds Council for Community Relations, had been dismissed for gross misconduct after leaving the firm without permission. Mr Oxley said that he had asked Mr Khaliq, a moulder, to work as a labourer for one day while there were staff shortages. This was in line with a union agreement and other members of staff had agreed to do this. However, Mr Khaliq refused to do a labouring job and, although he was given another chance to change his mind, he declined and went home. Mr Oxley denied that he had sworn at Mr Khaliq. Evidence was also given for the respondents by Mr P. Brunner, the Production Manager, who conducted Mr Khaliq's appeal against dismissal. Mr Brunner told the tribunal that in his view, he had felt it irrelevant to use an independent interpreter, since Mr Khaliq's witness, Mr Dad, would have been of little help to the appeal hearing as he had little command of English.

The tribunal unanimously decided that Mr Khaliq had been discriminated against and awarded him £50 compensation. The tribunal Chairman, Mr J. Morrish, said that there had been a breach of the Race Relations Act because, if an interpreter had been allowed, Mr Dad's evidence could have been of relevance to Mr Khaliq's case.

From: Tribunal Cases, *Employment Report*, Commission for Racial Equality, November 1980

FULL EMPLOYMENT IN A FREE SOCIETY

Twice in this century the onset of cyclical depression has been arrested by the outbreak of war, just after the culmination of an upward movement of the trade cycle. After the boom of 1913 employment had already begun to fall in 1914. After the half-hearted boom of 1937 employment fell in 1938. In each case an incipient depression was stopped or reversed, but it needed a war to bring this about. The test of statesmanship in the near future lies in finding a way to avoid depression without plunging into war.

That is the aim and hope of this Report. We cure unemployment for the sake of waging war. We ought to decide to cure unemployment without war. We cure unemployment in war, because war gives us a common objective that is recognized by all, an objective so vital that it must be attained without regard to cost, in life, leisure, privileges or material resources. The cure of unemployment in peace depends on finding a common objective for peace that will be equally compelling on our efforts. The suggestion of this Report is that we should find that common objective in determination to make a Britain free of the giant evils of Want, Disease, Ignorance and Squalor. We cure unemployment through hate of Hitler; we ought to cure it through hate of these giant evils. We should make these in peace our common enemy, changing the direction and the speed rather than the concentration and strength of our effort. Whether we can do this, depends upon the degree to which social conscience becomes the driving force in our national life. We should regard Want, Disease, Ignorance and Squalor as common enemies of all of us, not as enemies with whom each individual may seek a separate peace, escaping himself to personal prosperity while leaving his fellows in their clutches. That is the meaning of social conscience; that one should refuse to make a separate peace with social evil. Social conscience, when the barbarous tyranny abroad has ended, should drive us to take up different arms in a new war against Want, Disease, Ignorance, and Squalor at home.

Want, arising mainly through unemployment and other interruptions of earnings, to a less extent through large families, is the subject of my earlier Report on Social Insurance. It could without question be abolished by the whole-hearted acceptance of the main principles of that Report. The worst feature of Want in Britain shortly before this war was its concentration upon children. Wages were not and probably could not be adjusted in any way to family responsibilities; the various social insurance schemes for providing income when wages failed either ignored family responsibilities entirely – as in health insurance or workmen's compensation – or made inadequate provision for them – as in unemployment insurance. By consequence there followed a sinister concentration of Want on those who would suffer from it most helplessly and most harmfully. Nearly half of all the persons discovered in Want by the social surveys of British cities between the wars were children under fifteen. Nearly half of all the working-class children in the country were born into Want. It is certain on general principles and can be shown by experiment that the bodies and minds of children respond directly and automatically to better environment, that the citizens of the future will grow up taller, stronger, abler, if in childhood all of them have had good feeding, clothing, housing and physical training. Want and its concentration on children between the wars represented a destruction of human capital none the less real because it did not enter into any economic calculus.[1] The decision to destroy Want should be taken at once, for its own sake, to free Britain from a needless scandal and a wasting sore. That decision would deliver at the same time the first blow in the war against Idleness. The redistribution of income that is involved in abolishing Want by Social Insurance and children's allowances will of itself be a potent force in helping to maintain demand for the products of industry, and so in preventing unemployment.

---

1. 52.5 per cent of all children under one year of age in York were found by Mr Rowntree in 1936 to be in families with incomes below his standard of human needs (*Poverty and Progress*, p. 156). York was certainly not less prosperous than Britain as a whole, with less than the average of unemployment. The effects of environment on the height and weight of school children have been demonstrated repeatedly by the statistics published by the Corporation of Glasgow. Uniformly, for both sexes and at all ages, the children from larger homes are heavier and taller than those from one and two-room homes, and keep their advantage while children of all classes improve with rising standards of life.

From: W. Beveridge, *Full Employment in a Free Society*, George Allen & Unwin (1944)

REFERENCES AND BIBLIOGRAPHY

A comprehensive bibliography is given below. Those titles marked with an asterisk and a number will provide students with some useful further reading. The number refers to the relevant chapter.

ALLEN, V. L. (1977) 'The differentiation of the working class' in A. Hunt (ed.) *Class and Class Structure*, Lawrence and Wishart.

ADVISORY, CONCILIATION AND ARBITRATION SERVICE (ACAS), (1978) *Button Manufacturing Wages Council*, Report No. II, ACAS.

ASSOCIATION OF COUNTY COUNCILS (1979) *Gearing for the Future of Sheltered Employment*, ACC.

ATKINSON, A. B. (1975) *The Economics of Inequality*, Oxford University Press.

ATKINSON, A. B. (1981) 'Unemployment benefits and incentives', in J. Creedy (ed.) *The Economics of Unemployment in Britain*, Butterworths.

ATKINSON, A. B. *et al.* (1982) *Who are the Low Paid?*, Discussion Series No. 3, Low Pay Unit.

BACON, W. and ELTIS, R. (1978) *Britain's Economic Problem: Too Few Producers*, Macmillan.

BALDWIN, S. (1977) *Disabled Children – Counting the Costs*, Disability Alliance.

BARBER, A. (1981) *Labour Force Information From the National Dwelling and Housing Survey*, Department of Employment Research Paper No. 17.

BARRETT, M. and McINTOSH, M. (1980) 'The "family wage": some problems for socialists and feminists', *Capital and Class*, 11.

BECKER, G. (1975) *Human Capital*, Columbia University Press.

BENJAMIN, D. K. and KOCHIN, L. A. (1979a) 'Searching for an explanation of unemployment in interwar Britain' *J. Pol. Econ.*, **87** (3).

BENJAMIN, D. K. and KOCHIN, L. A. (1979b) 'Voluntary unemployment in interwar Britain', *The Banker*, February.

BENTLEY, S. (1976) 'Industrial conflict, strikes and black workers: problems of research methodology', *New Community*, V, 1–2.

BEVERIDGE, W. (1944) *Full Employment in a Free Society*, George Allen & Unwin.

BOGGS, R. (1982) 'Discrimination and law enforcement', in Runnymede Trust, *Racial Discrimination*, proceedings of a seminar at the University of Surrey, September.

BOSANQUET, N. and DOERINGER, P. B. (1973) 'Is there a dual labour market in Great Britain?', *Economic Journal*, 83.

BRENNER, M. H. (1980) 'Mortality and the national economy – a review, and the experiences of England and Wales 1936–76', *The Lancet*, 15, September.

BRESLAU, N., SALKEVER, D. and STARUCH, K. S. (1982), 'Women's labour force activity and responsibilities for disabled dependents: a study of families with disabled children', *Journal of Health and Social Behaviour*, 23, June.

BUCKLE, J. R. (1971) *Work and Housing of Impaired People in Great Britain*, HMSO.

BURGHES, L. (1980) *Living from Hand to Mouth*, Poverty Pamphlet 50, Family Service Units and Child Poverty Action Group.

BURTON, J. (1977) 'Employment subsidies – the cases for and against, *National Westminster Quarterly Review*, February.

BYRNE, D, *et al.* (1983) 'Low wages in Britain', *Low Pay Review*, 12, February.

CAIN, G. C. (1976) 'The challenge of segmented labor market theories to orthodox theory: a survey', *J. Econ. Lit.*, **14**(4), September.

CAMPBELL, B. (1982) 'Women: not what they bargained for', *Marxism Today*, March.

CASSON, M. (1979) *Youth Unemployment*, Macmillan.

CENTRE FOR ALTERNATIVE INDUSTRIAL AND TECHNOLOGICAL SYSTEMS (CAITS), (1978) *Alternatives to Unemployment – New Approaches to Work in Industry and the Community*, CAITS Conference Papers, November.

CLARK, G. (1982) 'Recent developments in working patterns', *Employment Gazette*, July.

COHEN, B. G. and JENNER, P. J. (1969) 'The employment of immigrants: a case study within the wool industry', *Race*, **10**.

COLLEDGE, M. and BARTHOLOMEW, R. (1980) *A Study of the Long Term Unemployed*, MSC.

COMMISSION FOR RACIAL EQUALITY (CRE), (1982) *Annual Report*.

COMMUNITY DEVELOPMENT PROJECT POLITICAL ECONOMY COLLECTIVE (CDPPEC), (1979) *The State and the Local Economy*, CDPPEC.

COMMUNITY DEVELOPMENT PROJECT POLITICAL ECONOMY COLLECTIVE (CDPPEC), (1980) *Back Street Factory*, CDPPEC.

COMMUNITY RELATIONS COMMISSION (1974) *Unemployment and Homelessness*, HMSO.

COOPER, S. (1980) *Social Security, Welfare and Benefit Schemes 1980–81*, Policy Studies Institute Research Paper 80/2.

COOTE, A. and CAMPBELL, B. (1982) *Sweet Freedom*, Pan Books.

COULSON, M., MAGAS, B. and WAINWRIGHT, H. (1975) 'The housewife and her labour under capitalism – a critique', *New Left Review*, 89.

COULTER, A. (1981) *Who Minds About the Minders?* Low Pay Unit, July.

COUSSINS, J. (1979) *The Shift-Work Swindle*, National Council for Civil Liberties, pamphlet.

COUSSINS, J and COOTE, A (1981) *The Family in the Firing Line*, Poverty Pamphlet 51, Child Poverty Action Group, March.

CRAIG, G. *et al.* (1979) *Jobs and Community Action*, Routledge & Kegan Paul.

*[1]CRAIG, C., RUBERY, J., TARLING, R. and WILKINSON F. (1982) *Labour Market Structure, Industrial Organisation and Low Pay*, Cambridge University Press.

CRINE, S. (1979), *The Hidden Army*, Low Pay Unit, November.

CRINE, S. (1980) *Legal Minimum Wages*, WEA, July.

CRINE, S. (1981a) *The Pay and Conditions of Homeworkers*, Submission to the House of Commons Select Committee on Employment, Low Pay Unit, February.

CRINE, S. (1981b) *The Great Pay Robbery*, Low Pay Report 8, October.

CRINE, S. (1982) *A Cut Below the Rest*, Low Pay Report 9, February.

DANIEL, W. W. (1968) *Racial Discrimination in England*, Pelican.

DANIEL, W. W. (1974) *A National Survey of the Unemployed*, Political and Economic Planning.

DANIEL, W. W. (1981a) *The Unemployed Flow*, Stage 1, Interim

Report, Policy Studies Institute, May.

DANIEL, W. W. (1981b) 'Why is high unemployment still somehow acceptable?', *New Society*, 19 March.

★³DANIEL, W. W. (1981c) *The Nature of Current Unemployment*, British-North American Research Association Occasional Paper 6.

DAVIES, R., HAMILL, L., MOYLAN, S. and SMEE, C. H. (1982) 'Incomes in and out of work', *Employment Gazette*, June.

DAVOUD, N. and KETTLE, M. (1981) *Multiple Sclerosis and its Effects upon Employment*, Multiple Sclerosis Society, London.

DAWES, L., BEDEMAN, T. and HARVEY, J. (1982) 'What happens after YOP – a longer term view', *Employment Gazette*, January.

DEACON, A. (1976) *In Search of the Scrounger*, Bell.

DEACON, A. (1978) 'The scrounging controversy: public attitudes towards the unemployed in contemporary Britain', *Soc. and Econ. Admin.*, **12** (2), Summer.

DEACON, A. (1981a) 'Unemployment and politics in Britain since 1945', in B. Showler and A. Sinfield (eds) *The Workless State*, Martin Robertson.

DEACON, A. (1981b) 'The duration of unemployment benefit under the National Insurance Act 1946', in L. Burghes and R. Lister (eds) *Unemployment: Who Pays the Prices?*, Child Poverty Action Group Pamphlet 53, November.

DEPARTMENT OF EMPLOYMENT (DE) (1972a) *Unemployment Statistics: Report of an Interdepartmental Working Party*, Cmnd 5157, HMSO, pp. 23/4 (quoted in Pond, C., *op. cit.*).

DEPARTMENT OF EMPLOYMENT (DE) (1972b) *Training for the Future: a Plan for Discussion*, HMSO.

★⁸DEPARTMENT OF EMPLOYMENT (DE) (1973) *Sheltered Employment for Disabled People*, HMSO.

DEPARTMENT OF EMPLOYMENT (DE) (1981) *A New Training Initiative: A Programme of Action*, Cmnd. 8455, HMSO, December.

DEPARTMENT OF EMPLOYMENT (DE), (1981) *New Earnings Survey*.

DEPARTMENT OF EMPLOYMENT (DE), (1982) *Young Workers Scheme*, PL 678 (Rev).

DEPARTMENT OF EMPLOYMENT and DEPARTMENT OF HEALTH AND SOCIAL SECURITY (DE and DHSS), (1981) *Payment of Benefits to Unemployed People*, (Report of the Joint DE/DHSS Rayner Scrutiny 1980), March.

DEPARTMENT OF THE ENVIRONMENT (DoE), (1977) *Policy for the Inner Cities*, HMSO.

DEPARTMENT OF HEALTH AND SOCIAL SECURITY (DHSS), (1980) *Inequalities in Health*, Report of a Research Working group.

DEPARTMENT OF HEALTH AND SOCIAL SECURITY (DHSS), (1981) *Care in Action*, HMSO.

DEX, S. (1978) 'Measuring women's unemployment', *Soc. and Econ. Admin.*, **12** (2), Summer.

DEX,S. (1979) 'A note on discrimination in employment and its effects on black youths', *J. Social Policy*, **8** (3).

DOERINGER, P. B. and PIORE, M. J. (1971) *Internal Labour Markets and Manpower Analysis*, Lexington Books.

DOERINGER, P. B. and PIORE, M. J. (1975) 'Unemployment and the "dual labour market', *The Public Interest*, 38.

DRUMMOND, P. (1980) 'In search of new egg baskets', *Health and Social Services Journal*, 12 September.

DUMMETT, A. & MARTIN, I. (1982) *British Nationality*, National Council for Civil Liberties.

DUNCAN, S. S. (1976) 'Self-help – the allocation of mortgages and the formation of housing sub markets', *Area*, **8** (4).

DURWARD, L. (1981) *That's the Way the Money Goes*, Disability Alliance, September.

DURWARD, L., LONSDALE, S., MORTON, J., WALTON., D. and WILSON, J. (1980) *Cuts in Local Authority Spending on Personal Social Services*, Social Priorities Alliance, July.

ECONOMIST INTELLIGENCE UNIT (1982) *Benefits for Partial Disability*, April.

EEC (1981) *Official Journal of the European Communities*, No.c77/27, 6 April.

ELIAS, P. (1980), 'Labour supply and employment opportunities for women' in Lindley, M. *Economic Change and Employment Policy*, Macmillan.

ELLIOT, D. (1977) *The Lucas Aerospace Workers Campaign*, Fabian Society.

ELLIOT, R., GLUCKLICH, P., MACLENNAN, E. and POND, C. (1981) *Women in the Labour Market: A Study of the Impact of Legislation and Policy Towards Women in the UK Labour Market During the Nineteen Seventies*, Report prepared for the International Institute of Management, Berlin.

EMPLOYMENT GAZETTE (1978) 'Measures to alleviate unemployment in the medium term: work-sharing', April.

EMPLOYMENT GAZETTE (1979) 'The development of special employment measures', November.

EMPLOYMENT GAZETTE (1983) June.

EQUAL OPPORTUNITIES COMMISSION (EOC), (1979) *With all my Worldly Goods I Thee Endow . . . Except my Tax Allowances*, EOC.

EQUAL OPPORTUNITIES COMMISSION (EOC), (1980) *The Experience of Caring for Elderly and Handicapped Dependants: Survey Report*, EOC.

EQUAL OPPORTUNITIES COMMISSION (EOC), (1981a) *Job Sharing, Improving the Quality and Availability of Part-time Work*, EOC, July.

EQUAL OPPORTUNITIES COMMISSION (EOC), (1981b) *Job Sharing: Alternative Working Arrangements*, EOC.

★5EQUAL OPPORTUNITIES COMMISSION (EOC), (1982a) *Caring for the Elderly and Handicapped: Community Care Policies and Women's Lives*, EOC, March.

EQUAL OPPORTUNITIES COMMISSION (EOC), (1982c) *The Job Splitting Scheme*, EOC, December.

EQUAL OPPORTUNITIES COMMISSION (EOC), (1982b), *Caring for the Elderly and Handicapped*, EOC, March.

FAGIN, L. H. (1979/80) 'The experience of unemployment in the culture of unemployment', *New Universities Quarterly*, **34** (1), Winter.

FAGIN, L. (1981) *Unemployment and Health in Families*, DHSS.

FIELD, F. (ed.), (1977), *The Conscript Army*, Routledge & Kegan Paul.

FIELD, F. (1981) *Inequality in Britain: Freedom, Welfare and the State*, Fontana.

FIELD, F. *et al.* (1977) *To Him Who Hath*, Penguin.

FINCH, J. and GROVES, D. (1980) 'Community care and the family: a case for equal opportunities', *J. Soc. Pol.*, **9**, 4 October.

★5FINCH, J. and GROVES, D. (1983) *A Labour of Love eg: Women, Work and Caring*, Routledge & Kegan Paul.

FOGARTY, M. P. (1975) *Forty to Sixty*, Centre for Studies in Social Policy, Bedford Square Press.

FOGARTY, M. P. (1980) *Retirement Age and Retirement Costs*, Report No. 592, Policy Studies Institute, December.

★7FOGARTY, M. (1982) *Retirement Policy: The Next Fifty Years*, Heinemann.

FRIEND, A. and METCALFE, A. (1981) *Slump City*, Pluto Press.

FULOP, C. (1971) *Markets for Employment*, Institute for Economic

Affairs, Research Monograph 26, November 1971.

GARDINER, J. (1975) 'Women's domestic labour', *New Left Review*, 89.

*[3]GARRATY, J. (1978) *Unemployment in History*, Harper & Row.

GENERAL HOUSEHOLD SURVEY 1980 (1982) HMSO.

GLASNER, A., KELLY, A. and ROBERTS, B. (1981) *The Labour Market and the Labour Process*, Discussion paper presented to the Annual Conference of Sociologists in Polytechnics.

GLENDINNING, C. (1980) *'After working all these years'*, Disability Alliance, November.

GLUCKLICH, P. and SNELL, M. W. (1982) *Women: Work and Wages*, Low Pay Unit, Discussion Series No. 2.

GLYN, A. and HARRISON, J. (1980) *The British Economic Disaster*, Pluto Press.

GORDON, D. M. (1972) *Theories of Poverty and Underemployment*, Lexington Books.

*[1]GORDON, D., EDWARDS, R., and REICH, M. (1982) *Segmented Work, Divided Workers*, Cambridge University Press.

GOUGH, I. (1979) *The Political Economy of the Welfare State*, Macmillan.

GRANT, J. (1982) 'Running for Shelter during the recession', *The Guardian*, 22 June.

GREENWOOD, G. (1981) 'Unemployment and its effect on health', *J. Inst. Health Educ.*, **19** (4).

GREGORY, J. (1982) 'Equal pay and sex discrimination', *Feminist Review*, 10.

GRIEW, S. (1964) *Job Redesign*, OECD.

*[8]GROVER, R. and GLADSTONE, F. (1981) *Disabled People – A Right to Work*, Bedford Square Press.

Guardian (1982), 28 July.

HAKIM, C. (1978) 'Sexual divisions within the labour force: occupational segregation', *Employment Gazette*, **86** (11).

*[5]HAKIM, C. (1979) *Occupational Segregation*, Research Paper No. 9, Department of Employment.

HAKIM, C. (1980) 'Homeworking: some new evidence', *Employment Gazette*, October.

HAKIM, C. (1981) 'Job segregation: trends in the 1970s', *Employment Gazette*, December.

HALBERSTADT, V. and HAVEMAN, R. H. (1981) *Public Policies for Disabled Workers: Cross National Evidence on Efficiency and Redistributive Effects*, Institute for Research on Poverty, University of Wisconsin-Madison.

HANSARD (1978) House of Commons, WA c709–12, 13 July.

HANSARD (1980) House of Commons, WA 488, 2 June.

HANSARD (1981a) House of Commons, WA c181, 5 February.

HANSARD (1981b) House of Commons, AC c342–3, 8 December.

HARRIS, A. *et al.* (1971) *Handicapped and Impaired in Great Britain*, Vol. 1, HMSO.

HARRIS, J. (1972) *Unemployment and Politics*, Oxford University Press.

HARRIS, J. (1977) *William Beveridge: A Biography*, Oxford University Press.

HART, B. (1982) *Unemployment Insurance and the Firm's Unemployment Strategy: A European and United States Comparison*, Wissenschaftszentrum, Berlin.

HAYES, J. and NUTMAN, P. (1981) *Understanding the Unemployed*, Tavistock.

HIGGINS, J. *et al.* (1983) *Government and Urban Poverty*, Basil Blackwell.

HILL, M. (1981) Unemployment and Government Manpower Policy', in B. Showler and A. Sinfield, op. cit.

HILL. M. J., HARRISON, R. M. SARGEANT, A.V. and TALBOT, V. (1973) *Men Out of Work*, Cambridge University Press.

HIMMELWEIT, S and MOHUN, S. (1977) 'Domestic labour and capital', *Cambridge Journal of Economics*, **1** (1).

*[6]HIRSCH, D. (1983) *Youth Unemployment*, Youthaid.

HITNER, T. *et al.* (1982) *Racial Minority Employment : Equal Opportunity Policy and Practice*, Department of Employment Research Paper No 35.

HMSO (1975) *Racial Discrimination*, Cmnd 6234.

HMSO (1977) Ninth Report of the Committee of Public Accounts, Minutes of Evidence.

HOLLAND, J. (1980) *Work and Women*, Bedford Way Papers 6, University of London Institute of Education.

HOPE, E., KENNEDY, M. and DE WINTER, A. (1976) 'Homeworkers in North London', in D. L. Barker and S. Allen (eds), *Dependence and Exploitation in Work and Marriage*, Longman.

HUGHES, M., MAYALL, B., MOSS, P., PERRY, J., PETRE, P. and PINKERTON, G. (1980) *Nurseries Now*, Penguin.

HUNT, A. (1978) *The Elderly at Home*, HMSO.

*[2]HURSTFIELD, J. (1978) *The Part-time Trap*, Low Pay Pamphlet No 9.

HURSTFIELD, J. (1980) 'Part-Time Pittance', *Low Pay Review*, 1, June.

INCOMES DATA SERVICES (1981) *Young Workers' Pay*, Study 254, November.

IRVINE, J. and EVANS, J. (eds), (1979) *Demystifying Social Statistics*, Pluto Press.

JAEHNIG, W. (1973) *'Seeking out the disabled'* in K. Jones (ed.) *Yearbook of Social Policy in Britain*, Routledge & Kegan Paul.

JAIN, H. C. and SLOANE, P. J. (1980) 'The structure of labour markets, minority workers and equal employment opportunity legislation', *Int. J. Social Econ.*, 7 (3).

JOLLY, J. and MINGAY, A. (1978) 'Employment, age and civil rights', *Department of Employment Gazette*, July.

JOLLY, J., MINGAY, A., and CREIGH, S. (1978) 'Age qualifications in job vacancies', *Department of Employment Gazette*, February.

*[7]JOLLY, J., CREIGH, S. and MINGAY, A. (1980) *Age as a factor in employment*, Unit for Manpower Studies, Research Paper No. 11, DE, April.

JORDON, B. (1982) *Mass Unemployment and the Future of Britain*, Basil Blackwell.

LABOUR RESEARCH DEPARTMENT (1981) *Long Suffering British Workers*, July.

LAND, H. (1977a) 'Sex role stereotyping in the social security and income tax systems', in J. Chetwynd and O. Hartnett (eds), *The Sex Role System*, Routledge & Kegan Paul.

LAND, H. (1977b) 'The child benefit fiasco', in H. Jones (ed.), *The Yearbook of Social Policy in Britain 1976*, Routledge & Kegan Paul.

*[5]LAND, H. (1980a) 'Social policies and the family in Great Britain', in R. S. Ratner (ed.), *Equal Employment Policy for Women*, Temple University Press.

LAND, H. (1980b) 'The family wage', *Feminist Review*, 6.

LAYARD R., PIACHAUD, D. and STEWART, M. (1978) *The Causes of Poverty*, Background Paper No. 5 to Report No. 6, *Lower Incomes*, Royal Commission on the Distribution of Income and Wealth, HMSO.

LEICESTER, C. (1982) 'Towards a fully part-time Britain', *Personnel Management*, June.

LEWIS, J. (1983) *Women's Welfare, Women's Rights*, Croom Helm

LINDLEY, M. (1980) *Economic Change and Employment Policy*, Macmillan.

LISTER, R. (1980) 'Taxation, women and the family' in Sandford, C. *et al.*, *Taxation and Social Policy*, Heineman.

LITTLE, A. (1977) 'The Race Relations Act 1976' in K. Jones (ed.),

The Yearbook of Social Policy in Britain 1976, Routledge & Kegan Paul.

LITTLER, C. R. (1982) *The Development of the Labour Process in Capitalist Societies*, Heinemann.

LLOYDS BANK ECONOMIC BULLETIN (1982) *Working Women's Uneven Progress*, June.

LONSDALE, S. (1980) 'Sickness – who pays?' *Low Pay Review*, 3.

★8LONSDALE, S. (1981) *Job Protection for the disabled*, Low Pay Report, 6.

LONSDALE, S. (1982) 'Weak commitment to the disabled', *Low Pay Review*, 9, May.

LONSDALE, S., FLOWERS, J., and SAUNDERS, B. (1980) *Long-Term Psychiatric Patients: a Study in Community Care*, Personal Social Services Council.

LONSDALE, S. and WALKER, A. (1982) *Labour Market Policies Towards People with Disabilities in the UK*, Report for the Wissenschaftszentrum, Berlin, March 1983.

LOW PAY UNIT (1980) 'Low Pay and Unemployment', *Low Pay Review*, 2, August.

LOW PAY UNIT (1982) 'Parliamentary Report', *Low Pay Review*, 9, May.

LOW PAY UNIT (1983) *Who Needs the Wages Councils?* Pamphlet No. 24, May.

MACAROV, D. (1981) 'Welfare as work's handmaiden', International Journal of Social Economics, **8**, 5.

MACKAY, D. J., MACKAY, R., MCVEAN, P. and EDWARDS, R. (1980) *Redundancy and Displacement*, DE, November

MACLENNAN, E. (1980) *Minimum Wages for Women*, Low Pay Unit and Equal Opportunities Commission.

★6MAKEHAM, P. (1980a) *Youth Unemployment*, Research paper No. 10, DE.

MAKEHAM, P. (1980b) *Economic Aspects of the Employment of Older Workers*, Research Paper No. 14, DE, September.

MAKEHAM, P. (1981) 'Older workers in the economy', *Employment Gazette*, January.

MAKEHAM, P. and MORGAN, P. (1980) *Evaluation of the Job Release Scheme*, Research Paper No. 13, DE, July.

MALLIER, A. T. and ROSSER, M. J. (1980) 'Part-time workers and the economy', *Int. J. of Manpower*, **1** (2).

MANPOWER SERVICES COMMISSION (MSC), (1977) *Young People and Work*, HMSO.

MANPOWER SERVICE COMMISSION (MSC), (1978a) *Young People*

and Work, HMSO.

MANPOWER SERVICES COMMISSION (MSC) (1978b) *Tops Review 1978*, MSC.

MANPOWER SERVICES COMMISSION (MSC) (1978c) *Developing Employment and Training Services for Disabled People*.

MANPOWER SERVICES COMMISSION (MSC), (1979a) *The Quota Scheme for the Employment of Disabled People. A Discussion Document*.

MANPOWER SERVICES COMMISSION (MSC) (1979b) *Review of the First Year of Special Programmes*, July.

MANPOWER SERVICES COMMISSION (MSC), (1980a) *Sheltered Industrial Groups*, EPL95,

MANPOWER SERVICES COMMISSION (MSC), (1980b) *Review of the Second Year of Special Programmes*.

MANPOWER SERVICES COMMISSION (MSC) (1980c) *Employment in Sheltered Workshops*, DPL 11.

MANPOWER SERVICES COMMISSION (MSC), (1980d) *Outlook on Training*, July.

[*4]MANPOWER SERVICES COMMISSION (MSC) (1981a) *Review of Services for the Unemployed*.

MANPOWER SERVICES COMMISSION (MSC), (1981c) *An 'Open-Tech' Programme*, May.

MANPOWER SERVICES COMMISSION (MSC), (1981d) *A Framework for the Future*, July.

[*4]MANPOWER SERVICES COMMISSION (MSC) (1981e) *Review of the Third Year of Special Programmes*, December.

MANPOWER SERVICES COMMISSION (MSC), (1981f) *A New Training Initiative: A Consultative Document*, May.

MANPOWER SERVICES COMMISSION (MSC), (1981g) *A New Training Initiative: An Agenda for Action*, December.

MANPOWER SERVICES COMMISSION (MSC), (1981h) *Employment Rehabilitation*, HMSO, July.

MANPOWER SERVICES COMMISSION (MSC), (1981i) *Review of the Quota Scheme for the Employment of Disabled People, A Report*.

MANPOWER SERVICES COMMISSION (MSC), (1982a) *Corporate Plan 1982–86*, April.

MANPOWER SERVICES COMMISSION (MSC), (1982b) *Annual Report 1981/2*, July.

MANPOWER SERVICES COMMISSION (MSC), (1982c) *Manpower Review*, July.

MANPOWER SERVICES COMMISSION (MSC), (1982d) *Annual Report 1981/2*.

MANPOWER SERVICES COMMISSION (MSC), (1982e) *Youth Task Group Report*, April.

MANPOWER SERVICES COMMISSION (MSC), (1982f) *Review of Assistance for Disabled People*.

MANPOWER SERVICES COMMISSION (MSC), (1982g) *Outline of the Proposed Structure for a Code of Practice on the Employment of Disabled People*, November.

MARRIS, P. and REIN, M. (1967) *Dilemmas of Social Reform*, Routledge & Kegan Paul.

MARSDEN, D. (1982) *Workless*, Croom Helm.

MARSDEN, D. (1983) 'Wage structure'; in G.S. Bain (ed.) *Industrial Relations in Britain*, Basil Blackwell.

MASSIE, B. (1981) *Aspects of the Employment of Disabled People in the Federal Republic of Germany*, RADAR

MERRITT, G. (1982) *World out of Work*, Collins.

METCALFE, D. (1980) 'Unemployment: history, incidence and prospects', *Policy and Politics*, **8** (1).

*⁴METCALFE, D. (1982) *Alternatives to Unemployment*, Report No. 610, Policy Studies Institute and Anglo-German Foundation, September.

MILES, R. and PHIZACKLEA, A. (1977) *The TUC, Black Workers and New Commonwealth Immigration, 1954–1973*, SSRC Working Paper on Ethnic Relations No. 6.

MILES, R. and PHIZACKLEA, A. (1978) 'The TUC and black workers 1974–1976', *Brit. J. Industrial Relations*, XVI, 2.

MOLYNEUX, M. (1979) 'Beyond the domestic labour debate', *New Left Review*, 116.

MORGAN, P. L. and MAKEHAM, P. (1978) *Economic and Financial Analysis of Sheltered Employment*, Research Paper No. 5, Department of Employment, November.

MOYLAN, S. and DAVIES, B. (1981) 'The flexibility of the unemployed', *Employment Gazette*, January.

MOYNIHAN, D. P. (1970) *Maximum Feasible Misunderstanding*, The Free Press.

NATIONAL ADVISORY COUNCIL ON THE EMPLOYMENT OF DISABLED PEOPLE (NACEDP), (1977) *Review of the Arrangements under which Sheltered Workshops Obtain Business from the Public Sector*, Report SEG6 to MSC.

NATIONAL ADVISORY COUNCIL ON EMPLOYMENT OF DISABLED PEOPLE (NACEDP), (1980) *Working Party Report on Wages Structure in Sheltered Employment*.

NATIONAL DEVELOPMENT GROUP FOR THE MENTALLY HANDI-

CAPPED (1977) *Day Services for Mentally Handicapped Adults*, Pamphlet No. 5, HMSO, July.

NISSEL, M. and BONNERJEA, L. (1982) *Family Care of the Handicapped Elderly*, Policy Studies Institute, No. 602.

OAKLEY, A. (1974) *The Sociology of Housework*, Martin Robertson.

OAKLEY, A. (1976) *Housewife*, Pelican.

ORGANISATION FOR ECONOMIC CO-OPERATION AND DEVELOPEMENT (OECD) (1982) *The Challenge of Unemployment*, Paris.

OFFICE OF HEALTH ECONOMICS (OHE), (1981) *Sickness Absence – A Review*, Briefing No. 16, August.

OPCS (1982) *General Household Survey 1980*, HMSO.

OPCS MONITOR (1981) Labour Force Survey, HMSO.

[*7]PARKER, S. R. (1980) *Older Workers and Retirement*, OPCS.

PARKER, S. R. (1981) 'Carry on working', *Employment Gazette*, January.

PERSONAL SOCIAL SERVICES COUNCIL AND CENTRAL HEALTH SERVICES COUNCIL (1978) *Collaboration in Community Care – a Discussion Document*, HMSO.

PIACHAUD, D. (1979) *The Cost of a Child*, Poverty Pamphlet 43, Child Poverty Action Group (CPAG), November.

PIORE, M. (1972) '*Notes for a theory of labour market stratification*', Working Paper No. 95, Dept of Economics, MIT.

[*1]PIORE, M. (1979) *Birds of Passage*, Cambridge University Press.

PIORE, M. (1980) '*Economic fluctuation, job security and labor-market duality in Italy, France and the United States*', *Politics and Society*, **9** (4).

POND, C. (1980) 'The structure of unemployment in Britain', *Int. J. Soc. Econ.*, **7** (7).

POND, C. (1981) 'Low Pay – 1980s style', *Low Pay Review*, 4, March.

POND, C. (1982) 'Youth unemployment: are wages to blame?'. *Low Pay Review*, 8, February.

POND, C (1983) *Wages Councils, the Unorganised and the Low Paid* in G. S. Bain (ed) Industrial Relations in Britain, Basil Blackwell.

POND, C, and MACLENNAN, E. (1981) *Insuring Poverty at Work*, Low Pay Report 6, April.

POPAY, J. (1981a) 'Unemployment: a threat to public health', in *Unemployment: Who Pays the Price?* Child Poverty Action Group Pamphlet 53.

POPAY, J. (1981b) *Ill Health and Unemployment*, Unemployment Alliance, Briefing Paper 2, November.

PORTER, M. (1982) 'Standing on the edge: working class housewives and the world of work', in J. West (ed.) *Work, Women and the Labour Market*, Routledge & Kegan Paul.

REARDON, S. (1982) 'Sheltering from the recession', *Employment Gazette*, May.

*[9]REES, T. (1979) 'Immigration policies in the United Kingdom', in C. Husband (ed.) *Race in Britain*, Hutchinson (1982).

REUBENS, B. (1970) *The Hard to Employ*, Columbia University Press.

RIGHTS OF WOMEN EUROPE (1983) *Women's Rights and the EEC*, Rights of Women Europe.

ROBERTS, K. *et al.* (1981) *Unregistered Youth Unemployment and Outreach Careers Work*, Department of Employment, Research Paper No. 31.

ROBERTSON, J. A. S. (1982) 'Does Job Release reduce unemployment?', *Employment Gazette*, May.

ROBINSON, O. (1979) 'Part-time employment in the European Community', *Int. Labour Review*, 118 (3).

ROUTH, G. (1980) *Occupation and Pay in Great Britain 1906–1979*, Macmillan.

ROUTH, G., WEDDERBURN, D. and WOOTTON, B. (1980) *The Roots of Pay Inequalities*, Low Pay Unit, Discussion Series No. 1.

RUBERY, J. (1978) 'Structured labour markets, low pay and worker organisation', *Cambridge J. Econ.*, 2 (1), March.

RUBERY, J. and WILKINSON, F. (1981) 'Outwork and segmented labour markets', in F. Wilkinson (ed.) *The Dynamics of Labour Market Segmentation*, Academic Press.

*[9]THE RUNNYMEDE TRUST AND THE RADICAL STATISTICS RACE GROUP (1980) *Britain's Black Population*, Heinemann Educational Books.

SCARMAN, LORD (1981) *The Scarman Report: The Brixton Disorders 10–12 April 1981*, Penguin.

SCORER, C. and SEDLEY, A. (1983) *Amending the Equality Laws*, National Council for Civil Liberties (NCCL).

SECCOMBE, W. (1974) 'The housewife and her labour under capitalism', *New Left Review*, 83.

*[2]SEDLEY, A (1980) *Part time workers need full time rights*, National Council for Civil Liberties.

SEMLINGER, K. (1982) *The Employment and Occupational Promotion of the Handicapped in the Federal Republic of Germany*, Conference Paper, International Institute for Management and Administration, Berlin.

SHEPPARD, H. L. (1976) 'Work and retirement', in R. H. Binstock and E. Shanas (eds) *Handbook of Ageing and the Social Sciences*, Litton Educational Publishing Inc.

SHOWLER, B. (1976) *The Public Employment Service*, Longman.

SHOWLER, B. (1982) 'Public Expenditure on employment', in A. Walker (ed.) *Public Expenditure and Social Policy*, Heinemann.

*[10]SHOWLER, B and SINFIELD, A. (eds) (1981) *The Workless State*, Martin Robertson.

SINFIELD, A. (1978) 'Analyses in the social division of welfare', *J. Soc Pol.*, 7 (2).

*[3]SINFIELD, A.(1981) *What Unemployment Means*, Martin Robertson.

SLATER, R. (1973), 'Age discrimination', *New Society*, 10 May.

SMITH, D. J. (1974) *Racial Disadvantage in Employment*, Political and Economic Planning, 544.

SMITH, D. J. (1976) *The Facts of Racial Disadvantage*, Political and Economic Planning, 560.

SMITH, D. J. (1980) 'How unemployment makes the poor poorer', *Policy Studies*, July.

SMITH, D. J. (1981) *Unemployment and Racial Minorities*, Policy Studies Institute, No. 594.

SNELL, M. W., GLUCKLICH, P. and POVALL, M. (1981) *Equal pay and Opportunities*, Research Paper No. 20, Department of Employment.

SOCIAL TRENDS (1983), No. 13, HMSO.

SORRENTINO, C. (1981) '*Unemployment in international perspective*', in B. Showler and A. Sinfield (eds) *The Workless State*, Martin Robertson.

TAYLOR, R. (1978) 'Work-sharing and worklessness', *New Society*, 23 November.

TITMUSS, R. (1958) *Essays on the Welfare State*, George Allen & Unwin.

TOMLINSON COMMITTEE (1943) *Report of Inter-Departmental Committee on the Rehabilitation and Resettlement of Disabled Persons*, Cmnd 6415, HMSO, January.

TOPLISS, E and GOULD, B. (1981) *Charter for the Disabled*, Martin Robertson.

TOWNSEND, P. (1976) 'Area deprivation policies', *New Statesman*, 6 August.

TOWNSEND, P. (1979) *Poverty in the United Kingdom*, Allen Lane and Penguin.

TOWNSEND, P. (1981) 'Guerrillas, subordinates and passers-by', *Critical Social Policy*, 1 (2).

TRADES UNION CONGRESS (TUC), (1981), *Unemployment and*

Working Time, TUC Consultative Document, February.

TUNNARD, J. (1978) *The Trouble with Tax*, Child Poverty Action Group, Pamphlet 35.

WAJCMAN, J., (1981) 'Work and the family in the Cambridge Women's Studies Group', *Women in Society*, Virago.

WALKER, A. (1980) 'The social creation of poverty and dependency in old age', *J. Soc. Pol.*, **9** (1), January.

WALKER, A. ((1981a) 'The level and distribution of unemployment', in L. Burghes and R. Lister (eds) *Unemployment: Who Pays the Price?*, Child Poverty Action Group.

WALKER, A. (1981b) 'Towards a political economy of old age', *Ageing and Society*, **1** (1), March.

WALKER, A. (1982a) 'The social consequences of early retirement', *Political Quarterly*, January.

WALKER, A. (1982b) *Unqualified and underemployed*, Macmillan.

WALSH, B. M. (1981) *Unemployment Insurance and the Labour Market: a Review of Research Relating to Policy*, OECD, MAS/WPS 81, 1, Paris.

WANSBOROUGH, N. (1980) *Sheltered Work, Open Employment*, National Schizophrenia Fellowship.

WEIR, S. (1981a) 'Our Image of the disabled, *New Society*, 1 January.

WEIR, S. (1981b) 'Notes', *New Society*, 11 June, p. 438.

WELLS, W. (1983) 'Relative pay and employment of young people', *Employment Gazette*, June.

WHELAN, E. and SPEAKE, B. (1977) *Adult Training Centres in England and Wales*, Revell and George Ltd, Manchester.

WHITE, M. (1980) *Shorter Working Time*, Policy Studies Institute, No. 589.

WHITE, M. (1981) *Case Studies of Shorter Working Time*, Policy Studies Institute, No. 597.

WOOTTON, B. (1962) *The Social Foundations of Wage Policy*, George Allen & Unwin.

WORSWICK, G. D. N. (ed.), (1976) *The Concept and Measurement of Involuntary Unemployment*, George, Allen & Unwin.

YOUTHAID WORKING GROUP (1981) *Quality or Collapse?* Report of a Review of the Youth Opportunity Programme.

YOUNG, K. & CONNELLY, N. (1981) *Policy and Practice in the Multi-Racial City*, Policy Studies Institute, 598.

ZIDERMAN, A. (1978) *Manpower Training: Theory and Policy*, Macmillan.

INDEX